DICK RAYMOND'S

LINDEN PRESS | *SIMON & SCHUSTER*
New York City   1985

GARDENING YEAR

BY DICK
RAYMOND

My special thanks to Richard Alther for all his energy and assistance on this project; to Joni Evans, for her inspiration and skill as editor *and* gardener; and to my wife, Jan, for her great help as my gardening partner, too.

Published by Linden Press/Simon & Schuster
A Division of Simon & Schuster, Inc.
Simon & Schuster Building
Rockefeller Center
1230 Avenue of the Americas
New York, New York 10020
LINDEN PRESS/SIMON & SCHUSTER and colophon
are trademarks of Simon & Schuster, Inc.
Photography by Dick Raymond/Paul Boisvert
Drawings by Norman Sevigny
Designed by Eve Metz/Irving Perkins Associates
Production by Jeanne Palmer
Manufactured in the United States of America
10   9   8   7   6   5   4   3   2   1

Library of Congress Cataloging in Publication Data

Raymond, Dick.
    Dick Raymond's gardening year.

    1. Vegetable gardening.   I. Title.   II. Title:
Gardening year.
SB321.R338   1985   635   85-18042
ISBN 0-671-50973-X
ISBN 0-671-60600-X (pbk.)

DICK RAYMOND'S
GARDENING YEAR

CONTENTS

APRIL

**Warm days . . .
soil's ready   62**

My foolproof "soil readiness" test; the first complete turning of the soil; applying fertilizers; appreciating the earthworm; transplanting and caring for seedlings; planting potatoes, lettuce and more peas outdoors and gambling on some early corn; also radishes and kale;

MIDDLE APRIL:

"hardening off" outdoors or in a coldframe; wide-row wonders;

LATE APRIL:

putting the first of your seedlings into the ground; planting hardy seeds; protecting your plants against the cutworm menace; building raised beds for rootcrops.

MAY

**Prime time
planting   90**

Planting a salad row; hardening off the last of my seedlings; hilling my potato patch; gambling on some tomatoes under protection; outwitting annual and perennial weeds from the beginning;

MIDDLE MAY:

planting my main-crop potatoes and corn; the marvels of the radish; plant shopping advice in a nutshell; my depth-planting chart; wide-row planting or single row—the rules of thumb; asparagus essentials;

LATE MAY:

the best system for planting tomatoes—on their sides; important but easy watering techniques; planting a pepper plantation; "pre-sprouting" melons and cucumber seeds; sweet potatoes.

JUNE

**Gardening care, done right,
takes less time   120**

Cultivating and weeding—in one step; watering—one inch per week; mulching—why, how and when; the weed-free garden; the best tools; my bug-control methods; tomato support systems—to stake or not to stake; first harvesting know-how; my crew-cut technique for harvesting lettuce, spinach, chard and other greens; some herb advice;

MIDDLE JUNE:

extra fertilizing by side dressing; mulching; container planting—the best space saver;

LATE JUNE:

harvesting asparagus, "suckering" tomatoes.

Contents   vii

JULY

Pick 'em young, tender and sweet! 148

How best to harvest peas; succession planting for fall is simple; training pole beans; how to overcome dry weather; how to blanch for the perfect cauliflower; the kohlrabi story;
MIDDLE JULY:
spraying and dusting—every week; more side-dressing;
LATE JULY:
setting melons on tin cans moves them 400 miles south; how to pick a perfect broccoli head; how to get six more cabbages from a single plant; harvesting some early potatoes, squash, zucchini and cukes; more spraying and dusting.

AUGUST

The lush harvest month 172

Knowing when to harvest; pick peppers as soon as there's something large enough to eat; final succession planting; pest control month; a raccoon raid—how to know if you need fencing; an important step to hasten the melon harvest—plucking the fuzzy ends; more dusting; prime-time harvesting of the onion crop;
MIDDLE AUGUST:
tomatoes are ready—for the slowpokes, try my special tricks; stripping leaves of Brussels sprouts gives strength to the plant; my corn-ripeness test;
LATE AUGUST:
personalizing pumpkins; my cardinal rule of harvesting—don't let most vegetables grow to full size; dusting and mulching; using weed-choking cover crops; the "inside story" on the vine crops.

SEPTEMBER

The bounty 196

When to harvest what, for peak flavor and best storage; melons, tomatoes, peppers, and corn in abundance; continuing with watering and cabbage-family bug control; potatoes, onions, sprouts and more in final stretch;
MIDDLE SEPTEMBER:
starting to put some of garden to bed; limas, eggplants, and dry beans;
LATE SEPTEMBER:
harvesting sweet potatoes and last of vine crops; stretching the fresh-eating season of broccoli, lettuce, cabbages and more.

OCTOBER

I don't let my garden get away with early retirement 214

Outwitting early frosts; essential garden clean-up; sowing cover crops once garden is finished; the best ways to store vegetables; how to extend the season;
MIDDLE AND LATE OCTOBER:
heavy-frost watch and my protection check list; root cellar storage.

NOVEMBER

Shape up garden soil 226

Improving soil with organic matter—leaves, grass clippings and brush; the compost pile . . . quick and easy ingredients; harvest kohlrabi, cabbage, turnips, chard, black radish and more . . . well into fall; more on soil-building cover crops; planning ahead—some raised beds for spring; the tool shed shutdown; root cellar serving tricks.

DECEMBER

I don't quit! 236

Gardening under snow—an insulating blanket; gifts from the garden.

Index 243

JANUARY

──────── *EARLY JANUARY* ────────
Review last garden
Decide on which vegetables

──────── *MIDDLE JANUARY* ────────
Select varieties

──────── *LATE JANUARY* ────────
Sketch out garden

FEBRUARY

INDOORS

──────── *EARLY FEBRUARY* ────────
Buy seeds
Reconsider garden site, size
Shop for fertilizers, soil test kit

──────── *MIDDLE FEBRUARY* ────────
Establish timetable
Gather supplies for indoor seed starting
Plant seeds: onions
        leeks
        celery

──────── *LATE FEBRUARY* ────────
Look over tools

MARCH

INDOORS

──────── *EARLY MARCH* ────────
Plant seed flats:
   more onions
   herbs
   annual flowers
   tomatoes
   early head lettuce
   early cabbage
   broccoli
   cauliflower
   Brussels sprouts
   peppers
   eggplants

──────── *MIDDLE MARCH* ────────
Seedling care: give onions a crew-cut;
   keep watered
Review protection devices for early
   outdoor planting

──────── *LATE MARCH* ────────
Plant seed flats: cucumbers, squashes,
   melons

OUTDOORS

──────── *LATE MARCH* ────────
Take soil test
Build a raised bed: early crops
Fertilize and cultivate: old asparagus
Gamble: early peas
Plant: early onion sets, spinach

APRIL

INDOORS

——————— *EARLY APRIL* ———————
Transplant seedlings:
   tomatoes
   eggplants
   peppers
   head lettuce
   cabbage family
Plant: more head lettuce
Trim: onions and leeks

——————— *MIDDLE APRIL* ———————
Care: water seedlings

——————— *LATE APRIL* ———————
Transplant a few early tomatoes a second
   time

OUTDOORS

——————— *EARLY APRIL* ———————
Turn soil
Lightly fertilize entire garden
Sow: maincrop peas
   early seed potatoes
   more onion sets plus seeds and plants
   kale
   garlic
   more spinach and leaf lettuce
   radishes
Gamble: early corn

——————— *MIDDLE APRIL* ———————
Harden off: cabbage family
       greens
       celery
       leeks
       onion plants
Ready coldframe, as option

——————— *LATE APRIL* ———————
Sow hardy maincrop seeds:
   spinach
   lettuce
   chards
   mustard greens
   turnips
   carrots
   beets
   peas
   onions
   radishes
   kohlrabi
   parsnips
Plant: onion plants, shallots, garlic,
   Jerusalem artichoke
Transplant to garden: cabbage, broccoli,
   Brussels sprouts, cauliflower, head
   lettuce, leeks, celery
Gamble: some seeds of squashes, melons,
   cukes under hotcaps or tunnels
Buy: early plants to set out if not raised

MAY

INDOORS

——————— *EARLY MAY* ———————
Care: sweet potato sprouts to plant
   outdoors later this month

OUTDOORS

——————— *EARLY MAY* ———————
Sow from seed: "multicrop" salad row
Harden off last of seedlings: tomatoes,
   peppers, eggplants, vine family crops
Hill: early potato patch
Gamble: tomatoes (under protection—
   hotcaps or tunnels)
Turn unplanted soil to destroy weeds

——————— *MIDDLE MAY* ———————
Plant: maincrop potatoes, maincrop corn
Onion plants: snap off seed pods
Buy and harden off: tomatoes, eggplants,
   peppers, cabbage-family crops, head
   lettuce, celery, vine crops, herbs
Cultivate and harvest-thin: some scallions
   from sets, beets, and all salad greens.
Cultivate and thin carrots
Harvest: asparagus, radishes
Side-dress and hill: potatoes (2nd hilling)

——————— *LATE MAY* ———————
Plant: tomatoes, eggplants, peppers, sweet
   potatoes, vine family plants
Plant seeds: melons, cukes, green and wax
   beans, squashes and other vines
Water: entire garden, weekly, inch
Harvest: radishes, spinach, lettuces, and
   greens

JUNE

OUTDOORS

——————— *EARLY JUNE* ———————
Cultivate and thin: seedlings ½-inch high
Uncover hotcaps
Replant: early corn skips in rows
Plant: maincrop corn
Dust: tomatoes, potatoes, and cabbage-
   family crops
Stake, cage, trellis or let sprawl: tomatoes
Sow: parsnips and winter squash (for
   winter storage), drying beans, rutabagas,
   okra, lima beans, herbs as plants, any
   remaining vine crops, peanuts
Side-dress and hill: early corn
Side-dress: head lettuce, chard
Harvest: more radishes and salad greens
Crew-cut: more looseleaf lettuce, spinach,
   chard, other greens
Patrol for bugs
Water: each week

——————— *MIDDLE JUNE* ———————
Side-dress: early tomatoes, leeks, potatoes
Mulch: tomatoes, peppers, eggplants,
   single-row or staggered and widely-
   spaced crops, if very dry
Hill: maincrop potatoes and early corn
   (2nd hilling)
Dust: potatoes every 10 days
Harvest: early Pixie tomatoes and first peas
Cut: looseleaf lettuce and other greens
Tie: tomato tops to supports
Water: each week

——————— *LATE JUNE* ———————
Sucker, tie, and mulch tomatoes
Harvest: asparagus, first peas, ongoing
   salad rows, a few early potatoes, head
   lettuce
Side-dress: early cabbage, broccoli, and
   cauliflower before they head, early corn
   again at tassel stage
Water: each week

Dick Raymond's Gardening Year   xi

JULY

OUTDOORS

──────── EARLY JULY ────────
Harvest: peas, chards, re-grown lettuces, greens, radishes, sprigs of herbs
Mulch, if necessary
Spray/dust: potatoes, tomatoes, cabbage-family and any insect-infested crops
Side-dress and hill: maincrop corn
Blanch: celery
Cultivate and thin: beets, carrots, chard, kale, collard greens and other wide-row planted vegetables
Side-dress: all squashes, peppers, eggplants, onions, cucumbers
Sucker tomatoes throughout this month
Succession-plant: beets, carrots, spinach, more lettuce in space of early completed crops
Train: pole beans up supports
Water: each week

──────── MIDDLE JULY ────────
Blanch: cauliflower
Spray/dust: potatoes, tomatoes, cabbage-family
Harvest: green and wax beans, kohlrabi, final peas, baby carrots and beets, first summer squashes, more early potatoes, early tomatoes
Side-dress: melons, tomatoes, broccoli, cauliflower if not yet done
Mulch: tomatoes if not yet done
Water: each week

──────── LATE JULY ────────
Harvest: broccoli heads, summer squash and zucchini, cucumbers, young cabbages
Spray/dust: cabbage-family, potatoes, tomatoes
Side-dress: Brussels sprouts
Hill: maincrop corn, if weedy
Train: climbing cucumbers
Water: each week
Plant: buckwheat as cover crop

AUGUST

OUTDOORS

──────── EARLY AUGUST ────────
Harvest: young peppers, cukes, green beans, early kale, tomatoes, zucchini, summer squash, early shallots, garlic and leeks, more cabbage, herbs throughout the month
Side-dress and hill: maincrop corn, final times
Spray/dust: cabbage crops
Harvest-thin: beets, onions, leeks
Succession-plant: more beets, carrots, late spinach, onion sets, radishes, greens, peas and beans
Pick: fuzzy ends off vine crops
Protect: garden from animal pests with fencing
Water: each week

──────── MIDDLE AUGUST ────────
Spray/dust: cabbage crops
Harvest: green beans, broccoli sideshoots, mid-season cabbages, cukes, okra, chards, shallots, corn, pole beans, early eggplant, more early peppers, carrots, beets, potatoes, tomatoes, onions, early leeks, early celery, more head lettuce
Strip leaves: Brussels sprouts
Side-dress: Brussels sprouts and okra
Cultivate and thin (or harvest-thin) succession plantings
Sample: early sweet potaotes
Water: each week

──────── LATE AUGUST ────────
Harvest: all ongoing crops
Sow: annual ryegrass cover crops
Topdress: onions
Spray-dust: cabbage crops
Water: each week

SEPTEMBER

──────── EARLY SEPTEMBER ────────
Harvest: tomatoes, peppers, large white and early red cabbages, corn, broccoli sideshoots, early rutabagas, okra, potatoes, carrots, more celery, all melons, continuing squashes
Strip: Brussels sprouts again
Spray/dust: cabbage-family crops
Clean: root cellar
Sow: black (winter) radish, more cover crops
Water: each week

──────── MIDDLE SEPTEMBER ────────
Crew-cut: late lettuce, chard, spinach and other greens
Harvest: all above from Early September, plus lima beans, eggplants, and dry beans (now through October)
Spray/dust: cabbage crops
Compost/turn under: crop residues, now through fall
Water: each week

──────── LATE SEPTEMBER ────────
Harvest: winter squashes, remaining summer vine crops, sweet potatoes, continuing broccoli sideshoots, sunflowers, early turnips, succession-planted peas and beans, early parsnips, green tomatoes for indoor ripening
Option: protect final tender crops from frost
Water: each week

OCTOBER

―――――― *EARLY OCTOBER* ――――――
Harvest: cabbages, pumpkins and gourds, beets, kale, spinach, lettuce, late onions, turnips, rutabagas, carrots, final dry beans, celery
Continue: crop residue spading-in or removal
Stock root cellar

―― *MIDDLE AND LATE OCTOBER* ――
Harvest: rutabagas, carrots, celery, leeks, kale, final cabbages of all varieties, Brussels sprouts, broccoli sideshoots, chards, radishes
Protect: final peas or lingering peppers and tender plants

NOVEMBER

Remove or spade under final crop residues
Make compost piles
Build up soil with collected organic matter
Harvest fall crops: carrots, all cabbages, turnips, kohlrabi, winter radish, leeks, onions (last call)
Mulch: carrots for winter harvest, parsnips for spring harvest
Make: a raised bed section for some early, drained spring planting
Clean and store tools
Eat from root cellar: first-to-go cabbages and celery

DECEMBER

Harvest: cabbages, chards, carrots, head lettuce, scallions, leeks, parsley, Brussels sprouts, turnips, and kale—under snow
Give: gifts from the garden

INTRODUCTION

If you've always wanted to know just *what* to do *when* in your gardening year, no matter where you live, I think you'll find this new book made to order for you.

You can join me month by month in *my* year of gardening. It starts January 1 with the arrival of those beautiful seed catalogs. That's all it takes to get me revved up about eating the best-tasting vegetables on earth. It ends in December with our tapping the bounty in the root cellar, and—would you believe?—*still* harvesting all kinds of delicious fresh vegetables from under snow!

January is planning month. So in that chapter (and February too) I review lots of ideas from my scrapbook of proven techniques. You can follow my checklist of considerations and begin thinking about (or reevaluating) your own garden design, location, size, and vegetable selections.

Dick Raymond's Gardening Year is meant to be your very own gardening coach. Because the lion's share of what you have to do for great results is the same no matter where you live, what's important here are the fundamentals. My way to transplant a tomato is going to get your earliest, juiciest, heal-thiest crop ever—from Maine to New Mexico. Wide-row planting, which I recommend for most vegetables, outwits the bulk of the weather, pests, moisture, and weed problems in every climate. You may be adjusting your garden activities somewhat ahead or behind mine here in Vermont. The important thing is: You have the same growing *sequence* as I do, from garden planning and seed starting right through to a bountiful harvest and stretching it to its limits.

Sun Belt gardeners are exceptions. You have spring gardens and fall gardens because the four months of June, July, August, and September are just too hot. When I'm starting off seeds indoors and planting my early, hardy crops outdoors in March, you're in December or January, two to three months ahead. I suggest you folks simply take a big leap as you follow my calendar. More advice for you as we proceed: Look for the Sun Belt symbol.

I think in monthly thirds. I start my tomato seeds indoors in early March . . . I'm fertilizing most vegetables mid-June . . . late September is final harvesting of tender crops. So, I've arranged my sequence of steps to share with you by dividing my activity into *Early, Middle,* and *Late* segments of each month.

On the first page of each month is a brief checklist of general gardening goals for that period. At the end of the month, I've included a checklist of reminders, plus a short preview of what's in store for the month ahead.

Basically, I show you what *I* do. You can pick and choose along the way. I also offer some advice on options in case you are less ambitious—or more!

Although I grow several gardens, from square-foot "salad bowl" patches in the lawn to big plots of melons and beans for drying, the specific vegetable or garden care advice applies to them all, whatever the shape or size of your garden.

If there's one thing that's constant in my help to gardeners, it's encouraging them to make the most productive use of their time and space. I'm going to show you how planting vegetables close together —my "wide-row" technique—will accomplish many good things. Sure, when seeds were scarce and land was cheap, it figured to treat seeds like little diamonds and space vegetables a foot or more apart. Now, seeds are abundant and a real bargain, but land is less available to us. You'll see many reasons to try what I call wide-row growing.

Your soil, no matter what shape it's in, is going to be much improved in texture and fertility if you follow what I do, especially during the second half of the gardening year. I'll share with you my harvesting know-how for each crop as it comes along.

For the beginner and veteran alike, I make *all* my garden steps easy and fun. I try to be smart enough to do all the work I *must* do, and lazy enough *not* to do any unnecessary work. For example, you'll see how I grow many crops as a "living mulch" where the peas, beans or lettuce become a blanket of vegetables. This method means so much less weeding and watering.

I can pretty much guarantee that the yields from a very modest amount of space, work and time are going to astonish you. My system makes a garden the source of beauty, pride, and joy it's meant to be.

So let's get growing!

D.R.

JANUARY

This is the month to daydream

EARLY JANUARY: ARMCHAIR GARDENING

Happy New Year. Early January, for me, is like the start of spring!

Indoor time is my chance to browse through the seed catalogs and to think up some new gardening ideas for the coming year. Having to wait a few months before I can dig into my soil doesn't stop me from dreaming about the beautiful vegetables I had last year and the new things I want to try . . . like a melon they say ripens one month earlier. Now that would be something here in northern Vermont! I've worked out an easy type of shelter —a plastic tunnel—for growing what I think could be my earliest tomatoes yet. I figure, what the heck, if I'm going to garden, why not gamble? This year I'm going to gamble even more and start some

things outdoors earlier than ever. I can make sure my early seedlings get the basics of light, heat, good rich soil, some nutrients, lots of water. Nothing to lose but a few seeds. At the very least, the more I experiment in my garden, the more fun I have, and the more I learn. I'm going to plant some sweet corn and peppers ahead of schedule. And my lima beans, which seem to take forever, are going to get an especially early start—if the weather is halfway decent.

How about you? Overall, were you satisfied with your garden? Which vegetables did you really succeed with? Any flops? This month you can join me as my wife, Jan, and I plan our actual list of vegetables.

My best advice: Start small. Keep your garden smaller rather than larger. Try a few ideas, but not all. When selecting vegetables, get mostly the tried-and-true varieties—not every eye-catching new one offered. As I browse through seed catalogs I can't wait to try the new things, but I'm not going to forget the old standbys. This year I'm going to plant more spinach and beets, and fewer kohlrabis. We Raymonds are fortunate to have a nice chunk of land here, so we raise some extra for our three grown and married daughters and their families. Although two of my daughters have their own gardens, we raise the potatoes, corn, and some of those sprawling squash and melon vines for all of them right here. But keep in mind that the most important help I offer gardeners is how to grow a lot in very limited space—sometimes only a few square feet.

My best idea from 40 years of gardening resulted from an accident

WIDE-ROW PLANTING

I can grow two to three times as much

Ages ago, I discovered, when I dropped a packet of peas, that a broad swath of them didn't need staking when the vines became long. I let them grow up in a cluster, and they supported themselves! Also, I didn't have to water, weed or cultivate—just plant and pick. That was only the beginning of the advantages I came to enjoy with a wide row of vegetables, compared to planting them ordinarily, in skinny rows, "single file." So why do seed companies continue to recommend single rows on their seed packets? It's easier to stick to the familiar.

Wide rows stagger your harvest. Since plants mature at somewhat different rates, slower-growing ones can expand into spaces left by the first-picked.

I plant all vegetables in wide rows except the following ones, which I do still plant in single rows: corn, potatoes, tomatoes, pole beans, and the sprawling squashes and cucumbers.

More on the details of my wide-row planting system later.

See how much taller this lettuce is growing, planted in a wide row? That's because the clustered plants keep the ground cooler—just what lettuce likes most.

As long as they stand "shoulder to shoulder" wide-row-planted crops shade the ground, conserve moisture, and form what I call their own living mulch.

Plants thrive in groups. Garden vegetables are no exception. See how this stand of green beans blocks sunshine and stunts these weeds?

Time to decide whether yes, no, or maybe . . .

	YES	NO	MAYBE
ASPARAGUS			
BEANS			
BEETS			
BROCCOLI			
BRUSSELS SPROUTS			
CABBAGE			
CAULIFLOWER			
CARROTS			
CELERY			
CHINESE CABBAGE			
COLLARDS			
CORN			
CUCUMBERS			
DILL			
EGGPLANT			
ENDIVE			
GARLIC			
HERBS			
KALE			
KOHLRABI			
LEEKS			
LETTUCE			
looseleaf			
head			
MELONS			

	YES	NO	MAYBE
MUSTARD GREENS			
OKRA			
ONIONS			
sets			
seeds			
PARSLEY			
PARSNIPS			
PEAS			
PEPPERS			
POTATOES			
PUMPKINS			
RADISHES			
RUTABAGAS			
SHALLOTS			
SPINACH			
SQUASH			
summer			
winter			
STRAWBERRIES			
SUNFLOWERS			
SWEET POTATOES			
SWISS CHARD			
TOMATOES			
TURNIPS			
ZUCCHINI			

> Next month I'll decide which vegetables to start in the garden from seed and which I'll buy or raise as young plants.

NO MORE EXCUSES!

Shady soil?

All vegetables need *some* sunshine. But many can grow in shady spots. I recommend concentrating on the cool-weather crops like greens—spinach, the chards, lettuce; and the cabbage family—including broccoli, Brussels sprouts, collards, cauliflower, and turnips. All of these prefer cooler, damper ground. Parsley and peas are other crops that are extremely hardy and forgiving in less-than-ideal conditions. The heat lovers (tomatoes, eggplants, beans, peppers) can grow in partial shade but must have at least half the day (about 5 to 6 hours) in sun. They will take longer to grow and reach maturity in shade than in full sun. You can also have a border of herbs—these don't need to grow as rapidly as fruiting vegetables.

Soil too hopeless to cope with?

Sorry, but that excuse flew out my window years ago. Most of us are stuck these days with everything from rock-hard clay to builders' fill. In upcoming months, I'll show you how I transform most any patch of ground into a fertile garden, with organic matter, some fertilizer, and a desire to grow vegetables!

Only time on weekends?

If you plant the garden my way, your upkeep is minimal. In fact, in July and August it will involve less than an hour a week.

On a slope?

For slopes over ten degrees, I like to build a simple terrace system. This does two things: it creates vegetable beds on a level that will prevent runoff of valuable topsoil, nutrients, and the washing away of the young plants themselves; and it makes it lots easier on the gardener to weed, tend, thin, and harvest, and I'm all for that. Please see page 29 next month for more discussion.

Don't want to dig up all your lawn for a garden?

Some narrow strips make good sense in that situation. It's easy to work in them from all sides. They are every bit as attractive, too, as beds of perennial flowers. To make a point of how much food can be grown in a concentrated area, in just *one square foot of turf* I've grown 144 onions from sets and an entire tomato plant.

Doubling Up Vegetables—*lettuce under broccoli: Each keeps the other cool. Broccoli grows best in cool weather—so I discovered that broadcast-sowing (as if you were sprinkling grass seed) some lettuce can produce a living mulch beneath broccoli plants. In addition, the tall broccoli serves as an "umbrella" over the lettuce and the lettuce cools the roots of the broccoli.*

Back-to-back rows—*I'm always trying to figure out how to keep my soil productive. Wide rows cut way down on the garden area taken up by walkways. And planting two of them, back-to-back, works even better. Much of the tending and harvesting is within arm's length of the lawn.*

IS SPACE A PROBLEM?

Tub farming—*In this patio planter box I've sown green beans and yellow wax beans, then added some marigolds for color. I put good, rich soil with some handfuls of compost in my planters, plus work in a little fertilizer—a spoonful per square foot—at planting time.*

Hanging baskets—*These cherry tomatoes make a hanging basket that is attractive as well as productive. Exposed to warm air as they are on all sides, containers require almost daily watering.*

MIDDLE JANUARY

MORE PLANNING

By now I've got a whole stack of seed catalogs. I stop browsing, and I start making a list for real. I generally buy some seeds by mail order—varieties I can't find locally or seeds I want to have on hand for early indoor sowing. But I also rely on the selections in our local garden-supply stores. They usually stock a more limited group of seeds, but they tend to carry the special varieties that do well in my region.

If you want a real early jump on spring, and the first possible crop, then I recommend you start some seeds indoors. This way, plants can be ready to set out when the weather's right, not when a local supplier may have them for sale. I begin to sow indoors in March (see page 44). Of course I also sow most vegetables from seed directly in the garden, April through June, for my main-crop summer garden. You may choose to skip the earlybird effort.

Most Florida and Texas and Southwest gardeners I know buy already started plants and do some indoor seed starting to get an early harvest and beat the heat of summer. They seed their hardy vegetables directly in the garden December through March.

For variety's sake, I do buy some plants at a local garden center. Later, on page 104, when I go shopping for them, I'll share the things I look for in an already started plant. I like to get my money's worth!

How to get the most from a seed catalog:

There's a lot of information tucked away in those pages between all the colorful photos.

My checklist for reading catalogs:

- *I make a note of "days to maturity."* First of all, I "guesstimate" my growing season—the number of days after the average date of *last* frost in the spring, to the average date of *first* frost in the autumn. It's about 120 days in my case (May 30 to September 30). You'll find a map in February which sets forth the average last-frost dates for the spring. But the best way to estimate the first *fall* frost is to ask around your immediate neighborhood. In a light-frost area the goal is to avoid the worst of blistering summer heat. Sun Belt gardeners look for varieties to begin growing in mid to late winter for their spring garden, and in late summer for their fall garden.

How much should I buy?

The amount of seed varies so greatly from packet to packet, depending on the packager, that I often get into hot water with readers asking me to recommend "numbers or portions of packets." I say: Buy one packet of seed of each vegetable variety for a family of three or four. But buy several packets of peas and beans so you'll have enough to plant in wide rows. Three to four pounds of onion sets would be right for a three-to-four-person household.

Zone maps are tricky, especially for the fall. Consider the difference between northern, central, and lower Florida alone. Frosts can vary widely in a six-mile area by as much as three to six weeks! What's good for Uncle Charlie across town might not apply to you. If you're near water (which retains heat) . . . or up a mountain . . . or in a valley . . . or exposed to the south mostly . . . you may have a completely different frost experience. I include that spring map on page 36 in February, a rough starting guide, for you. But I've not put one in for the fall, which is a much less important date.

I don't like hardiness zone maps. I think they limit our creativity as gardeners. As you'll soon see, I stretch the days of my growing season into months in both directions by taking a chance and by protecting my plants. As a matter of fact, I like to think I can keep something growing in the garden 365 days a year. Many Sun Belt gardeners do just that, stretching peppers for a few years. But this encourages disease problems, so gardeners really should replant annually.

- *I stick to the tried-and-true varieties*—the ones that sound familiar. Chances are, more problems are bred out of these hybrids. If you already grow good straight carrots, *then* you may want to experiment on optional sizes and shapes.
- *I pay attention to new varieties* to see if they offer me some advantage. But I try not to be dazzled. I experiment each year, but with just a few. If I'm careful with labeling, I can usually make some extra feet of a wide row available so I can test something out and not confuse it with my main crop. (See extra space between rows #8 and #9 in our upcoming 30- by 40-foot garden plan on pages 20–21, for this very purpose.) And try an oddball like spaghetti squash. It tastes terrific.
- *I look for the varieties* which are labeled on the packet or in the catalog as better resisting insect and disease damage. Choosing varieties which promise to solve such problems before they begin is giving me a real leg up as a gardener. Examples: a tomato "resistant to verticillium and fusarium wilt" and to "root knot nematode"; or, peas "resistant to downy mildew." A lot of work goes on in this area in our universities. Take advantage of it!

Carrot variety dimensions

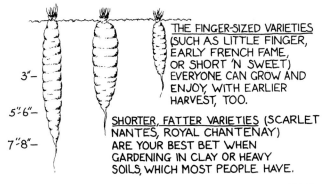

THE FINGER-SIZED VARIETIES (SUCH AS LITTLE FINGER, EARLY FRENCH FAME, OR SHORT 'N SWEET) EVERYONE CAN GROW AND ENJOY, WITH EARLIER HARVEST, TOO.

SHORTER, FATTER VARIETIES (SCARLET NANTES, ROYAL CHANTENAY) ARE YOUR BEST BET WHEN GARDENING IN CLAY OR HEAVY SOILS, WHICH MOST PEOPLE HAVE.

LONG, SLENDER VARIETIES (DANVERS, IMPERATORS) ARE GOOD FOR SANDY SOIL AND SOILS IN EXCELLENT, SPONGY TEXTURE.

Approximate days *from seed* to first harvest and maturity I show in the first column. You'll soon be learning that I like to harvest many vegetables when there's something large enough to eat (baby carrots, beet greens and turnip greens before the bulbs amount to much), so there's quite a range in the following numbers. The low number represents the quickest-growing variety; high number is late-season variety, often best for storage and sweetest flavor. Weather conditions vary from year to year, so these numbers are not hard and fast. In the second column I show approximate days to harvest from transplanting already started plants.

	FROM SEED	FROM TRANSPLANT
BEANS, snap	50–60	
BEANS, lima and butter	80–120	
BEANS, shell (dry)	65–110	
BEETS	60–90	
BROCCOLI	90–120	60–80
BRUSSELS SPROUTS	110–130	90–100
CABBAGE	90–120	80–100
CARROTS	80–120	
CAULIFLOWER	90–120	60–80
CELERY	120–150	80–100
CHINESE CABBAGE	70–90	
COLLARDS	60–70	40–50
CORN	60–110	
CUCUMBER	60–80	50–60
EGGPLANT	100–120	80–90
ENDIVE	80–90	
GARLIC, sets	60–100	
KALE	50–65	
KOHLRABI	50–70	
LEEKS	80–130	(same)
LETTUCE, head	75–90	45–65
LETTUCE, looseleaf	35–50	
MELONS	90–100	75–90
MUSTARD	35–45	

	FROM SEED	FROM TRANSPLANT
OKRA	50–55	
ONIONS, sets	30–45	
ONIONS, seeds	75–100	
ONIONS, plants (greentops)		50
ONIONS, plants (large varieties)		90–120
PARSNIPS	120–150	
PEAS, English	50–80	
PEAS, Southern	60–120	
PEPPERS	90–130	75–90
POTATOES	75–120	
PUMPKINS	100–120	
RADISHES	25–40	
RUTABAGA	80–120	
SHALLOTS, sets or plants	30–70	(same)
SPINACH	35–50	
SPINACH, New Zealand	75–80	
SQUASH, summer	65–90	50–80
SQUASH, winter	85–120	70–100
SUNFLOWERS	80–110	
SWEET POTATOES, slips	90–120	
SWISS CHARD	50–65	
TOMATOES	70–120	50–75
TURNIPS	40–100	
ZUCCHINI	50–60	50–60

Note on herbs: I recommend buying already started plants. Seeds are slow-growing (75–90 days). You can begin to snip from the plants right away (see page 134 for herb information).

Our favorites . . .

ONIONS: They're so easy to grow, and so many can be grown in a very limited space. Buy at least one pound of sets. In addition, already started plants are easy to plant and tend in a wide row. They get large and sweet. I'll also encourage you to grow some shallots, garlic, and leeks—just as carefree—and so full of flavor when homegrown.

TOMATOES: Plant a few varieties—early, mid-season, and late. But don't go overboard. I'd hate to tell you how many times I've seen a small backyard garden ending up like a jungle of tomato vines, producing enough fruit for half the town. Don't necessarily go for size. Generally, the larger the size the longer the ripening time. Flavor is what counts. I always include some Tiny Tim or cherry tomatoes. The plum-shaped tomato is meatier and good for making sauce. And the Pixie is my favorite for early ripening.

CORN: I have a soft spot for Silver Queen, the late-maturing white type. It is extra sweet because, like most vegetables, the longer the growing season, the sweeter and fuller the taste that is developed. Another bonus: birds don't like it as much as the yellow varieties.

LETTUCE AND OTHER SALAD GREENS (chard, spinach, mustard, kale, endive): A few plants go a long way, in a wide row of greens. If you keep them cut, as I'll be showing you in upcoming months, they'll just keep producing. Some varieties good for growing in hot weather are Slo-Bolt, Matchless, Summer Bibb, Buttercrunch or Black-Seeded Simpson. Grown in wide rows, they stay cooler.

BEETS: Besides the familiar hard dark-red globes, I usually plant the Lutz variety, too. They're larger, somewhat softer and sweeter—a cousin of the sugar beet.

SUMMER SQUASH: Most gardeners don't need me as a reminder of how these squashes pose a population problem if you include any more than six plants. Proceed at your own risk!

BEANS: I think the flavor of pole or "runner" beans is special . . . a nice nutty, crunchy taste. And they stay crisp and delicious over a much longer period than do the more popular bush varieties. So try pole beans. Later, I'll show you how to grow beans up a simple means of support. Saves on space, too.

PEAS: Here I offer the opposite advice from that I gave regarding quantities of tomatoes. Everybody loves peas, and often a family runs out just when there are many eager hands to help with picking and shelling. For every two people, get a half-pound of seeds (at least) so you can plant them in a wide block, as I will demonstrate this spring. A half-pound, which costs less than two packets, will produce 20 to 25 pounds of peas. Dwarf varieties do especially well in hot climates, as plants are closer to cool ground.

SUGAR SNAP PEAS: Those delectable edible-podded peas are in a class by themselves, along with snow peas, the flatter, crisper version popular in Oriental cooking. A gardener feels doubly good getting to eat the pods as well as the peas.

TURNIPS: Let's try to get the difference straight between turnips (one pictured here) and rutabagas. Turnips mature more quickly, and I think of them as a summer crop, especially for harvesting as greens. Rutabagas can look exactly like turnips—white to creamy-yellow flesh, reddish skins to plain. There are dozens of varieties of each, so it's confusing. But rutabagas can grow larger and into the fall. *Rutabagas are better for the root cellar*, and many think they're somewhat milder in taste than turnips.

BROCCOLI: All the "cole" family (I like to say cabbage family) crops—broccoli, cauliflower, cabbages, kale, collards, kohlrabi, Brussels sprouts, turnips and rutabagas—thrive in cool weather. Set out young plants *early*—even up to two to four weeks *before* last frost—late April, for me. Or plan them for a fall garden, sowing seeds in August for a really late crop in October and beyond. Or both. Red cabbage, by the way, is less bothered by the cabbage worm than the green, which makes this variety a real plus.

POTATOES: One of the chief thrills of gardening is to dig into soil and come up with a few handfuls of your own new potatoes. I'll be showing you how simple it is to plant and tend a crop of regular or sweet potatoes—so save a few feet in your garden.

CARROTS: All root crops need loose soil to expand in. Yet most gardeners have heavy or clay-type soil, and often get discouraged. A raised bed is my answer, which I show you all about in March.

CUCUMBERS: Yes, they sprawl. But you can train their vines up a trellis. All gardeners can enjoy this summer favorite even if pinched for space.

PEPPERS: Along with eggplants and tomatoes, these heat lovers need a real long growing season. Even gardeners in the Sun Belt (who *could* sow pepper, tomato, and eggplant seeds directly in the ground) prefer, like the rest of us, to set out started plants. The goal for all of us is a big harvest in a short time. In the North, we're in a race against fall frosts; in the South, you're avoiding those summer months.

EGGPLANTS: More and more people are growing eggplants. They're a meal in themselves but combine well with other flavors, too.

PUMPKINS: If you have the space, plan a pumpkin patch. I'll help you to cut down on the room these sprawlers take. I'll also show you how I "autograph" my grandchildren's names right on pumpkins so this fun vegetable brings the family even closer together at harvest time.

DECORATIVE GOURDS: I always plant a few. They're great to give away to garden visitors and as gifts during the holidays. *Any* gifts from the garden are a hit, we've found.

MELONS: I defy anyone to taste a sweeter melon than the one you grow yourself. If there's room, melons are definitely worth a try.

KOHLRABI: I call this the sputnik of the garden. Kohlrabi looks like a space machine, but peeled of its rather tough outer skin it is sweet and juicy inside—solid vegetable. I sometimes eat it like an apple. With its mild cabbage flavor, it's great lightly steamed (and tossed with some butter, of course).

Middle January   15

My space-saving high-yield tricks

CONSIDER THESE IDEAS BEFORE YOU MAKE YOUR FINAL VEGETABLE SELECTION

Succession planting: more fresh vegetables, well into fall

Provided my soil is in top shape (and I try to make sure it is), I often plant two crops in the same space over the course of one growing season. For example, when my first lettuce is finished bearing in July, I dig under the remains, rake smooth, and sow some carrots for the fall. My goal is to stretch the fresh-eating season for as long as I can. You may not want to stretch out the growing season that far. But come November, you'll see that we've got our helping of over a dozen fresh vegetables to eat—over two months *after* our average-date first frost in late September. Proper fertilization and good soil are my secrets for making this work, so don't be afraid to give succession planting a try. I'll let you know when I do this in the cycle of my gardening year. If you're game, you should order twice the amount of seeds you originally planned on. All hardy vegetables do well in succession planting: root crops; cabbage-family crops; lettuces and all leafy greens—like chard, mustard greens and spinach; onions and peas.

Block planting:

I don't plant my peas and beans only in a wide row. I sometimes plant them in a block ten feet square. After we harvest the peas in early July, I plant a block of beans in the very same section. This really takes advantage of my cultivated soil. (Details follow in planting time.) No weeding, cultivating, no lifting of a finger! No staking required for peas— the vines support themselves.

Multicropping:

What I call my "salad row" is five to six vegetables, all I'd need for a crisp salad, interplanted. Pull out a radish, or a carrot, and let a beet become a bit larger. Pull a young onion as a scallion, and the adjoining lettuce plant will keep growing into the space. I add some dill and basil, too, for flavoring

the dressing. It's a great idea to keep the salad bowl interesting—always a slightly different combination of ingredients. For planting instructions, see page 92. If multicropping appeals to you, plan to get some extra seeds.

Raised beds:

I can grow about the longest, straightest, juiciest carrots possible on raised beds. *All* root crops (beets, turnips, onions) have twice as much loose topsoil to expand in as do beds on the level. Raised beds are also good for heat-loving vegetables (tomatoes, peppers, etc.) in areas with short growing seasons because elevated beds stay warmer and drier, surrounded by air and sun on three sides. This is a real bonus for us New Englanders, Rocky Mountain gardeners, and the like. Above all, raised beds are great for gardeners with heavy soils that don't drain well, so they can get on with earlier planting of peas, onions, salad greens in the spring. Now, heavy and clay soil plagues gardeners *everywhere*. Nothing new about raised beds, but I think many people assume at first they take too much work. I'll show you how simple they are to form, with more of their advantages on pages 57 and 58.

Corn Blocks:

Corn grows best in blocks for pollination purposes. Each silk connected to a kernel has to be pollinated with some of the pollen from the plant's tassel. If it isn't, that's when you don't get filled ears. On a windy day, pollen on a single corn row could blow away; in a block it's more shielded and will filter on down through the rows.

I always include four or five rows' worth of corn in my main-crop 30- by 40-foot garden. But since I want to have enough to share with my daughters who don't have the room at their places, plus enough to can and freeze for ourselves, I'm planning on another whole section at my home just for corn. But for fresh eating on the cob for two or three people a block which measures about 10 by 15 feet is plenty.

Potato Patch:

Potatoes are easy to grow. You can even "rob" a few new potatoes in midsummer while the plant simply keeps on producing. You can also dig up a potato plant, take the large potatoes and replant it if you water it well. As with corn, I plant a great big section (100 feet by 40 feet) all to potatoes to keep the whole family supplied through winter. But I also sow 3 pounds of seed potatoes in just a 3-row patch (6 feet by 10 feet) in our main-crop 30- by 40-foot garden for fresh eating, which is plenty for two to three people. You'll find details of how I plant and tend seed potatoes, month by month, as I go through my gardening year.

This short section of a wide row is producing a half-dozen tangy-fresh herbs: parsley, dill, chives, sage, sweet basil, and thyme. As a matter of fact, this two-foot row is more than one family could consume. And nothing can match the flavor!

Flowers: *I enjoy marigolds here and there in our vegetable garden for splashes of color. We also plant a whole nice wide row of annuals for cutting flowers, including asters, strawflowers, zinnias, cosmos, and snapdragons. Soul food!*

Middle January   17

LATE JANUARY

FINAL VEGETABLE SELECTION AND SKETCH

I grow several complete gardens here at my place. I like to experiment with "salad gardens"—real small ones, for summer eating only—just to see how much I can raise in a few square feet. I grow some large patches of corn, potatoes, and squash, as I've already mentioned, to supply our daughters' families with these staples for freezing, and for their root cellars. The plan sketched on the following pages is for my 30- by 40-foot main-crop garden. It's what I think of as a typical garden for families of three or four people who want fresh eating all summer, with surplus to store as well as give away.

Last year, the harvest from this one garden amounted to over $1,200 worth at supermarket prices.

This is not a huge storage garden—that is, all the vegetables a family could eat fresh and preserve for a year. But it's close. Most gardeners I've found attempt to grow this much produce on plots three to four *times* this 1,200 square foot space.

Whether you have less or more space, you can use my plan (see pages 20–21) as a guide.

—**Onions** are one of the first things to plant. I plant lots of sets so I'll have plenty to pull as fresh scallions.

—**March and April spinach** will provide good salad ingredients for two months. Then I'll sow some looseleaf lettuce, then finally carrots and beets for a fall harvest.

—**Notice that my corn block** and pole beans, the tallest crops in this garden, are situated on the north border so they won't shade the shorter-growing things. Sunflowers, the very tallest, are interplanted in the final corn row.

—**When my block planting of peas** is finished bearing, about early July, I'll plant green beans in the same space.

—**Early beets** for the spring will be finished by midsummer and this good space will be planted to one of best-tasting fall crops—kale.

—**A small section of herbs** will go a long way. In just a 1½-foot section I have chives, parsley, sage, basil, and dill.

—**The lima beans** are going to take all summer. When they're finished, after Labor Day, I'll sow a little annual rye grass there as a quick-growing cover crop to protect the soil over winter.

—**It may seem that a lot of the garden is just walkways.** I have to allow for the vine-family sprawlers, and hilling potatoes and corn. But I keep the walkways to an absolute minimum, from 16 to 36 inches depending on the crop. By harvest time, very little soil will be showing.

—**Continuously harvesting outer chard leaves** will keep this vegetable strong and productive to the very end of the year—even after several killing frosts.

—**I always leave some extra space** for experiments. How about Indian corn, popcorn, or peppergrass? Or something especially for the kids like a few "ground-hogging" Big Max pumpkins?

—**There's space for four to six pepper varieties.**

—**Don't YOU plant ten EACH of summer squash and zucchini.** A half-dozen will be tops, ordinarily. Unless, like me, you have many chances to give away your extras.

—**Tomatoes in a row this long** will produce more than enough to eat fresh. So if you don't want to can the surplus, plant half a row.

If all goes well, this is what our 30- by 40-foot main-crop garden will look like in early summer.

—There are many "extras" in this 30- by 40-foot garden. If you cut out sweet potatoes, pole beans, sunflowers, melons of two kinds, succession-planted fall greens and root crops, pickling cukes, shell beans for drying, ruta-bagas, kohlrabi, Brussels sprouts, herbs, and okra (whew!) . . . there would be a garden half this size still producing 30-odd vegetables—all the noncontroversial family favorites!

Notice that for my original plantings, I have three feet of wide-row beets, in three different locations, a total of nine feet. They were planted several weeks apart to stagger the harvest.

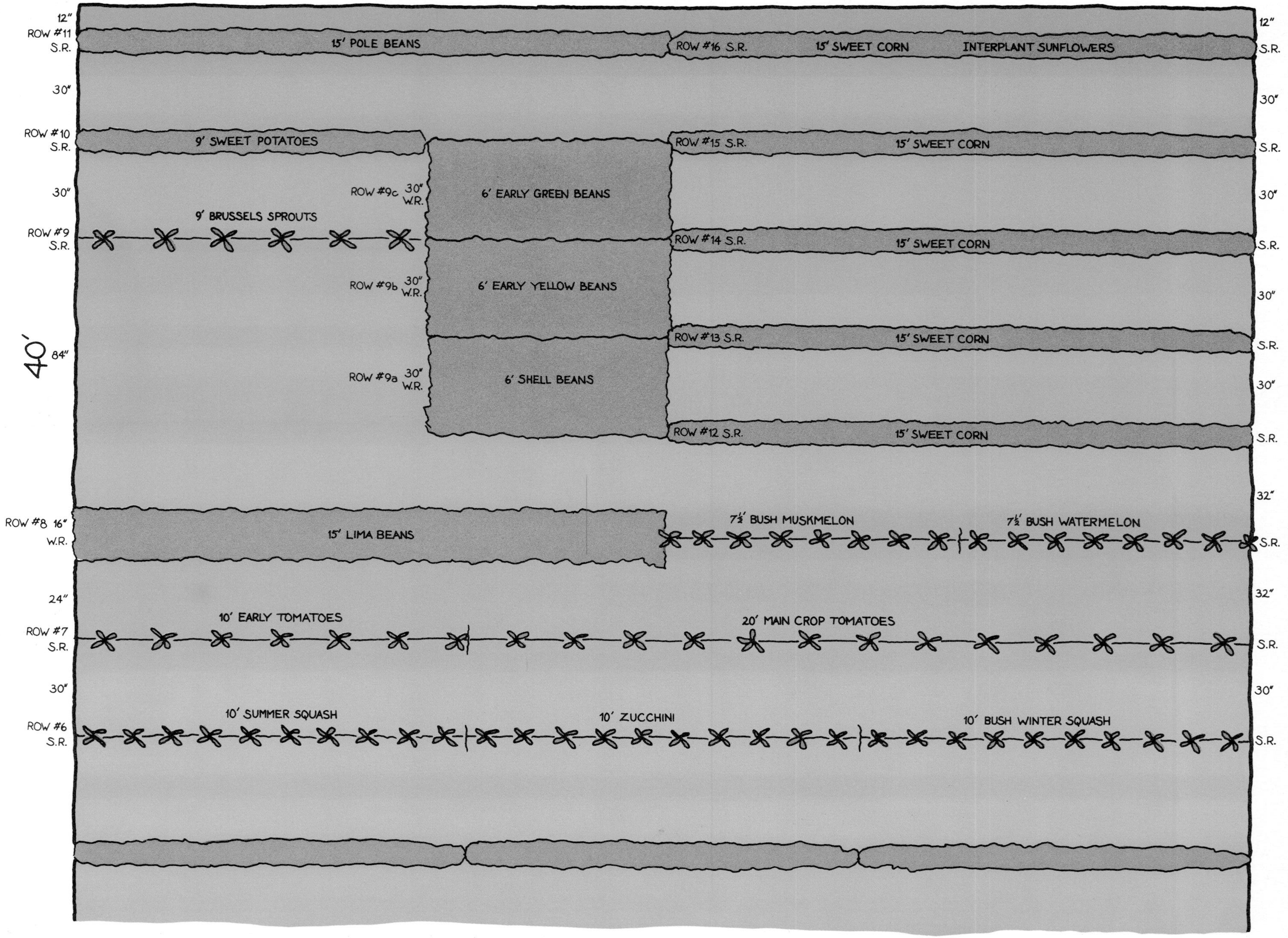

40'
12"
ROW #11 S.R.
15' POLE BEANS
ROW #16 S.R.
15' SWEET CORN
INTERPLANT SUNFLOWERS
30"
ROW #10 S.R.
9' SWEET POTATOES
ROW #15 S.R.
15' SWEET CORN
30"
ROW #9c 30" W.R.
6' EARLY GREEN BEANS
9' BRUSSELS SPROUTS
ROW #9 S.R.
ROW #14 S.R.
15' SWEET CORN
ROW #9b 30" W.R.
6' EARLY YELLOW BEANS
84"
ROW #13 S.R.
15' SWEET CORN
ROW #9a 30" W.R.
6' SHELL BEANS
ROW #12 S.R.
15' SWEET CORN
32"
ROW #8 16" W.R.
15' LIMA BEANS
7½' BUSH MUSKMELON
7½' BUSH WATERMELON
S.R.
24"
32"
ROW #7 S.R.
10' EARLY TOMATOES
20' MAIN CROP TOMATOES
30"
ROW #6 S.R.
10' SUMMER SQUASH
10' ZUCCHINI
10' BUSH WINTER SQUASH

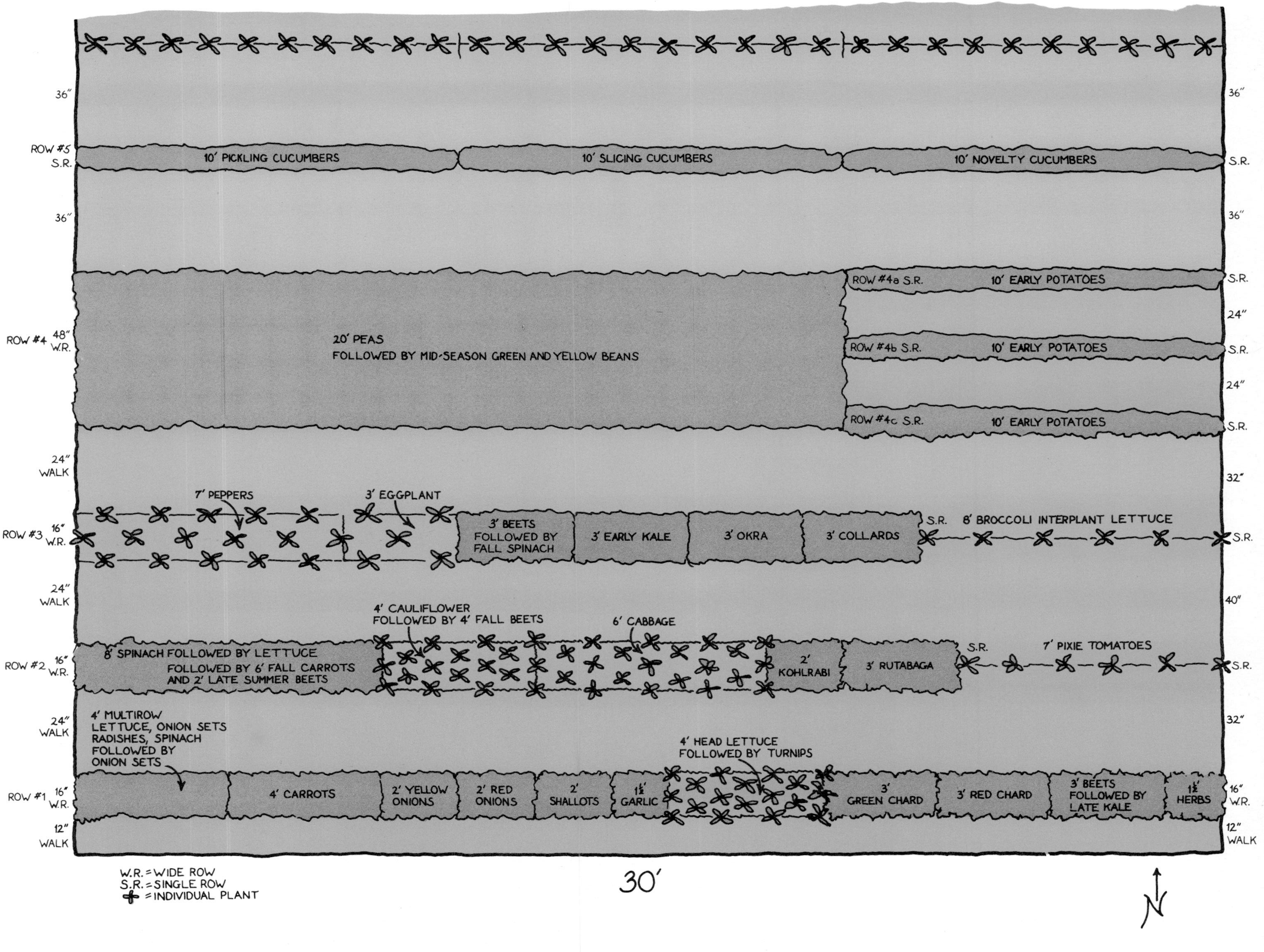
36"
ROW #5 S.R.
10' PICKLING CUCUMBERS
10' SLICING CUCUMBERS
10' NOVELTY CUCUMBERS
S.R.
36"
ROW #4 48" W.R.
20' PEAS
FOLLOWED BY MID-SEASON GREEN AND YELLOW BEANS
ROW #4a S.R.
10' EARLY POTATOES
24"
ROW #4b S.R.
10' EARLY POTATOES
24"
ROW #4c S.R.
10' EARLY POTATOES
24" WALK
32"
7' PEPPERS
3' EGGPLANT
ROW #3 16" W.R.
3' BEETS FOLLOWED BY FALL SPINACH
3' EARLY KALE
3' OKRA
3' COLLARDS
S.R.
8' BROCCOLI INTERPLANT LETTUCE
24" WALK
40"
4' CAULIFLOWER FOLLOWED BY 4' FALL BEETS
6' CABBAGE
ROW #2 16" W.R.
8' SPINACH FOLLOWED BY LETTUCE
FOLLOWED BY 6' FALL CARROTS
AND 2' LATE SUMMER BEETS
2' KOHLRABI
3' RUTABAGA
7' PIXIE TOMATOES
24" WALK
32"
4' MULTIROW LETTUCE, ONION SETS RADISHES, SPINACH FOLLOWED BY ONION SETS
4' HEAD LETTUCE FOLLOWED BY TURNIPS
ROW #1 16" W.R.
4' CARROTS
2' YELLOW ONIONS
2' RED ONIONS
2' SHALLOTS
1½' GARLIC
3' GREEN CHARD
3' RED CHARD
3' BEETS FOLLOWED BY LATE KALE
1½' HERBS
12" WALK
W.R. = WIDE ROW
S.R. = SINGLE ROW
= INDIVIDUAL PLANT
30'
N

A note on crop rotation—sounds like a farm technique, but here's how it adapts simply to the garden.

There's a strain on the soil when you grow the same crop year in, year out. This practice also invites more disease and insect problems, many of which overwinter in that spot—especially cabbage worms and corn borers.

Here are some specific pointers that I follow: Each year I like to rotate my cabbage-family crops (which include cabbage, broccoli, cauliflower, Brussels sprouts), my "nightshade"-family crops (tomatoes, peppers, and eggplants), and my vine-family crops (cucumbers, squashes and melons). For me,

these are the crops most likely to get a fungus disease, so some rotation helps. The greens (spinach, chard, mustard), onions, and root crops are all pretty hardy, and don't seem to put stress on the soil as much as the three families of vegetables I just mentioned.

Don't get overly concerned about insects and diseases. Remember, healthy plants are the most insect-and-disease resistant. If you follow my month-by-month steps for soil care, I wager you'll have your most bountiful, trouble-free garden ever. So what if the bugs claim a bite or two? You'll have plenty left.

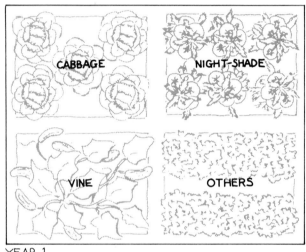

YEAR 1

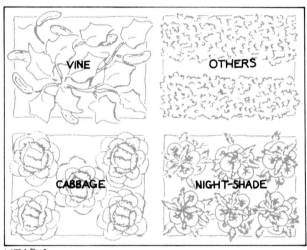

YEAR 2

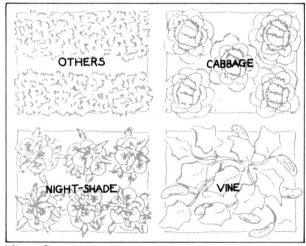

YEAR 3

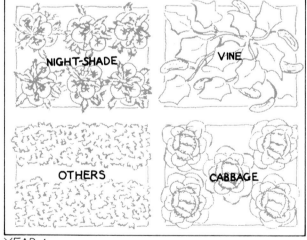

YEAR 4

CABBAGE (CABBAGE, BROCCOLI, CAULIFLOWER, BRUSSELS SPROUTS, ETC.)
NIGHT-SHADE (TOMATOES, PEPPERS AND EGGPLANTS)
VINE (CUCUMBERS, SQUASH AND MELONS)
OTHERS (LEAFY GREENS, ONIONS, CARROTS, BEETS, ETC.)

January reminders . . .

- Review the list of vegetables on page 6. Decide between "musts" and "maybes."
- Sketch garden on paper, with "musts." Enough room for "maybes"?
- Do a preliminary seed-shopping list for the year, including extra packets for those vegetables you want to succession-plant.

Brewing for February . . .

- Equipment preview
- Fertilizers and soil basics simplified
- Vertical gardening and space-saving ideas
- Assembling supplies for starting seed indoors—for those who can't wait to get dirt under their nails!

- Purchasing seeds—through the mail or at the store

- Reconsidering garden site and size

- Checking out my tool shed

- Understanding soils and fertilizers while there's time

- Assembling seed-starting supplies if you want to start early

FEBRUARY

Seeds in hand . . . we're on our way

Here I'm buying my peas and beans by the poundful. *When a store offers vegetable seeds this way, you know you're dealing with an outfit that takes home gardening seriously. And their selections are likely good ones for you.*

EARLY FEBRUARY

SEEDS OR PLANTS

Here's my list of seeds to sow directly in the garden:

peas	collards
beans	kale
radish	rutabagas
looseleaf lettuce	corn
head lettuce	vine crops
greens (mustard, spinach, chard)	onion sets
carrots	okra
beets	dill
turnips	

The big benefit from direct garden seeding is avoiding the shock of transplanting to tender young plants. They won't be nearly as early, but they'll be hardier. And of course this is an easier, less time-consuming way to do it. So it depends on your situation. Unless you live in the Sun Belt, you can't (or shouldn't) sow peppers, eggplants, or tomatoes directly in the garden. They need *heat*, and seed will likely rot in damp, cool garden soil while waiting to sprout. The vine-family crops are also tender, but later, I'll share a trick for speeding up vine-crop germination to allow those seeds to be sown directly in the garden.

Here are the vegetables I buy as young plants:

If you decide not to start any vegetables from seed indoors, which is true for most gardeners, you can shop for the following young plants in a few months:

tomatoes	onions
celery	leeks
eggplant	peppers
cauliflower	parsley
cabbage	chives
broccoli	dill and other herbs
Brussels sprouts	vine-family crops (cukes, melons
head lettuce	and squashes)

I also buy "seed potatoes"—very solid specimens with plenty of eyes selected especially for this purpose. I'm not sure what category these fall into. They're available locally as well as through the mail. This applies also to sweet potatoes and onion plants.

Don't skimp on seeds

If you're like most gardeners, you receive more seed catalogs than you can shake a stick at. Even if you're not planning to buy seeds by mail, hold onto those catalogs. They often contain a wealth of information—sometimes more for a particular variety than you'll find printed on the seed packet itself. If you don't receive any in the mail, buy a national gardening magazine and send away for catalogs of the advertisers.

Last month, I made a plan. Now it's time to pick actual varieties.

Keep a close eye out for "days to maturity," as I mentioned last month. Using the catalogs and the tentative list of vegetables that I want to raise, I begin to zero in on the varieties. *I take my lists to the local stores* and see how much of what I'd like is available right there. If the store only carries one variety, say Nantes carrots, chances are that Nantes is a good bet for me, too. Instead of spelling out all the specific varieties I use here in Vermont, I'm recommending that you be guided by what's on your local shelves.

If you're going to try my wide rows, you're going to need more seed for those crops than you may be used to. Less space is wasted on nonproductive walkways. Weeding and harvesting time will be cut way down. Wide-row-planted vegetables actually choke out weeds. What weeds do sneak through are easy to spot. And so much more harvest is within arm's reach. So don't skimp on seeds. (For quantities, see page 11.)

For an early start—seed indoors

If you decide to buy these vegetables as *started plants*, no need to get these as seeds. We'll buy them in flats a few months from now: tomatoes, celery, eggplant, cauliflower, cabbage, broccoli, head lettuce, onions, leeks, peppers, the vine-family crops (cukes, melons, squashes).

There are reasons I start vegetable plants from seed indoors:

1. The only difference between indoor and outdoor-started vegetables is timing, not taste. By starting plants inside, I gain four to six weeks over starting these crops from seed in the ground. It's a way to get some *real early* crops. When I count days to maturity from seed, it means I can't enjoy the slow-growing, heat-loving vegetables until nearly fall. Starting from seed indoors, I *know* I'll harvest some tomatoes and cucumbers by July. Starting the cabbage-family crops this way (cabbage, broccoli, cauliflower, etc.) lets me get them into the garden early, so they'll mature in late spring. Broccoli and head lettuce and all the cabbage-family crops prefer cool weather, so I can give them more of that by timing most of their growth in early spring. It works better this way in all parts of the country.

2. Another reason for indoor seed-starting is to get varieties that aren't available locally as started plants—hot Jalapeño peppers, Bermuda onions, and other interesting items.

3. It's cheaper to grow your own started plants than to buy them.

"TREATED" SEEDS

To be *sure* I get an early crop, treated seeds make sense. (Treated seeds are always marked on the package.) I like my corn seeds treated because I plant them *months* earlier than recommended for my area (early April, instead of June 1). The coating prevents rotting while seeds are waiting for soil to warm. It also increases the germination rate—an answer to lingering cold spells. Some of the seeds we buy are not treated, but it's easy to treat them yourself. Buy a packet of "seed treatment" or "seed protectant." Rip off the corner of the seed package, then take a book match and dip it into the pow-

der. A small amount will cling to the matchstick. Then slip the whole match into the seed packet and shake it up. An option: simply plant more seeds to ensure a good stand of vegetables, if treated seeds are not for you.

Here are my final choices . . .

	YES	NO	FROM SEED INDOORS	SEWN DIRECTLY IN GARDEN	BUY AS PLANTS
ASPARAGUS	X				X
BEANS	X			X	
BEETS	X			X	
BROCCOLI	X		X		X
BRUSSELS SPROUTS	X		X		X
CABBAGE	X		X		X
CAULIFLOWER	X		X		X
CARROTS	X			X	
CELERY	X		X		X
CHINESE CABBAGE	X				X
COLLARDS	X			X	
CORN	X			X	
CUCUMBERS	X		X	X	X
DILL	X		X	X	X
EGGPLANT	X		X		X
ENDIVE	X				
GARLIC, sets	X			X	
HERBS	X				X
KALE	X			X	
KOHLRABI	X		X	X	X
LEEKS	X		X		X
LETTUCE	X				
Looseleaf	X			X	
Head	X		X		X
MELONS	X		X	X	X

	YES	NO	FROM SEED INDOORS	SEWN DIRECTLY IN GARDEN	BUY AS PLANTS
MUSTARD GREENS		X			
OKRA	X			X	
ONIONS	X				
Sets	X			X	
Seeds	X		X		X
PARSLEY	X				X
PARSNIPS	X			X	
PEAS	X			X	
PEPPERS	X		X		X
POTATOES	X			X	
PUMPKINS	X		X	X	X
RADISHES	X			X	
RUTABAGAS	X			X	
SHALLOTS	X			X	
SPINACH	X			X	
SQUASH	X				
Summer	X		X	X	X
Winter	X		X	X	X
STRAWBERRIES		X			
SUNFLOWERS	X			X	
SWEET POTATOES	X		X	X	X
SWISS CHARD	X			X	
TOMATOES	X		X		X
TURNIPS	X			X	
ZUCCHINI	X		X	X	X

Notice that for many vegetables, it's possible to use more than one way to start them off.

Protein on the shelf. *Because I've got the room, I grow some beans for drying: yellow eye, soy, soldier, navy, and others. It's at this time of year we rely on our stored produce, and we're glad we're gardeners. You'll see how I plant, harvest, and "thresh" dry beans (see page 128), and may want to try a small patch yourself. They're very easy.*

SEEDS SELECTED . . . LET'S TALK SOIL

Think twice about garden *location* and *size*—well before planting.

The ideal garden site has a gentle slope to it—up to 5 percent—enough so that excess rains drain off rather than puddle up. Plants need to breathe, just like we do. We want rain to sink into the roots where they'll do our vegetables the most good. That means *not* having the water stand there in puddles. This chokes off the supply of oxygen to plant roots, and they can drown.

If a slope is *too* steep (15 percent or over) rainfall can wash off much of the topsoil and fertilizer.

Full sunshine all morning and afternoon is also ideal. Plant shorter crops on the south side, and taller ones on the north. That way all plants will receive the maximum sunshine.

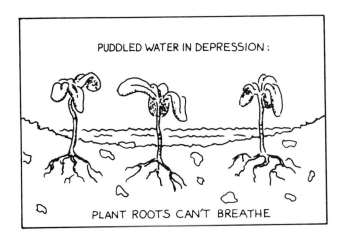

PUDDLED WATER IN DEPRESSION:

PLANT ROOTS CAN'T BREATHE

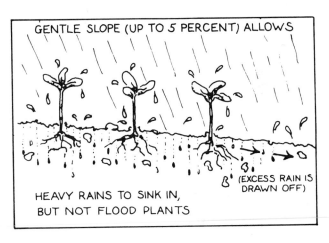

GENTLE SLOPE (UP TO 5 PERCENT) ALLOWS

HEAVY RAINS TO SINK IN, BUT NOT FLOOD PLANTS

(EXCESS RAIN IS DRAWN OFF)

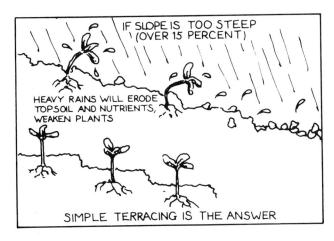

IF SLOPE IS TOO STEEP (OVER 15 PERCENT)

HEAVY RAINS WILL ERODE TOPSOIL AND NUTRIENTS, WEAKEN PLANTS

SIMPLE TERRACING IS THE ANSWER

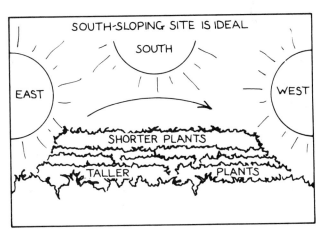

SOUTH-SLOPING SITE IS IDEAL

SOUTH

EAST

WEST

SHORTER PLANTS

TALLER PLANTS

Improving the soil texture by adding organic matter compensates for minor limitations of the terrain.

If I have access to some well-rotted manure, piles of old leaves, grass clippings, or any decomposing vegetation, the best use for any of these will be to build up my soil. It will help to make my soil spongelike and allow it to hold more moisture. If I don't have these materials, now is the time to purchase peat moss or bagged manure.

Then, as early as possible before planting, hopefully even by next month, I till or spade under this good soil-building material into the earth, along with the top layer of turf (in the case of a new garden). There are always some days in early spring that get unusually warm and dry out the soil. I have my own tillers, and so may you, but they're easy to rent or borrow.

Basically, rototillers are powered machines with revolving tines that chop and churn the earth, burying the crusted upper layer and bringing soft, crumbly soil to the surface. A good old spade and elbow grease accomplish the same thing. The machine simply makes it easier.

The earlier I can do some initial turf breaking and soil building before actual spring planting, the better. (This applies to old gardens as well as new. *All* garden soils need to get replenished.) In a few months, *most* (but not all) of that valuable organic matter will be broken down. By planting time,

when I work the soil again, I'll have a brand new seedbed that's much better textured and more fertile than one I break up right at the time of planting. I add some extra fertilizer in this last case, because the soil life and microbes are so busy breaking down the organic matter (turf, sod, etc.) that, for a time, they've used up many of the available nutrients, especially the nitrogen. So my plants will need an extra dose.

At least this is what *I* do when starting to garden in a new area. In fact, when I get the chance, it's best to dig up the new bed the previous autumn. This allows for over half a year before planting— plenty of time to build up the soil, remove large stones, and break up tough clods and vegetation into fine particles. As you'll see in October, this is also what I do to my established gardens.

The size of a garden depends on how many vegetables you want to plant. Last month you saw the plan for our 30- by 40-foot summer garden—a garden which will amply feed three or four people fresh vegetables for half the year, with surplus to store and share. That's growing just about every vegetable in the book. A space 30 by 20 feet, or 600 square feet—the size of the average backyard American garden—is plenty for most families, *especially* using my high-yield wide rows.

If you're really short on space, *you might try my idea of planting some edibles to decorate your lawn, foundation areas, or even a square-foot patch like this one of lettuce.* Anyone can garden, anywhere!

FERTILIZERS— THE SIMPLE FACTS

I remember when all we had on the farm was horse manure. My father always told me which pile was which—fresh as opposed to aged. But I must have forgotten. After I spread the weed-seed-filled, fresh manure on a part of the garden, my father made sure that patch was mine to tend. I learned my lesson. The weeds were impossible! Also, acids can be too strong in fresh manure and burn seeds and seedlings. Manures should be aged at least a few months. Decomposition in a heaped pile builds up enough heat to actually "cook itself," weed seeds included. If you can get *decomposed* animal manures for fertilizer, use them.

We are asking a lot of our garden soil when we expect it to provide us with food in a compact amount of space unless we add to the soil's own supply of nutrients (which normally doesn't support much growth other than low-demand crops like grass, wildflowers, and weeds). So *some* fertilizer is necessary, organic or inorganic, to keep our soil healthy.

I am *not* a "hard-liner" about organic versus non-organic (commercial) fertilizers. I believe the plant takes up the nutrient and doesn't question the source. As I've tried to explain, it's mostly a question of *timing*. I use them all, and *always* in moderation. Too many chemicals can harm plants and soil life. Fertilizers are really plant food. *Organic* fertilizers are materials formed naturally—from decayed plant matter—which are highly concentrated in the elements plants need as nutrition. I'll explain these nutrients in a moment. *Inorganic* fertilizers accomplish the same thing, but are synthetically produced chemical compounds in even *more* concentrated form. As such, they can be stored and handled in much smaller volumes. They're readily available.

Compost is the end product of decomposing organic matter—grass clippings, leaves, crop residues, yard debris, vegetable kitchen waste, and any greens free of pests and diseases. It's rich in basic nutrients. It's often bagged and for sale, along with various composted animal manures. They too get labeled as to their estimated nutrient content—usually much lower than the manufactured fertilizers.

All you need to know about commercial fertilizers, organic or otherwise, is those first three numbers on the bag. They represent the percentage of nitrogen, phosphorus, and potassium—in that order—the important nutrients plants need to grow.

Nitrogen encourages plants to produce dark-green leaves. This is the chief staple in the diet of most vegetable plants. Yellowing leaves means the plant isn't getting enough nitrogen from sources already in the soil. But it only takes a *little* to do the job. We don't want overgrown stems, bushy leaves, and little or no fruit.

Phosphorus stimulates root growth. All plants need it to get their root foundation off to a vigorous start and for growth, but root crops need it especially.

Potassium is critical to the continuing good health of all plants, especially during the second half of the life cycle, in setting blossoms and bearing fruit.

I stick to 5–10–10 or 10–10–10 for my vegetable garden. These are well-balanced fertilizers and are widely available in the stores.

Too much fertilizer is one of the most common mistakes in backyard gardening.

Used in moderation, fertilizer is going to give my plants the boost they need at two critical points: taking off from seedling into healthy young plant; and nearly mature plant getting ready to flower. You'll be using it by the *spoonful*, if you follow along with me.

For every 100 square feet or 10- by 10-foot section of garden, I sprinkle (broadcast) a quart of 10–10–10 or 5–10–10. A 25-pound bag should be plenty for the average gardener, which allows for fertilizing or side-dressing vegetables (applying fertilizer next to the plant, then working it in) twice during the course of their growing season.

Keep in mind that to equal every *tablespoonful* of 10–10–10, I need a handful or two of compost. Most gardeners don't have the time or materials to make compost in sufficient volume to supply all their needs. I use my compost mostly under transplants to gently feed and cushion the root ball.

I think of compost as improving the soil's *texture* (in the short term) more than its fertility. Of course, in *any* garden, you cannot break down clay or help bind together loose, sandy soil without relying on huge quantities of vegetation: chopped-up residues, grass clippings, mulches, and organic material of all sorts. But the immediate *fertilizing* effects of nutrients released in all this decomposition are less reliable than sprinkling a tablespoon of chemical fertilizer, say, around a pepper plant just as it sets blossoms. This is the *only* time peppers need a boost. Otherwise they grow too bushy. More on when and how I use various fertilizers in upcoming months.

I never use purchased chemical fertilizers without organic matter in the garden overall. All I'm saying is, neither can do the gardener's job by itself.

If I get the right pH of 6.5, my vegetables will grow like gangbusters.

pH measures alkalinity/acidity in the soil. Alkaline means sweet, acid means sour. You don't want either sweet or sour soil, but something in between. Below 7.0 on the pH scale is acid; above is alkaline. I remember an old gent when I was a kid who used to taste the soil, ponder it, spit it out, and know whether or not to get out the limestone.

Myself, I prefer a simple soil-test kit available at any local garden center. Some are fancier as kits than others, but all I really need to know is: If pH is too low, how much lime do I need to add to make the soil more alkaline and less acid? If it's too high, how much sulphur do I need to add to lower the pH?

Ground limestone (lime) is also at your garden supply store. It is alkaline and generally is needed to raise the average soil's pH—to the ideal range for most vegetables of around 6.5. The only exception is potatoes, so I stay away from using lime in that section of the garden.

Sulphur in powdered form is available in drugstores. It only takes a half-pound or so to lower the pH of 1,000 square feet of soil one percentage point. But before you do this, I strongly recommend you take a soil sample to a professional—your county extension service agent will know where for your area. It is less likely to have soil that is too alkaline, so it's best to get a specific reading before you add sulphur.

If the pH isn't close to this mid-range, the fertilizer you put in won't work at its best. This has to do with soil chemistry, which I can't explain, so please take my word. The little soil-test kit has all the necessary instructions, so I won't repeat those here and confuse you. (You can—for a few dollars—send a sample of your soil to your state agricultural extension service for a pH test to obtain the most accurate reading.) Next month, I'll show you how I use mine.

I mention fertilizers and lime here, while we're not especially rushed with other garden chores, so we can shop for these supplies and have them right on hand.

We see Mother Nature grow lush forests without interference, so why not a little garden?

Just consider the fact that the leaves of the forest, packed with nutrients drawn from the depths of the subsoil, are not removed as harvested crops. Forests "recycle" their own fertilizer (falling leaves). Home gardening is a little more artificial. Our soils rely on us for amendments. In nature, vegetation that does well in a particular soil ends up flourishing there. Our backyard soil was not necessarily designed for tomatoes, peas, onions, corn, and other demanding plants.

Wood ash instead of lime

The snow's gone for the moment, and since I'm a saver in general, I always have this urge to spread my potassium-rich fireplace ashes over my garden. It's true, ashes are a good substitute for lime. But I recommend going easy with them. One or two

pails per 1,000 square feet is plenty, and just once a year—otherwise the pH level of the soil will be raised too high. Wood ashes will help lawns turn a dark glossy green and keep it that way all summer.

Composters worry less about "trace minerals."

What about nutrients other than the big numbers on fertilizer bags? Zinc, copper, boron, and so forth? Be guided by the actual upcoming results of your soil test—but my experience shows that the vast majority of gardeners have all they need in the way of trace minerals. Gardeners who make compost are breaking down a variety of materials from far-off places, and that's good. Compost is generally rich in trace elements and makes up for the limited composition of a particular region's soil. If there's a problem in your area, telephone your county extension agent, and take in a soil sample for a more thorough test. If you (and your neighbors) simply can't grow a certain vegetable, my advice is to forget it and concentrate on the crops that do well. Gardening is for fun . . . it doesn't have to become a chemistry class.

Some other shopping list items while I'm at it . . .

Here are more things I like to have on hand. In six weeks, I'll be too busy to want to run to the store.

Root crops (carrots, beets, turnips, parsnips) and bulb crops (onions, garlic) and potatoes are especially heavy feeders on phosphorus. About the cheapest and best source of that nutrient is superphosphate (0–20–0). You can buy a bag to have on tap. Bone meal is an organic fertilizer high in phosphorus, and releases its nutrients very slowly. I simply rake it into the soil before planting root crops, and side-dress onions with it for an extra large and succulent harvest. Onions need a lot of nitrogen, too, for big bulbs. More advice on that later.

Soil is the foundation of the garden. Yes, to some extent, we're stuck with what we have. But we can build on it—or build it up, I should say. Remember, people have gardened and grown vegetables just about everywhere on earth.

Organic matter is the key to loose, crumbly soil . . . where heavy rain sinks in deeply to plant roots, yet drains away where it is in excess. Ideal soil sponges up enough moisture to water the plant during the dry spells, yet is porous enough to allow a good flow of oxygen in to plant roots and hard-working microbes.

Clay soil packs down, becomes shiny when wet, and baked tight when dry. Structurally it is formed by flat discs which can be separated by organic matter to allow for a freer flow of air, water, and nutrients.

Sandy soil, on the other hand, is formed by particles which can't cling to each other. Rain and nutrients leach away too readily. Hard, smooth pebbles of sand are *bound together* by organic matter in this case.

Either way I hope you have a better idea of why organic matter is well worth collecting or buying and adding to all garden soils. More on this later.

"Clay" soil (on the left) . . . and "sandy" soil. I have them both.

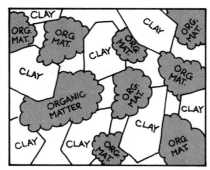

CLAY SOIL PACKS DOWN, BECOMES SHINY WHEN WET, BAKED TIGHT WHEN DRY.

FLAT DISCS OF CLAY ARE SEPARATED BY ORGANIC MATTER.

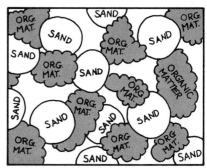

SANDY SOIL PARTICLES CAN'T CLING TO EACH OTHER. RAIN AND NUTRIENTS LEACH AWAY.

HARD, SMOOTH PEBBLES OF SAND ARE BOUND TOGETHER BY ORGANIC MATTER.

The life and times of a Pixie tomato plant:

Just to keep me going, I sow some seeds of the Pixie tomato variety in January. They do a super job for me, seed to harvest in just two months, right indoors. It's a good-sized fruit, two or three times the cherry types . . . up to the size of a plum, say. These tomatoes do not grow very leggy, and the thick, fleshy stem will support a vigorous growth of sideshoots and blossoms. They make an attractive hanging basket, too. You'll find specific advice for indoor seed starting on pages 44–45 in EARLY March, when I begin this activity for real, with many vegetables.

January . . .

February . . .

and March!

MIDDLE FEBRUARY:

I figure if I don't lose some vegetables each year, I know I'm not planting early enough!

I like one never-ending harvest to keep all the space in a garden productive continuously—starting early, then succession planting. We eat fresh from the garden close to three-quarters of the year. I start gardening in early spring as soon as I can prepare a seedbed. This is usually sometime in March, in a warm spell after several dry days. I have to be Johnny-on-the-spot, or else such a break in the normally wet spring weather might not come about for weeks and weeks ahead.

I keep an especially close watch on the first-to-drain parts. If there's an unseasonably warm day that has dried up the soil crust, even in late February or early March, I try to take advantage of it. I roll out the tiller or grab the spade and work up a seedbed for the first crop to go in. And I keep planting, on and off, through summer. There's rarely a section of my garden that sits idle, because I spade under or compost my crop residues, fertilize, then plant a follow-up crop.

My average date of last frost is May 25—roughly, Memorial Day weekend. But I'm a gambler and try to plant about *two months before this point.* Goodness, if I waited till Memorial Day, I'd just have a summer salad garden.

Here's a photo of what my main-crop garden looked like last Memorial Day, to give you a better idea of how far my garden had progressed to that point.

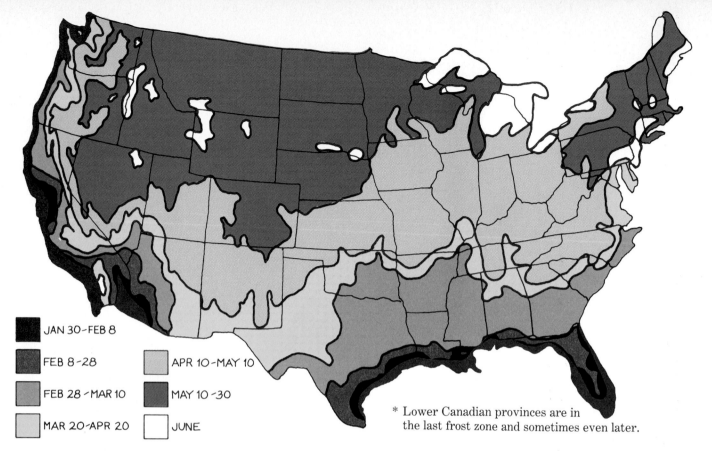

JAN 30–FEB 8

FEB 8–28

FEB 28–MAR 10

MAR 20–APR 20

APR 10–MAY 10

MAY 10–30

JUNE

* Lower Canadian provinces are in the last frost zone and sometimes even later.

Average Dates of *LAST FROST* Each Spring

The next two months, watch me as I plant and *protect* my first seedings and seedlings. I rig up different kinds of simple sheltering devices ("mini-climates") so that those seeds and transplants get fooled into thinking they're taking off in the tropics! I hope all you readers will find the ideas interesting even though you may not use them yourself —just yet! You certainly don't *need* to do all that I do for a bountiful garden. You may choose to plant all in one single day come May or June (January to March in the Sun Belt).

The point I'm trying to make, here in mid-February, is that if I get organized . . . do a fairly detailed plan . . . check out my power equipment and tools . . . have my seeds and supplies on hand . . . I'm ready to go, and really get a jump on spring. You can, too, if that's your goal.

I've got a few more ideas up my sleeve:

Edible landscaping: *Another way to make more productive use of my place. Who's to say rhubarb isn't every bit as attractive as a hedge?*

Container gardening: *How many vegetables are planted in this tub? Well, there's broccoli, cabbage, head lettuce, looseleaf lettuce, spinach, onions, radish, carrots, parsley, peppers, and a tomato plant! In June, I'll show you how I do my outdoor patio planters.*

36 Dick Raymond's Gardening Year

Partners in space-saving: *I always grow some pole beans up a "tepee" of four long poles. Grown this way, there's always room for this deliciously flavored bean. But I found I could even utilize the center space at the base of the poles—for growing a few kinds of lettuce. As the beans develop, they'll shade the lettuce so the greens, shielded, can flourish longer into hot weather.*

Trellises: Help vegetables grow up, instead of out.

Members of the vine family love wrapping their coiling tendrils around the nearest forms of support. I tie them with cloth to get them started. To save space in a garden, I've made this trellis of two-by-twos and chicken wire.

Middle February   37

SUPPLIES FOR STARTING PLANTS INDOORS

Gardeners ask me, "Dick, do I need a pile of expensive supplies to start some of my vegetable plants from seed indoors?"

Absolutely not. If I have a sunny window, that's all it takes to get me started, which I'm going to do next month. (I'll also illustrate using electric grow-lights which are optional and do involve some investment in equipment.) I start with potting soil or potting soil mix. I prefer the mix—part soil and part filler or inorganic binder material, which helps fluff up the mixture. Pure potting soil can be heavy, and seedlings want a nice, loose medium. I add peat moss to stretch any potting soil mix even further.

I always have handy a dark waterproof marking pencil, some little stakes, some kitchen bags or plain plastic food wrap, and regular houseplant fertilizer.

Finally, I need some containers at least a couple of inches deep for planting—peat pots, "Jiffy Sevens," cut-off milk cartons, plastic jugs, Dixie cups, or tin cans. The seedlings are only going to be in these purchased or homemade flats for a few weeks before I transplant them into larger, deeper, *non-cardboard* containers, which won't rob the mois-

ture and quickly rot, as would cardboard egg cartons. (Quart and half-gallon milk cartons are an exception, because they are wax-coated.)

"Todd Planters" are my favorite commercial product. Basically, since the space is a wedge-shaped pyramid, the seedling will slip right out without disturbing its roots, with the main tap root aimed downward for a fast start after transplanting. See page 108 for how these planters work.

Milk cartons are great because I can peel away the sides without knocking apart the root ball and soil. The less shock to the plant, the better. Also, they're deep enough to permit lots of root growth.

Individual pots, being larger, allow for additional growth for the seedlings. But of course, they are bulkier to tend and take up more room than trays of little compartments. Vine crops do not like "their cages rattled," so I generally give them a separate pot.

Be creative. Use up your odd jugs and cans before you buy too much. The truth is, the amount of sunny space you have indoors will determine how many containers you need.

For Sun Belt gardeners

If you're in a warmer section of the country, with no danger of hard frost 30 to 50 days from now, you can start many seeds right now. As a matter of fact, that applies to any phase of my gardening year. I hope you'll feel free to browse ahead at all times and adjust your calendar to mine however it suits you. The basic idea here is the *sequence* of how I go about my gardening.

It is time to start my longest-growing plants from *seed* indoors: onions and leeks (up to 130 days) and celery (up to 150 days). They'll have been indoors about 3 months—90 days—when I set them into the garden in mid-May, for early first harvesting in July and August. If you intend to do the same, follow my easy seed-starting technique, which is explained at the beginning of next month. The seeds of these plants are extremely tiny and don't fare well in garden soil no matter where you live.

Sun Belt gardeners anticipating a long, hot summer . . .

- *Get your crops in as early as possible* and then concentrate on a fall garden. Much of the spring harvest can be enjoyed before the height of summer. And the next plantings won't come into full production until fall, when the sun sets lower in the sky.
- *Definitely plan on wide rows,* with as little walkway space as possible. Let vegetables form a shady canopy over the soil to prevent the harsh, evaporating effects of the sun.
- *Plant lettuce and spinach* under tepees of pole beans, in partial shade. Try some cabbage-family crops between the corn rows. In each case, the taller vegetable is the heat lover, while the shaded crop needs cooler conditions.
- *Don't stake your tomatoes:* Let them sprawl as vines on the ground. This will limit the amount of moisture loss they would suffer as standing plants constantly exposed to the dehydrating wind.
- *Use windbreaks around your garden* for the same purpose: to help your plants and soil hold water.
- *Consider eliminating the thirstiest plants*—corn, potatoes, the vine crops. Greens and root crops are less demanding in terms of water consumption. Celery is about the thirstiest of vegetables. Peas and beans are moderate.
- *Avoid lots of fertilizers in the beginning* of the year, unless mixed deep into the soil. They could encourage roots to form near the surface and become more dependent on regular watering—since soil closer to the surface dries out faster.

LATE FEBRUARY

A trip to my toolshed

It's none too early for me to slip out there at the first signs of spring. What tools need sharpening or other attention? I'll show you how I tend to this next month; for now, I'm just snooping around. Like most gardeners, I'm afraid I've collected more tools over the years than I really use and come to depend on.

I reach for my old reliables so often because they are light. If a tool is too heavy, people won't bother with it.

Basically, all the tools gardeners need for garden care are

an ordinary shovel (a spade)
a good iron rake
a nice, light hoe
and a strong trowel.

Always clean garden tools after use and store them in a dry shed or garage. Rusty tools mean a short life and harder work.

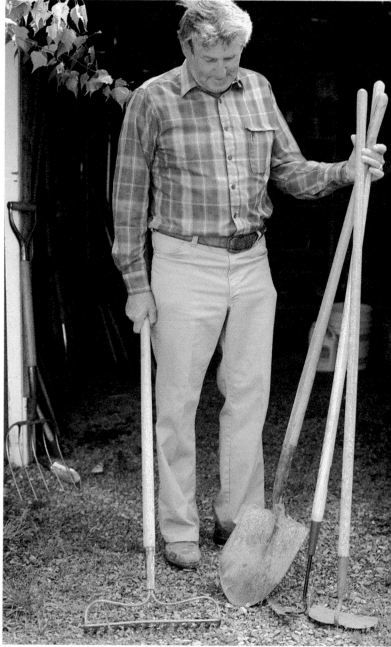

My "must haves" for tools are the really light ones.

For those in the market for power tools . . .

If you've got upward of 1,000 square feet of garden, you probably have considered equipment larger than hand tools. A powered machine like a good rotary tiller does ten times the quality of soil preparation in a fraction of the time it takes me to do it by hand. I said earlier a spade can accomplish the same thing as a tiller. *It* can, but the gardener usually cannot. I've worked all my life. I get plenty enough exercise bustling around in my garden, cutting the lawn, playing some golf, and going fishing.

Because I cultivate large areas of land, I'm delighted to use my powered machines on occasion, but many gardeners often have more horsepower than they need, and so confusion sets in. I'll introduce you to my equipment throughout the upcoming seasons. I did feel readers should know I use labor-saving help when it makes sense. I'm into gardening for the joy of it. If there's a way to make it easier, I go for it.

More on tools later; this is just a winter preview.

Reminders for February . . .

- Complete selection of vegetables. Place mail orders and/or buy seeds locally.
- Browse through a good garden-supply center and get a soil-test kit and the fertilizers you need.
- Gather seed-starting supplies if you plan that activity.

Brewing for March . . .

- Starting, tending, and transplanting indoor seedlings
- Planning pest protection
- Taking that soil test
- More ways to jump the gun on spring, for those so inclined
- Gambling in the garden on peas, onions, and greens!

- Getting indoor seeds and seedlings off to a good start
- Readying for the bug battle
- Planting hardiest crops—onions are indestructible, peas about as tough

- Sharpening tools—a must
- Soil testing
- Building raised beds for guaranteed success

MARCH

First planting—indoors and out

EARLY MARCH Seed starting for an extra

 Remember: this is for earlybirds only . . . to really extend the season. Flats of seedlings will remain indoors from six to eight weeks. Gardening is not an exact science. I could set outside an onion plant that was four weeks old or 12 weeks old—either way it would represent a head start. Approximately three months before my average date of final frost (May 25) is when I begin most of my seeds indoors.

If you don't want to get involved with gardening this early in the game, you have lots of time to buy plants and start seeds directly in your garden, many weeks and even a few months from now. We'll do it together in May in my main-crop garden.

I'm going to start these seeds right now:

Long-growing: Herbs, annual flowers, and some more onions. Celery, and leeks I've already started in mid-February along with the first onions. If I had not, I could start them now. Cantaloupes, watermelons, cucumbers, and squashes need a few weeks less before I set them out; I'll plant these in flats in March.

Extra-hardy (cold-tolerant): Pixie tomatoes; early head lettuce; early cabbage; broccoli; cauliflower.

Main crops: Hot and other varieties of peppers I can't buy locally; main-crop tomatoes; remaining cabbage-family plants; more head lettuce; and eggplants. By saying six to eight weeks indoors, I'm indicating that some plants will be candidates for transplanting outdoors as early as mid-April. If weather was unusually warm, I could put the hardier ones in even earlier, with protection. In a cold, wet year, they may not make it into the garden until mid-May—ten weeks from now. But that's okay. They'll just be larger transplants, with more developed root systems. It's hard to pin down exact timings, and it isn't necessary. The rhythm of gardening changes each year—that's part of the excitement. I try to be ready as early as possible, but try not to fret if Mother Nature plays havoc.

Here's my step-by-step, no-fail system:

Those dreams in the seed catalogs can become reality. Although this may look easy (and it is!) there's always a bit of magic in dropping those tiny seeds and picturing the big, beautiful vegetables a few months later.

Fill the flat with the premoistened potting soil mix you bought last month. (First moisten mix in separate, larger container—it's so light and airy, it can otherwise float away.) Level with a small piece of wood to form a flat surface. Then gently sprinkle seed over the flat—not too thickly. One container of each vegetable is usually enough. (Save the rest of the seeds—many of them you'll be using outdoors, too.)

Press seeds into surface of mix to make good, firm contact. This will speed germination. Then sprinkle more soil mix on top of pressed-down layer —enough to cover the seeds with four times their diameter. For these lettuce seeds, that's about a quarter-inch.

Then place the flat inside a plastic bag and tie it. This way you won't need to water until the seedlings sprout. Don't rest the flat in a drafty spot or in one that's too warm. The top of the fridge is good. *Never* park them on a windowsill *until* the seedlings have sprouted. Look for a home away from sunlight. Strong light will either dehydrate

Here's a diagram to actual scale of how I sow my tiny lettuce seeds.

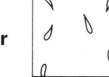

SPACING FOR LETTUCE SEEDS BROADCAST OVER A WIDE ROW.

early harvest

the flat or produce too much trapped moisture, which could rot the seeds before they sprout.

Mark your seedling flats (variety of vegetable and date of planting) with a waterproof pen. One of the most rewarding things about starting seeds is comparing varieties and coming up with new favorites. So, you want to keep them straight as well as record such notes for future reference.

Once seeds become seedlings, they will need full sun. I happen to have a big and sunny south-facing window (I planned the room that way). Others may not have such a window, and may decide to invest in some fluorescent-lighting equipment.

Grow-lights in place of windows:

CONSTANT, STEADY LIGHT TO SPEED SEEDLINGS:

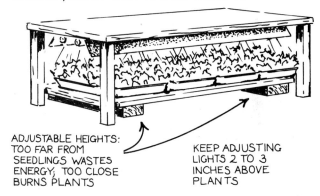

ADJUSTABLE HEIGHTS: TOO FAR FROM SEEDLINGS WASTES ENERGY; TOO CLOSE BURNS PLANTS

KEEP ADJUSTING LIGHTS 2 TO 3 INCHES ABOVE PLANTS

I prefer the cool white bulbs to the more expensive grow-lamps, these latter designed for flowering houseplants. Make sure the lights stay just two to three inches above the plants—not too close to burn, and not so far away that the light effect is weak and wasting its energy on nongrowing areas. The lights should be kept on 16 hours a day and off for eight. Plants need to rest and sleep just like people.

My Seedling Care Tips

- Remove the flats from their plastic "hothouses" as soon as the seeds sprout and break through the surface.
- Seedlings should emerge within two weeks; ten days is average. If they haven't, don't panic. They *can* take up to three weeks, from too much moisture or from being in too cold or drafty a location. No luck is not the end: Replant a flat and improve the germinating-period conditions. Or *buy* them later as started plants!
- Keep the flats watered. Try to check every day. Press with fingertip and if soil is not moist, water. Use water at room temperature to lessen chances of shocking the seedlings.
- Don't drown tender seedlings. Water from the bottom, setting flats within a larger waterproof

dish or tray. Or mist with a fine spray. Otherwise you could knock down the tiny seedlings.
- Add some houseplant fertilizer to the water once a week, but not until three to four weeks after sowing—when they are established and need it.
- Avoid extremes of temperature and keep out of drafts. Seedlings should stay warm, like infants. Pull back from windows on frosty nights. A heat tape (literally, a strip of tape with fine wires inside, which plugs in to become toasty warm) is reasonable to buy at a hardware store and can be set underneath the flats to provide even, moderate warmth—a miniature electric blanket if your house is real chilly and you want to refine this process.

Timetable: As I mentioned, the seedlings will be indoors for March and most of April—about eight weeks—and some will be transplanted to larger containers at least once. They'll be kept outdoors for most of the day for another two weeks—and then, into the garden, sometime in early May.

Greenhouse Gardeners: You are concentrating heat and light (and therefore doing more watering) and could be on a faster schedule than sunny-windowsill gardeners. You should either start later or be prepared to transplant earlier to the garden.

I keep track of the dates I plant from seed—you can, too, at the back of this book.

The best thing about keeping track of planting times, to me, is trying things a bit *earlier* for the following year . . . for gambling on how much sooner we can harvest fresh vegetables. Jot down the dates your seeds sprouted, the first transplanting to larger containers, and so forth. If you complete the back pages of this journal, this time next year it'll be like having your very own gardening book—the closest idea of exactly what you should do and when.

"Sweet potatoes up North?"

For me, gardening has become a lot more than sticking seeds and plants in the soil and hoping for the best. There are so many ways I've found to give a particular plant what it needs. I don't mean to force Mother Nature's hand—it's more working *with* her. My experience is that most plants coop-

erate fully, if given their special requirements.

Sweet potatoes need a long growing season (120 days), so I give them a real head start. I buy or sprout young sweet-potato plants, to have them ready when my soil is.

Sprouting sweet potatoes is this easy . . .

I buy some sweet potatoes at the store and split them. Then I wedge them, cut side down, into a few inches of potting soil mix in an aluminum tray, and soak them well.

The tray is tucked inside of a plastic bag, and I handle it just like my other flats of germinating seedlings. Tender leaves will sprout in a few weeks, and then I'll set this tray in a sunny win-

dow and water it. In about two months, I'll have sweet-potato "slips"—young plants—ready for the garden. Watch for this process in the upcoming sections of the book.

Gardens are appealing to more than humans.

The concentrating of lots of delicious plant material in one place is bound to invite insects of some sort. Just about every gardener will need a duster or sprayer sometime, whether to apply "home remedy" sprays of soap or garlic and hot peppers or a commercial pesticide. Whatever you rely on to keep your plants flourishing, the sprayer or duster had better be reliable. I prefer the smaller equipment that's easy to handle and clean. Gardeners with just a few plants can get self-contained cans of dust and shake it on. But equipment makes sense for all others.

To spray or to dust? Sprays are concoctions we make or buy and generally have to dilute with water. They can be in either liquid or powder form before mixing with water. Dusts, of course, are powdered pesticides and are squeezed or pumped into a fine puff onto plants.

Here's my "two cents' worth" on the sprayer and duster I use. I like this 2-gallon plastic sprayer. It easily hand-pumps up the pressure . . . I can mix a small amount of spray so it's not wasted . . . it's

carried easily by hand or on my back . . . and it rinses out quickly. The "trombone" duster is handy for "spot dusting." I can put the powder inside and leave it in the shed until next time. I don't have to use it all up, as with liquid sprays (which must be made fresh).

PLAIN TALK ON PESTICIDES

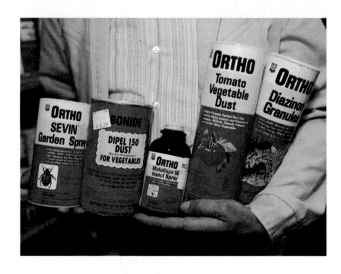

Before I use any pesticides, I follow these basic pointers to beat the bugs (I'll refer you back to this common-sense checklist, in early summer) . . .

- Hand-pick and destroy bugs. An early-morning tour catches them awake, eating, and off guard.
- Choose insect-resistant varieties (so labeled on packets and in catalogs) and healthy transplants at the store.
- Keep weeds under control. The stronger the vegetables, the more insect-resistant to damage they will be.
- Follow the crop-rotation idea I suggested in January planning section. Plant in wide rows; colonies of vegetables are hardier.
- Plant early crops. They tend to be more insect-resistant than midsummer ones.
- Remove and burn or destroy damaged leaves and fruit.
- Always turn under or compost crop residues and weeds—they are breeding grounds and winter hibernation quarters for many insects.

You'll find some of my bug-chasing "home brews" listed in June, on page 132.

Preventive dusting or spraying every other week means big, beautiful vegetables that taste better, too. I'm not satisfied with homegrown vegetables only a little bit better than what we can buy. I like to raise them to the peak of perfection (or at least aim for that). This does involve a few sprayings or dustings, but I should remind you that such a home-gardening pesticide program is nothing compared to the practices of commercial growers. Their sprays are not only much more powerful sub-

stances, but are applied every few *days*. In my lectures I always get questions from strictly organic gardeners. I try to encourage them in their goals, while explaining that reasonable use of chemicals generally produces vegetables fuller in flavor, vitamins, resistant to scab, rotten spots, and insect spoilage. My hunch is that gardening my way, which I know is safe, results in more harvest to eat fresh and to store, plus longer-lasting root-cellar crops—more vegetables in the diet, overall.

Most folks are willing to buy and eat commercially processed vegetables ten months a year yet don't think their backyard supply requires this type of attention.

These 5 products are my basics:

Sevin spray or dust (for chewing damage from bugs you can see)
Dipel spray or dust (for worms—tomato and cabbage family)
Malathion spray or dust (stronger, when Sevin doesn't work)
Tomato and vegetable dust (for tomato flea beetles and potato beetles)
Diazanon (for root maggots and sucking insects like aphids: granules mixed into soil near crops)

I'll discuss these pesticides and a few others (Rotenone and Pyrethrum) more completely on pages 132–33, when I begin using them in June. But it may be convenient for you to buy these now to have on hand.

Dipel, by the way, is a must. It's a nontoxic, bacteria-based material that paralyzes the stomachs of cabbage worms. It can be used without any danger to humans right up to harvest. At last—worm-free broccoli and beautifully formed cabbage!

ANIMAL PESTS?

When uninvited guests turn my wonderful garden into a combat zone . . .

I try some of the following tricks before investing in a fence.

- Rabbits: Black pepper on transplants will cause them to sneeze. Moth crystals will insult their sensitive noses, too.
- Woodchucks: Moth crystals, liquid creosote, used motor oil dumped into their holes (usually close to the garden) will cause them to move on.
- Raccoons: Moth crystals spread at edge of corn patch, *before* they get a taste of corn. Once they do, an electric fence is only answer.
- Birds: Protective netting over corn when just planted and berries near harvest time.
- Mice: Avoid weed-seed-infested mulch. Keep a cat!

- Dogs and Skunks: Fencing should do. You don't want to try to trap a skunk, for obvious reasons!
- Deer: Very tall fencing is required for this intruder—at least six feet. Bags of human hair are thought to repel deer.

I mention this subject now, because fencing—the ultimate animal-protection device—takes time and money, and you may want to plan for (as well as build) it at this time. I've found fencing that is built to last is worth its cost . . . in worry-free abundant harvests. No reason to go ahead, however, unless you *know* you have an animal problem.

MIDDLE MARCH
I'm getting itchy to plant outdoors

I'm keeping a close watch on the moisture content of my soil, especially in those first-to-drain areas. I want to plant as soon as I can.

Most folks simply pick up a ball of soil and decide it's ready to be planted if they can tap the lump apart. Please see EARLY April, page 64, for a demonstration of my foot-stepping method to determine soil readiness—to my mind, a more reliable indication. Sometimes I take a rake and break only the topmost layer of soil that I know is still too wet so as to let some drying air get in there. I repeat this a few days later, going deeper. Even when it rains a lot, there are always a few hours of warm, drying air. So I manage to prepare *some* section very early for my first onions and peas, as well as to build a raised bed for additional early sowings of lettuce, other salad greens, radishes, carrots, and a hardy Pixie tomato.

Onions are the first crop I plant. I'm not really gambling when I plant them very early. As I've often said, you can't kill an onion with a hammer! It must be the sheer force of that bulb, determined to expand, set forth a seedpod, and reproduce itself. I'm all in favor of this amazingly rugged vegetable.

STORAGE TIPS FOR NEWLY ARRIVED SEEDS AND ONION SETS

(a) *Keep bunched onion plants* in refrigerator until ready to plant, so they won't continue growing. Or you can heel them in (digging a shallow trench and covering loosely with soil) in an idle corner of the garden.

(b) *Store onion sets* in cool, dark, and *dry* place. It's hard to "turn them off," but they'll do just fine in their sprouted form, too. Onions are always eager to grow. I usually stagger the planting of onion sets and plants to have a continuous supply of pencil-thin scallions.

(c) *Keep your seed packets* away from an overheated place until planting time. Heat and sun can do damage; cold will not. Best to keep them where it's cool, dark, and dry.

Buying onion sets . . . the convenient way.

Planting an already started onion bulb, called a set, accelerates onion growing. Sets are commercially grown, and I rely on them myself for my main crop because it takes four or five months to produce onions from seed to mature onion. Sets can save up to two months. Don't buy the largest sets. They could split and divide their energy into two lesser onions. Or, because of their head start, they will grow too quickly and attempt to go to seed real fast.

Starting onions from seed . . . huge and juicy are the payoffs.

But I always start off a few of my favorite onion varieties in seed flats with the technique I've already demonstrated. I do that in MID to LATE February, EARLY March at the latest. Transplanted into the garden by late spring, I can count on these onion plants (as opposed to the sets) to develop an especially vigorous root system. They grow nice and large and will be fully mature in September.

I give my onion seedlings a crew cut. *This forces bottom growth and a strong root system.*

Shallots—*the "gourmet" onion with a milder, slightly nutty flavor.*
White Onions—*they grow big and sweet, especially if started early.*
Red Onions—*the large "hamburger" Bermuda types, with tangy flavor.*
Garlic—*to me, homegrown garlic has more punch than store-bought, and is just as easy to grow as its onion cousins.*
Yellow Onions—*not so large, but firm, and keeps best of all for winter storage.*

The next thing I do with my seed flats:

Water, each day if necessary . . . watch how they're coming along. I take the extra trouble to use water at room temperature. Then there's less danger of shocking the seedlings. It looks like they won't be ready for transplanting into larger containers until early April. I let them grow two to four inches first. If yours are ahead of mine, skip to that section—EARLY April—for my transplanting advice.

If seedlings are leggy: don't worry. You'll be transplanting them deeper, next month.

If soil is moldy: don't worry. It won't bother plants. It's due to a tiny fungus in your soil mix, and seedlings soon grow up farther into sunny, well-circulating air space, away from the damp soil.

Another sowing of lettuce

I like to grow several types of head lettuce, crisp and fresh, early in the season. So I usually sow a second, sometimes a third, flat indoors, every few weeks at this time of year. There are tight-growing heads of lettuce (Iceberg) and loose-growing heads (Buttercrunch, Oakleaf, Bibb, Boston). Looseleaf is another term we all use in describing these loose lettuces. Starting next month, I also sow *all* types of lettuce seed directly in the garden in wide rows. These sowings I do *not* try to thin and harvest as individual heads. Much more on this to come.

Time to sow flats of vine-family crops

Toward the end of March I start off my cucumbers, melons, summer and winter squashes. See page 54 for specifics.

Best ten minutes I could spend this month:

DID YOU REALIZE MOST HOES ARE SHARPENED ON THE <u>WRONG</u> SIDE?

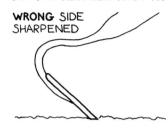

WRONG SIDE SHARPENED

THE ANGLE AND ACTION OF HOEING IS DIFFICULT BECAUSE THE HOE "RIDES" THE SOIL—IT WON'T GO IN. THE WORK OF BREAKING UP THE SOIL ISN'T HAPPENING, SO MORE FORCE IS APPLIED. THE DANGER OF DISTURBING PLANTS AND THEIR ROOTS IS INCREASED.

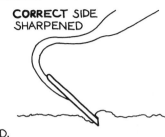

CORRECT SIDE SHARPENED

SHARPENED <u>THIS</u> WAY, LIKE A BEVELED WOOD CHISEL, THE HOE SLIDES INTO THE SOIL, TO BREAK IT UP. THE USER GETS LESS TIRED, AND MORE HOEING GETS DONE!

PLANT PROTECTION MATERIAL I USE . . .

I'll be ready when the good weather arrives (good for planting, but still quite chilly for tender transplants). So I look for material that will retain heat, transmit light and trap moisture, but protect young plants against unfavorable weather.

Hot caps

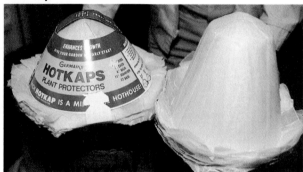

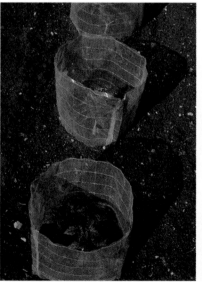

Newspapers and pieces of plastic about the house and shed are always available to hold in heat and moisture. But I think neatness counts too. So I have a supply of these heavy waxed paper caps that are molded just right for the job, featuring a flat brim on which to pile the surrounding dirt as anchor. They're very reasonable in cost and available at most garden centers.

Three-foot chicken wire within heavy plastic sheeting

On a grander scale, this flexible material can make a nice long tunnel or a mini-greenhouse or a collar to protect transplants. I buy this convenient covering at a retail garden center. This is just one of several interesting new plant-covering materials and products. I'll show you next month how easily I put this idea to work.

LATE MARCH:

The most appreciated perennial vegetable—
ASPARAGUS

Many visitors to my place in midsummer stare at asparagus ferns and wonder how in the dickens the spears grow! I figured the basic story was worth repeating.

After the few months of spear harvesting—from mid-May to early July for me—it's important to give the roots a chance to rest. This allows the spears to grow up into tall stalks and ferns, which in turn replenish and strengthen the roots and crowns for yet another upcoming spring harvest season.

Now is the one chance all year to . . .

Cut and shred the old stalks. Here in March, the plant material from last year has turned brown and died, its job complete. But very shortly the crowns will start again to send up spears. So before they do, and so as not to injure them or interfere, I cut down the old stalks. This makes for a much cleaner, disease-resistant bed.

Do a thorough weeding. For the same reasons, this is the chance to loosen the soil, destroy weed seeds, and take out weeds that might compete with the asparagus.

Stir up soil with a rake before new shoots appear. Perennials are difficult to cultivate in general. But asparagus is easy at this moment in time. Its roots need oxygen and cultivated soil the same as all plants.

Work in fertilizer for the upcoming crop. Anyone who has an asparagus bed doesn't need reminders to harvest it! Asparagus gets a workout, and deserves its annual feeding. I broadcast ten quarts of commercial fertilizer every 50 feet of row (or one quart for every five feet). I sprinkle a half-foot from the crowns in all directions. Again, this is the month to do it, with dormant crowns or budding shoots still a good two or so inches under cover.

To plant a *new* asparagus bed, see my suggestions on page 110, in May.

"SOD-POT" SEED STARTING

Before the days of plastic trays, my family simply started their seedlings from upside-down cubes of cut-up lawn sod. We called them "sod pots," and they work with any kind of seed. Since cucumbers and the vine-family crops are especially sensitive to having their roots disturbed, I often use this method—one-step seeding; then they go right into the garden.

Vine crops do well in sod pots.

1. First I cut the sod from an out-of-the-way edge of lawn into squares. The roots of grass hold the top two inches of sod together, so the sod "pots" are about two inches deep. They look like pieces of sheet cake. (Don't buy commercially grown sod for this—it's just an idea, if you have lawn sod available, to save time and money.)

2. Then I shove the seed down into the soft, spongy side of the sod, and cover with the grass roots and loose soil. I use treated seed, as there are so many live organisms in the sod.

3. I put them in a flat and soak the sod cubes . . .

4. . . . then cover, as I do all my seed flats, in plastic bags.

5. They'll sprout within a week to ten days.

When the cuke or melon plants are well-established, six or so weeks from now, they are all ready for direct transplanting. ▶

SOIL TEST NOW—SUPER HARVEST LATER

I take several trowelfuls of soil, digging down about six inches, to get a representative sample and mix them up in one pail.

A simple soil test comes with easy instructions. It takes only a minute or two. This is as close to scientific as gardening ever has to get! Adjusting the soil pH to approximately 6.5, which most vegetables prefer, is like baking a dish at the oven temperature stated in the recipe. It's something easy —not intimidating—that gardeners can do to increase chances for a successful outcome.

I keep my seedlings well watered. Vegetables grow like jungle plants. In a very short period of time they go from seed to fully mature crops. This process consumes *lots* of moisture, so make sure they have it, indoors or out.

I'm sure I grow more plants than the average reader. Soon, I'm going to have this many plants to tend in flats and pots, so . . .

The easy art of sun-trapping

This arrangement is a little elaborate for most gardeners, but I thought readers would find it useful for two reasons: (1) It shows what you can do to give plants a big leap before planting with just some plastic and a south-facing exposure, and (2) it shows you don't need a fancy, multi-thousand-dollar unit if you're serious about greenhouse gardening. Jan and I sure enjoy puttering around in this toasty little cottage filled with greens.

The same concept can work inside your house on a scale of a few feet.

Arrange your indoor vegetable plants in south-facing windows. Put a table near the window for this month and next, to give them more room. At night, build a cover of plastic around your plants, without bending them, to keep them warmer.

. . . I came up with my low-cost "sunpit-greenhouse."

Pamper them! They'll love it and will do just great. (Don't *you*, with some extra attention?)

My sunpit works on the same principle as an outdoor cold frame, to use another term. If a cold frame was slightly submerged and backed up against a south-facing wall or foundation or earth mound, it would be a miniature version of my rig. But I can't work with plants outdoors for another month yet.

56   Dick Raymond's Gardening Year

First thing I do when my soil is workable: I build some

RAISED BEDS

Please refer to page 64 next month for my footstep soil-readiness test. The whole garden need not be ready now to use this easy, helpful technique, just a three- by five-foot section.

I could grow *any* crop on a raised bed. But they are especially appropriate for *early* crops, *root* crops, and *heat-loving crops*.

Here are the many reasons I've revived this age-old gardening idea:

(1) Elevated beds stay eight to ten degrees warmer than soil at ground level. So they dry out faster, too. Good news for early tomatoes.
(2) Raised vegetables don't get the beating from mud splatter and heavy spring rains.
(3) Creates drainage ditch for excess rain.
(4) Doubles the depth of loose, crumbly topsoil— so these beds are great for all root crops trying to expand into soft earth.

(5) Clay soil sufferers: here is the best remedy I've found for growing long, straight, juicy carrots and the largest, best bulb crops.
(6) Perfect for wide-row planting. Kneeling next to raised beds to plant, tend, and harvest makes gardening as easy as reaching to your lap.
(7) Avoids compacting adjacent soil . . . helps vegetable plant roots and soil organisms get all the oxygen they need to flourish.

Sun Belt gardeners: try reversing this scheme and plant in the lower, cooler "walkways," in combination with trench irrigation.

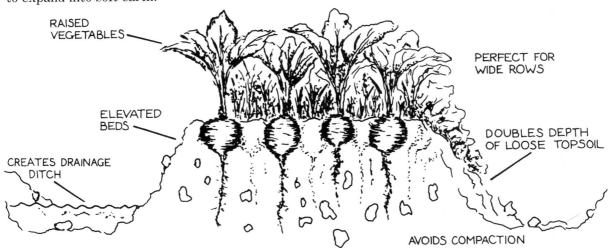

RAISED VEGETABLES

PERFECT FOR WIDE ROWS

ELEVATED BEDS

DOUBLES DEPTH OF LOOSE TOPSOIL

CREATES DRAINAGE DITCH

AVOIDS COMPACTION

Follow me step-by-step

First of all, I give my soil the best texture I can. I till it thoroughly with a powered machine or I spade it at least eight inches deep. The extra time and effort spent in soil preparation is well worth it, considering all the advantages of raised beds. In early spring I can only do this on my driest garden section.

3. *The seedbed is formed by lightly dragging the flat end of the rake over the crown of soil—right along the center.*

1. *I set up two sets of stakes with string to mark off a 24-inch wide row. Then I go down one side of the row and pull loose soil up and into the central portion of the row. Then I switch sides, standing in the area where I took the soil, and draw soil up and into the row opposite me.*

4. *You can see the bed is elevated to about one-half the width of the rake—over eight inches. That's all there is to it.*

2. *I follow this easy procedure down the length of the row for as far as I'm planning a raised section.*

5. *High and dry after spring rain.*

And now I plant my first outdoor crops—peas and onions on a raised bed.

Usually, before I plant anything, I *lightly* broadcast some fertilizer like 10–10–10 over the entire garden. I didn't have a chance in this case, because my soil is still pretty wet. So I added some directly to this particular seedbed . . . not much . . . about a handful for every two to three feet of wide row. I worked this fertilizer into the top of the seedbed, a few inches deep, to avoid direct contact with the seeds I'm planting. (Seeds would be burned by the harsh chemicals.)

I always gamble on a very early sowing of peas. They're tough seeds and can tolerate a cool (or cold!) wet spring start. Raised beds keep them higher and drier. I don't side-dress peas for a later boost—they don't need much fertilizer.

As I think you can see, I hand-cast the seed over the entire row, trying to keep the peas approximately two to three inches apart in all directions. I used "treated" seed (see page 27). Using the back of a hoe, I tamp the peas down firmly into the soil to make solid contact. Finally I draw loose soil from each side of the raised bed to cover the peas to about four times their diameter, or one inch. Then I firm the seedbed again. (See pages 70–71 next month when I sow my main crop of peas in a block.)

Wide-row planting on a raised bed:

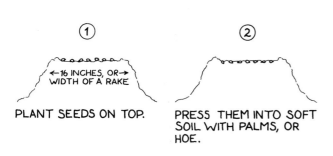

① PLANT SEEDS ON TOP.
← 16 INCHES, OR → WIDTH OF A RAKE

② PRESS THEM INTO SOFT SOIL WITH PALMS, OR HOE.

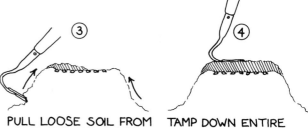

③ PULL LOOSE SOIL FROM WALKWAYS AND SIDES, TO COVER SEED TO 4 TIMES ITS DIAMETER.

④ TAMP DOWN ENTIRE SEEDBED SO SEEDS MAKE CLOSE CONTACT WITH SOIL AND MOISTURE.

I'm going to put in a few feet of onion sets on the rest of that raised bed. (It's too early to plant the onions I'm starting from seed, or those purchased as young onion plants. The hard, dry sets are much more rugged and further along in their development.) I sometimes plant 144 onion sets in one square foot of soil. We'll pull two out of three of them (96) to eat as scallions, eat 24 mid-season, and still leave 24 to grow to full size for storage. Onions are *very* heavy feeders. You'll be seeing that I add fertilizer to my onion rows every two weeks, for superlarge bulbs.

I take the onion set firmly by the pointed end and shove it completely into the loose soil to the full depth of the set. However deep I plant the onion set is as far down as the onion is going to grow. As it expands, it will wind up with the bulb being two-thirds above the ground, which is good. But many people think in order to leave room for that expansion the set should only be partially sunk. No. You

want lots of earth contact for vigorous root development. I often crowd them, at least one every three or four inches, and usually as close together as one or two inches. As I said just before, I'll be pulling most of them as scallions before they elbow each other, anyway. As a matter of fact, the "harvest-thinning" of scallions in a wide row actually helps to aerate and loosen the soil for the remaining, maturing bulbs. So don't worry about overcrowding.

Then I tamp down all the sets with the flats of my palms. This way, the rooted end of the onion makes good contact with the soil and its moisture—and it will take hold and sprout new roots that much faster.

March is none too early for me to plant my *first* sowing of some spinach seeds—the hardiest green of all. Please see pages 77–78 next month for my wide-row hardy seed planting instructions.

Reminders for March . . .

- Risk a little spoilage—your early harvest will be worth it. Peas, onions, spinach and lettuce are my first crops to go in.
- Keep seed flats watered and warm.
- Keep an eye peeled for first-to-dry garden areas.
- Build a raised bed—for wet-soil and heavy clay problems especially.

Brewing for April . . .

- Soil preparation, for real
- Progress in my gambler's garden
- Foolproof transplanting to larger containers
- "Block planting" main-crop peas
- Wide-row planting more hardy seeds and greens
- Direct seeding in my outdoor "plant bank"
- The three-foot salad row!

- ✔ Preparing soil as soon as ground is dry enough

- ✔ Adding some fertilizer—carefully

- ✔ Transplanting indoor seed flats to individual containers

- ✔ Understanding the basics of my wide-row planting system

- ✔ Garden-planting the early crops: salad row, root crops, more onions, cabbages, potatoes, and peas by the "block"

- ✔ Speeding up seedlings: cold frames and ideas to try

1. The time I spend spading (or tilling) the garden is the most productive thing I do in the garden.

2. There's no special technique to thoroughly spading the soil. Just patience and elbow grease. But a deep seedbed really pays off. More on this shortly.

3. I like to mix the soil as much as possible while spading. Here I'm placing the shovelful onto the previously dug section. I don't trample this soil and pack it back down.

4. I wait to rake smooth right until just before sowing seeds. It's easier to break down those clumps in heavy soil even further, once they air-dry.

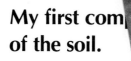

My first com[plete] of the soil.

Last month when I ga[rdened] of peas and onions, I [ ] in a fast-to-dry area o[ ] 30- by 40-foot main-cr[op] plots free for two impor[tant] the soil several times [before] planting; and I'll be able [to] so vegetables all at once [ ] tion of the soil.

Of course, power equipme[nt] tion much easier and fas[ter] tiller, I overlap half (taking [ ] only half the width of the se[ ] the soil even finer.

Early April

APRIL

Warm days . . . soil's ready

My easy "soil readiness" test

NO *Footprint leaves shiny surface, indicating too much moisture content near surface to till or spade soil.*

YES *Footprint looks dull, meaning excess water has drained away.*

Broadcasting lime.

Last month I discussed
wet or dry-and-workable
foot-stepping test is mo[re]
If my soil test indicat[es]
add that now, if I didn't
the test last month. I spr[ead]
ground limestone for ever[y]
erally my garden require[s]
four to five years. Sandy s[oils]
often. I prefer to lime in th[e]
too, when we are most act[ive]
anytime before, during, or j[ust after till]
ing. Lime is just ground lim[estone]
soils, and won't interfere with
Since the limestone takes a [while to settle]
down, the full effect won't rea[ch the gar]
den for many months. To repe[at]
expensive soil test kit, avail[able at garden]
stores, is really worth it. If y[ou are plan]
recommend you do it now. Cauti[on:]
ning to plant potatoes, leave tha[t area alone]
as potatoes love acid soil.

Whether by hand or machine, it's important to go seven to eight inches deep.

I always get my seedbeds worked a good seven to eight inches down. I want my seedlings and young plants to be able to *sink* their roots as easily and quickly as they can. In a finely prepared seedbed, more moisture and nutrients can make contact with tiny root hairs. Can I do a better job by hand, with my spade? Not really. If you want my honest opinion, I find a machine is worth the expense and effort to break up tough clods and to bring lower soil to the top. A powered rototiller with rotating blades can save hand-digging if you have a large enough garden.

Should you own a powered garden machine?

Soil preparation is the most important job of gardening, by far. So I recommend not skimping on this task. You can put in the hand labor yourself or rent or borrow a tiller. No need to purchase a machine for a garden much under 1,000 square feet.

For larger gardens, what size tiller?

If your soil has been worked before, and is in pretty decent shape, get something *light* in weight (three to four horsepower)—a tiller you and other members of your family can comfortably handle. I've used them all, and I say most gardeners saddle themselves with more engine horsepower than they usually need. (I use six-, seven-, and eight-horsepower tillers because I'm handling several gardens, some a quarter-acre each.) If you're confronting perennial weeds, tough sod, untilled earth, heavy or clay soil . . . rent or borrow a heavier-duty, rear-tined tiller for the initial work. Such tillers chop up and bury material far more easily than other types with tines mounted in the front. But you'll likely only need a smaller machine with less horsepower for seedbed preparation and cultivation thereafter. Many people hire a custom tilling service to do their spring ground-breaking, then rely on hand tools for the balance of the season.

All soil contains millions of weed seeds. Turning the earth brings seeds to the surface where, at this time of year, some will be destroyed by the weather and others will sprout and be uprooted by a subsequent tilling or spading.

THE HIDDEN GARDENERS

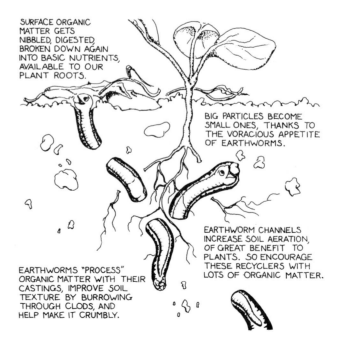

SURFACE ORGANIC MATTER GETS NIBBLED, DIGESTED, BROKEN DOWN AGAIN INTO BASIC NUTRIENTS, AVAILABLE TO OUR PLANT ROOTS.

BIG PARTICLES BECOME SMALL ONES, THANKS TO THE VORACIOUS APPETITE OF EARTHWORMS.

EARTHWORM CHANNELS INCREASE SOIL AERATION, OF GREAT BENEFIT TO PLANTS. SO ENCOURAGE THESE RECYCLERS WITH LOTS OF ORGANIC MATTER.

EARTHWORMS "PROCESS" ORGANIC MATTER WITH THEIR CASTINGS, IMPROVE SOIL TEXTURE BY BURROWING THROUGH CLODS, AND HELP MAKE IT CRUMBLY.

The earthworm is a gardener's best friend. Don't worry if, when you are rototilling or spading your soil, you happen to cut some of them in half. You really won't harm that many.

Have you ever noticed when you're spading, digging for fishworms for instance, that the first shovelful you take out is full of worms, the next one only has a few, and as you go on, fewer and fewer? Well, the reason is that as you are jarring the ground, you're actually driving the earthworms down. This is the same thing that happens when you prepare your soil. And even if you do cut them in half, the section with the head will usually go on and live.

Earthworms work 24 hours a day, seven days a week, breaking down organic material and depositing nutrient-rich castings. All you need to do is give them a little bit to eat—leaves, grass clippings, soft crop remains—and they'll multiply very fast. Don't *buy* them. With food, they'll come to you in droves.

In October and November you'll see me do a lot to enrich my garden with large doses of organic matter.

Surface organic matter gets nibbled, digested, broken down again into basic nutrients, available to our plant roots.

Earthworms "process" organic matter with their castings, improve soil texture by burrowing through clods, and help make the soil crumbly.

Big particles become small ones, thanks to the voracious appetite of earthworms.

Earthworm channels increase soil aeration, of great benefit to plants. So, encourage these recyclers with lots of organic matter.

With commercial fertilizer, I broadcast and work into the top four to six inches of soil about a quart for every 100 square feet. In other words, an ordinary ten-quart pail will hold enough for 1,000 square feet of garden.

I generally use 5–10–10 for this chore. Then there won't be *too* much nitrogen. As I've mentioned, the biggest mistake gardeners make regarding fertilizers is being too heavy-handed in their use. Throughout the upcoming months I'll recommend moderate use of additional fertilizers, crop by crop, both during planting and as side dressing, once the plants are established.

A high-phosphorus fertilizer like bone meal (organic) or superphosphate (chemical) gives onions and root crops extra strength. This, too, could be worked into the seedbed, about six inches deep, just before seeding.

Quite often it's 8–16–16 or 6–8–8 that's available in various regions. Go with your local supplier. The advantages of chemical fertilizers, as I mentioned earlier, are ease of handling and instant availability of nutrients for plants.

With organic fertilizers, which I also use, I work them in several weeks before planting, so the worms and soil microbes can break down the material into smaller nutrient units. Organic matter creates a slow release of nutrients, not necessarily timed to the needs of the plant cycle. If the organic matter was "fresh," then the soil microbes would have to work overtime using up most of the soil's nutrients.

I prefer not to rely on manures, although they are wonderfully good for the soil and I believe in recycling wastes. But too many weed seeds are in-

I lightly fertilize the entire garden each spring.

gested by animals. If you do have a source for manure, make sure it's well composted—at least two months old. Otherwise, it, too, like chemicals, can burn seeds and plants with its strong acids. And the *heat* of the manure while it's decomposing in the soil can prevent the germination of seeds.

The best things about organic fertilizers are that they greatly improve the *texture* and sponginess of the soil and they make valuable use of otherwise discarded material such as grass clippings.

I try to add my organic fertilizer just before planting with chemical fertilizer—or a day ahead. If done much sooner, some of the nitrogen, especially, will have leached away. It's important to mix the fertilizer in to avoid burning seeds and tender transplant roots.

Early April 67

Time to transplant my tomatoes into larger containers.

If there are any leaves on the little stem, I snap them off. I only do this on tomatoes during indoor transplanting; not on eggplants, peppers, and others. Tomatoes are very rapid growers and at this stage I want to favor development in the underground side.

I set the young seedling all the way down on the bottom of the carton . . .

. . . and fill it almost full with a soil mix, firming the soil down so that little root clump makes good contact with its new environment. I soak the cartons well, then set them in trays and place them back in my sunny window, or in my sunpit-greenhouse. I'll keep you posted on their progress, so you'll have a good idea when the tomatoes outgrow these containers and are ready for the next. As with all transplants, don't forget to water gently.

It's been four to five weeks since I planted my tomato seeds. Common sense says when flats of seedlings need more "shoulder room." If they are not transplanted into larger containers once they're four to six inches tall, they'll grow leggy—stretching to reach the light. And they'll be spindly, competing for the available nutrients and moisture.

With most vegetables, I'll do this transplanting just once during their indoor stay. But I like to transplant my early tomatoes *twice* before they go in the garden. This way, I know I'm forcing the largest, deepest ball of roots, and strongest, thickest stem. Foliage and fruit are not the goals at this point. In other words, planting them deeper sets them back, halts the development of leaves and reconcentrates the effort toward strengthening those roots and the stem.

I do the same now with eggplants and peppers.

In my part of the country, if I'm going to grow these heat-loving, heavy-producing vegetables, I find another transplanting now into individual containers will really reward me with a big crop. Once I've set up to transplant my tomatoes, it's no more effort to do the peppers and eggplants, too.

- *Head lettuce* I plant indoors every few weeks, to have a continuous supply on hand. Lettuces grow quickly and dependably.
- *Melons and squash* can be started now. You can use my sod-pot idea I illustrated last month (on page 54), or whatever method is handy. But if you don't want to start vine-family members indoors, I've got an easy trick I'll share with you later for speeding them up in direct garden seeding. Most gardeners direct-seed vine crops.
- *Celery, onions, and leeks* I sowed *thinly* in flats in order to *avoid* the effort of transplanting them to larger containers—they are such tiny seedlings to handle.

These well-established celery plants had a long head start indoors.

NOTHING BEATS THE TASTE OF
NEW POTATOES

As you can see in my 30- by 40-foot plan, I sow three ten-foot rows, 36 inches apart. This crop is my *early* crop—it will yield about two bushels, enough for three or four people to eat fresh for a few months. My main crop will go in in May.

Potatoes are so satisfying to grow. They let me "steal" some early tubers, which the plant replaces while pumping more energy into the ones already formed. They'll be a real success if I purchase good certified seed potatoes. I don't want to rely on those left over and sprouting in the root cellar. Planted, these are apt to carry some disease.

To try different varieties, sometimes it's fun to buy regular potatoes at the market to use for planting, like Idaho bakers for us gardeners in the east. I leave them in a cardboard box in the sun for about three weeks before planting, which triggers them to grow. Once they've sprouted, I can plant them. They form small green clusters, which start growing fast when planted. Purchased seed potatoes don't need this three-week preplanting boost; they haven't been treated with a sprouting inhibitor.

Make a furrow *with a tilted hoe in well-prepared soil. As you can see, I use those stakes and string to allow for three feet between rows. That way there's plenty of soil for hilling up the plants later on. The new potatoes form in the ground above the seed potato. So, the lower that furrow, and the looser the surrounding soil, the heavier the harvest.*

If the seed potato is small, *I don't cut it up. Large ones I usually cut into quarters—just so there are two or three "eyes" per quarter or piece of seed potato. Coating each of the seed potatoes (cut up or whole) with sulphur, available at drug stores, helps to prevent rotting and also makes the soil a little more acid, or "sour," as I say, which potatoes favor. To do this, I simply shake the seed potato and the pieces in a small paper bag of sulphur. Buy the smallest amount you can—¼ pound is enough —but don't worry if you have a surplus because it stores well.*

Next, a quarter-handful of superphosphate *(0–20– 0) goes into the furrow at ten- to 12-inch intervals —the distance between the seed potatoes. Bone meal would also be good. This adds an extra dose of phosphorus for root growth, as I explained on page 33 back in February. (You can also use low-nitrogen 5–10–10.) Remember I already added a balanced fertilizer over the entire garden plot, so one of these phosphorus-rich sources is in addition.*

It's important to cover fertilizer *with a few inches of soil so the seed potato won't make direct contact with it. The soil should be dry at this point, so there's little danger of its rotting the potatoes.*

Notice that the cut side *is planted down, so that the eyes, or sprouted buds, are aiming upward toward the direction of their potential growth. By the way, I cut the larger seed potatoes a few days before planting, which gives them a chance to heal and to be less vulnerable to disease organisms.*

Cover with four to five inches *of loose soil and tamp down the row. Just as soon as the first leaves sprout through the soil, I'll "hill them up"—but more on that later.*

How to seed a block planting of peas or beans by hand

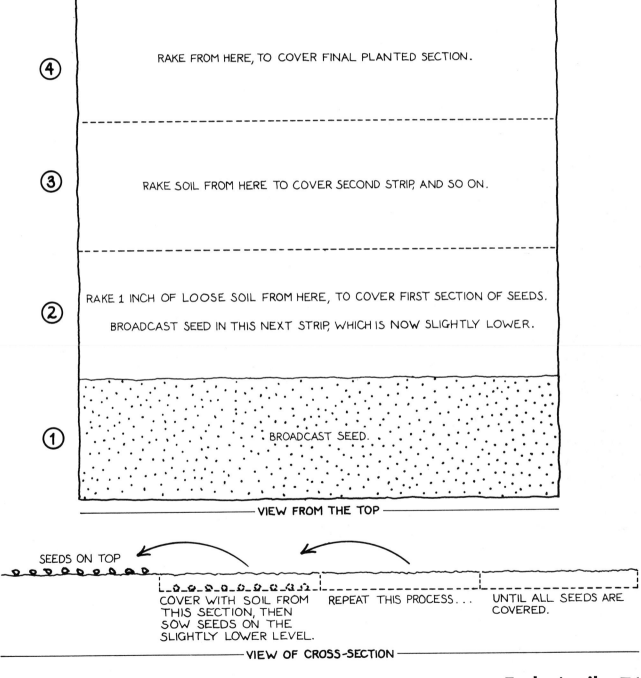

④ RAKE FROM HERE, TO COVER FINAL PLANTED SECTION.

③ RAKE SOIL FROM HERE TO COVER SECOND STRIP, AND SO ON.

② RAKE 1 INCH OF LOOSE SOIL FROM HERE, TO COVER FIRST SECTION OF SEEDS.

BROADCAST SEED IN THIS NEXT STRIP, WHICH IS NOW SLIGHTLY LOWER.

① BROADCAST SEED.

— VIEW FROM THE TOP —

SEEDS ON TOP

COVER WITH SOIL FROM THIS SECTION, THEN SOW SEEDS ON THE SLIGHTLY LOWER LEVEL.

REPEAT THIS PROCESS...

UNTIL ALL SEEDS ARE COVERED.

— VIEW OF CROSS-SECTION —

NOTHING BEATS THE TASTE OF *NEW POTATOES*

As you can see in my 30- by 40-foot plan, I sow three ten-foot rows, 36 inches apart. This crop is my *early* crop—it will yield about two bushels, enough for three or four people to eat fresh for a few months. My main crop will go in in May.

Potatoes are so satisfying to grow. They let me "steal" some early tubers, which the plant replaces while pumping more energy into the ones already formed. They'll be a real success if I purchase good certified seed potatoes. I don't want to rely on those left over and sprouting in the root cellar. Planted, these are apt to carry some disease.

To try different varieties, sometimes it's fun to buy regular potatoes at the market to use for planting, like Idaho bakers for us gardeners in the east. I leave them in a cardboard box in the sun for about three weeks before planting, which triggers them to grow. Once they've sprouted, I can plant them. They form small green clusters, which start growing fast when planted. Purchased seed potatoes don't need this three-week preplanting boost; they haven't been treated with a sprouting inhibitor.

Make a furrow *with a tilted hoe in well-prepared soil. As you can see, I use those stakes and string to allow for three feet between rows. That way there's plenty of soil for hilling up the plants later on. The new potatoes form in the ground above the seed potato. So, the lower that furrow, and the looser the surrounding soil, the heavier the harvest.*

If the seed potato is small, *I don't cut it up. Large ones I usually cut into quarters—just so there are two or three "eyes" per quarter or piece of seed potato. Coating each of the seed potatoes (cut up or whole) with sulphur, available at drug stores, helps to prevent rotting and also makes the soil a little more acid, or "sour," as I say, which potatoes favor. To do this, I simply shake the seed potato and the pieces in a small paper bag of sulphur. Buy the smallest amount you can—¼ pound is enough —but don't worry if you have a surplus because it stores well.*

Next, a quarter-handful of superphosphate *(0–20–0) goes into the furrow at ten- to 12-inch intervals —the distance between the seed potatoes. Bone meal would also be good. This adds an extra dose of phosphorus for root growth, as I explained on page 33 back in February. (You can also use low-nitrogen 5–10–10.) Remember I already added a balanced fertilizer over the entire garden plot, so one of these phosphorus-rich sources is in addition.*

It's important to cover fertilizer *with a few inches of soil so the seed potato won't make direct contact with it. The soil should be dry at this point, so there's little danger of its rotting the potatoes.*

Notice that the cut side *is planted down, so that the eyes, or sprouted buds, are aiming upward toward the direction of their potential growth. By the way, I cut the larger seed potatoes a few days before planting, which gives them a chance to heal and to be less vulnerable to disease organisms.*

Cover with four to five inches *of loose soil and tamp down the row. Just as soon as the first leaves sprout through the soil, I'll "hill them up"—but more on that later.*

We love peas so much, I plant them by the "block"—the widest of my wide rows.

For years, we never seemed to have enough peas—those sweet and extra-early treats from the garden. Sowing my peas in block formation—anywhere from three or four to ten feet wide, by ten feet long—gives us the harvest we all enjoy. But as I'll be showing you, there is absolutely no work involved—which I'm happy to skip. You'll see I'm about to plant a 4- by 20-foot block in our 30- by 40-foot garden. A diagram seems simpler than photos for demonstrating this technique.

All I do is plant and pick!

As legumes, peas and beans are really self-fertilizing. In fact, they leave more nitrogen in the soil than they use up because small nodules on their roots manufacture and store it. So when I plant them very close together like this, I know I'm not overtaxing my soil.

Peas seem nearly indestructible. But I give mine a little boost. I toss them in "inoculant"—actually a bacterial powder—which speeds up the nitrogen-fixing process on their roots. It's available in garden centers.

Of course peas can be planted in one of my wide rows (see pages 77–78, a little bit further along this month, for my detailed wide-row planting instructions). Either wide-row or block-planted, peas don't need staking or trellising. Yes, some of the vines on the outside edges flop over and yield slightly less. But overall, production per square foot of garden is greatly increased. They're kept cooler, weed-free, and are self-supporting.

I keep my indoor flats and pots well watered. On sunny days they get thirsty. Seedlings should be a few inches high by now, so they can be watered from the top. Reminder: For those of you planning to buy some flats of started vegetables, I'll be giving you some shopping advice next month, on page 104, closer to when you'd likely start your summer garden. Remember, my indoor plants about to go into the garden are for an especially early harvest.

Onions don't take long to get a foothold. And there are no weeds yet.

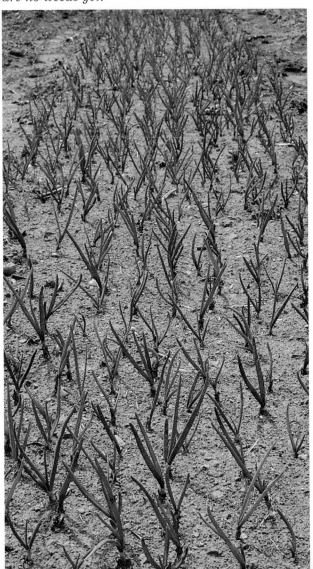

I'm about to gamble on some early corn . . . even though this spring has been the worst! I don't expect the best harvest from it, but I always like to try. I'll be showing you next month how I plant—and protect—my corn in order to harvest about the earliest crop possible. Those suggestions are on pages 100–101, in May, if you want to look at them and join me *now*, for a real gamble. If this first sowing isn't 100 percent successful, I'll still get some harvest. I never know when the weather will be in our favor, and if I didn't plant some corn *extra early*, I'd have to say, "Gee, I wish I'd planted . . ." Some years I've had corn seedlings freeze three times, die back, resprout, and still yield corn!

More early vegetables I plant—

Radishes	Garlic
Onion sets and seeds	Spinach
Kale	Leaf lettuce

If some soil is workable in one of my many garden plots, these are the next crops I try to slip in. If you, too, want to do this, skip ahead to pages 77–78 of this month where I illustrate in detail my wide-row planting technique, appropriate for each of these crops. In a few weeks, I won't be gambling when I again plant these vegetables and many others in my 30- by 40-foot main crop garden.

Early April   73

I practically *guarantee* a great garden with my "plant bank."

I thought you'd like to see this, whether or not you try it yourself.

I decided it would be good to come up with a mini-greenhouse that was easy and cheap and effective for the starting of plants right in the garden, as an option to indoor gardening. I wanted an arrangement where I could crowd lots of seedlings into one compact area, then cover it with plastic. The photo below shows what the plants will look like several weeks after sowing seeds. I sowed all the vegetables out here that I did indoors: onions, celery, leeks, all the cabbage-family crops and head lettuces. But don't start tomatoes, eggplants, peppers or the vine crops here—the soil, even under cover, is still too cool in April.

Here's how simple this is to do:

First I get some half-inch black plastic piping. It comes in a roll. I simply bend arches so they'll be about two feet high in the center and insert them into holes drilled into two-by-four framing on the ground. Plastic is stretched over this easy-to-make structure. By the way, I work in extra organic matter (peat moss will do) so that when seedlings are eventually dug up, their roots will stay more intact. I can crowd the seedlings because they're going to be transplanted elsewhere when they are a few inches high. So, there's *no* thinning! I just sprinkle seeds of one variety over one square foot.

Covered up for a few weeks, my plant bank will retain all the heat from the ground and sun, plus the moisture. Blanketed this way, the soil can't freeze as it still could in surrounding areas. With this much space to start out seeds, I have plenty of chance to raise annual flowers, too.

But I'll be sowing those later. They're tender.

In no time, I'll have ready-to-plant seedlings. This method of seed starting doesn't give me seedlings and ripe crops earlier than those I start from seed indoors. But because the seeds have been started outdoors in garden soil, they are exceptionally rugged, cold-tolerant, and healthy. I always have a few extra seedlings to share, something all gardeners enjoy doing.

MIDDLE APRIL
Just before the busy season

 Right about now I'm doing lots of indoor transplanting into individual containers. That's why I mix up a batch of what I call "my soil bank."

I dig up some of my best topsoil, well-rotted compost, perhaps some sandier soil if it seems too heavy, and mix it all together. Plants at all stages of their growth appreciate loose, rich soil. It makes sense.

How much time did this take? Ten, fifteen minutes. And I enjoyed the crisp early-spring air. I try to inspect my trays of seedlings every day. The larger plants need watering almost daily.

My sweet-potato halves are beginning to produce shoots, or slips. Some may say it is too much trouble to keep these watered. I do buy many of my seedlings, but I always enjoy a few projects like this just to watch the expression on the faces of my grandchildren as the plants finally form.

I gambled and lost. These peas I sowed in March in this particular patch had to survive three solid weeks of rain. Many seeds rotted and weeds came up in their place.

No problem with losing the first round. There are more peas that were started a little later, and they're coming on strong. I sow peas thickly, and once sprouted, weeds can't compete with them.

If you look close, to the right of the onion, you'll see nibbled leaves. The radishes are always so abundant that their bushy leaves distract insects from chomping on the other crops. We're now eating the radishes and first crisp leaves of spinach. The lettuce is still too small.

Progress in the salad row . . .

some protected situation like under a hot cap or a tunnel, need a transition period to accustom them to being totally exposed to the elements.

I wouldn't spend all day in the sun first time out after winter or I'd burn to a crisp. I allow my plants the same caution. This process of acclimatizing is called "hardening off."

I set my plants outside in full or partial sun for two to three hours the first day, then bring them in. Next day, I put them out in the sun for three or four hours, then set them in the shade for another few hours. A windbreak is important; the plants are tender and can snap. After three or four days of gradually increasing their exposure to sun, I leave them out all day long. I don't have to water them as often outdoors because there's more humidity outside than indoors. By the second week, it's safe to leave them outside all night, if it doesn't freeze.

Plants will respond to a little care. Try it and see!

Now is the time to harden off the rugged cabbage-family members, plus the greens, celery, leeks and onion plants. As planting time draws close, every few days I check to see if it's warm enough to bring some flats of heat-loving seedlings outside for a morning or afternoon.

 ## "Hardening off."

Just remember that plants can sunburn, windburn, overheat, freeze, and go into stress—just like us. If we keep remembering that plants are like people, we end up way ahead as gardeners. Transplants raised indoors, or purchased from a garden center (greenhouse-raised), or otherwise grown in

---

My hay-bale cold frame.

Another option: this mini-greenhouse is nothing more than a half-dozen or so hay bales and an old window sash. Clear plastic, secured with stones or bricks, works also. The biggest difference between this and my sunny window is that a cold frame makes for lower nighttime temperatures, which toughens young plants faster. It allows the trapping of more heat on a sunny day and more moisture than is generally available indoors. Placing a cold frame against a northern windbreak and facing it horizontally toward the south helps, too.

I've set some seedling trays in here to harden off. But you could also sow some seeds, like spinach, onions, and lettuce, directly in the soil for later transplanting.

Midday ventilation is a must! A thermometer tucked inside is the safest way to prevent overheating of plants. Prop up the cover or remove it when it hits 80 degrees or higher inside the cold frame. On the other hand, on very cold nights,

cover the entire cold frame with an old blanket. This should prevent the inside temperature from falling any lower than the mid-forties.

LATE APRIL

I use the same basic technique of *wide-row planting* for sowing most of my hardy crops

Planting time for hardy seeds (spinach, head and looseleaf lettuce, chards, turnips, carrots, beets, peas, and onions)—if the weather's on your side

I'm going to plant the rest of the "salad seeds" in our 30- by 40-foot garden, now that I've had the chance to work the whole plot into seedbed condi-

tion. Most years, Jan and I start eating when the seed packets tell us to plant. But spinach, lettuce, and the chards do not mind a light, lingering frost.

1. Set up string and stakes.

This may seem like more work, but it actually saves time. I use two good-sized wooden stakes and a heavy twine that unwinds easily without getting tangled. String-and-stake guidelines help me to make the very most of a given amount of garden space. They keep me organized.

2. Drag rake along string the length of the row.

This accomplishes the "marking" of a wide-banded row, over which I scatter the seeds. Rakes are usually 16 inches wide, so that's the width that has suited me for most purposes. This step also smooths out the seedbed and brings nice moist soil to the surface.

3. Sow the seed over the whole 16-inch band.

How thick to broadcast the seed? Don't worry. My way to thin is easy if you've been too heavy-handed with the sowing. That situation is easier to correct than sowing a sparsely seeded row. More seed is better than less seed also in terms of guaranteeing an *early* crop . . . the survival rate is higher, should there be some frost damage.

Important: Just don't use much more than a *few feet* of a wide row for any one crop. You'll be amazed at the quantity a wide row produces.

Late April   77

4. Firm down seeds so they make contact with the soil.

The steady downward pressure of my hands is good enough for this step—or I also can press down with the back of my hoe.

You can prevent the over-sowing of tiny seeds like lettuce and carrots using an old garlic shaker or a large-holed saltshaker. Thinning carrots by hand is time-consuming, so this trick helps control their sowing to a reasonable spacing. Think of sowing grass seed when sowing a wide row: moderate, even coverage is the idea.

5. Draw soil from the sides, enough to cover the seeds four times their diameter. That means about a quarter-inch for fine seeds like lettuce, dill, carrots . . . a half-inch for larger ones, like beets and chards . . . one inch for peas and beans. Then firm again.

6. Then water with a fine spray to get the ground damp.

See my Easy Seed and Plant Depth Planting Guide, in early May, pages 96–97.

CROPS TO PLANT IN GARDEN WIDE ROWS:

from seed:

—all of the greens: looseleaf lettuce, mustard greens, endive, chard, spinach, kale, collards
—the root crops: carrots, beets, rutabagas, turnips, parsnips, radishes
—kohlrabi
—okra
—all peas and beans
—basil, sage, chives, dill, and many other herbs
—all onions: from seed, plants, and sets, including shallots, garlic, and leeks
—almost all flower seed, too

as started plants:

—celery
—all other cabbage-family crops (except kohlrabi): cauliflower, broccoli, Brussels sprouts, Chinese cabbage, cabbages themselves
—head lettuce
—peppers
—eggplants
—onion plants

I use radishes as row markers.

Many of the crops I sow directly in the garden take their time to germinate and develop. Radishes sprout fast and are ready to eat in a few weeks. Sowing them broadcast-style right in my wide rows along with parsnips, carrots, chard, and many other vegetables, I can see clearly the outlines of my rows. But that's just the start of their bonus benefits . . .

You can see how much more mature are the radish plants than these slower-growing melons. Radishes make a protective—not to mention edible—border, keeping out accidental footsteps.

Harvesting the radishes interplanted in wide rows frees up extra space for the oncoming vegetables to develop. And the abundant radish foliage (first to appear in the spring garden) distracts insects from its tender younger vegetable neighbors. You'll see more ways I use my friend the radish as we proceed.

I demonstrated building a raised bed last month (pages 57–58). As you could see, a raised bed automatically becomes an elevated wide-row platform. I've never grown straighter carrots or plumper, juicier beets than when I combined these two great planting techniques. Notice, I always mix my carrots with white icicle radishes.

◀ *And I generally plant all of my root crops in wide rows on raised beds. Remember that for the largest, juiciest roots and bulbs you can add bone meal or superphosphate to the soil. To get this buried a half foot, I sprinkle it over the row on ground level, before pulling soil from the two sides to form the elevated platform.*

Carrots in a 16-inch-wide row on a raised bed

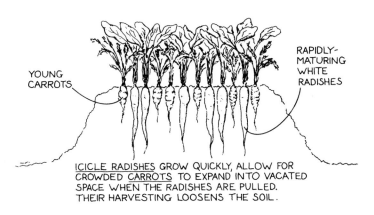

YOUNG CARROTS

RAPIDLY-MATURING WHITE RADISHES

ICICLE RADISHES GROW QUICKLY, ALLOW FOR CROWDED CARROTS TO EXPAND INTO VACATED SPACE WHEN THE RADISHES ARE PULLED. THEIR HARVESTING LOOSENS THE SOIL.

Time to do final indoor transplant of tomatoes—

The only vegetables that I transplant twice

Peel off the old container—don't yank plant out.

Pinch off all but topmost leaf cluster. Leaf growth isn't as important to the tomato plant at this stage as its root system. By stripping off most leaves and burying former "stem," most of the length of the plant, now underground, will sprout roots and greatly strengthen the foundation.

Place the plant into the new container, then fill it with soil mix so that just the top leaf clusters are showing. The whole stem and root ball must be submerged. Otherwise, the plant will grow tall and leggy, with cramped roots. Here's the before and after of what we've just accomplished. Cut-off plastic jugs are good for this project, too. Now, back they go to my greenhouse. Or your sunny window. Or whatever.

The next transplanting step will be out into the garden!

My way to transplant tomatoes aims for the sturdiest, healthiest plants possible.

Using nice large containers like half-gallon milk cartons lets that young tomato plant have lots of room to develop a rugged root system.

Try to disturb root system as little as possible. The less shock, the faster the plant will take hold in new container.

Don't forget to firm the soil. And water regularly. Once a week add some ordinary houseplant fertilizer such as Miracle-Gro, or anything that dissolves in water.

A word on celery, leeks, and other small-seeded, slow-growing crops . . .

Celery needs lots of water as its roots are close to the surface. To force strong roots, I generally transplant celery somewhat deeper than it was originally. As for my onion plants and leeks, I keep the scissors handy and keep them trimmed to about four or five inches: I want those bulbs and lower stems to get fleshy.

I use radishes as row markers.

Many of the crops I sow directly in the garden take their time to germinate and develop. Radishes sprout fast and are ready to eat in a few weeks. Sowing them broadcast-style right in my wide rows

along with parsnips, carrots, chard, and many other vegetables, I can see clearly the outlines of my rows. But that's just the start of their bonus benefits . . .

You can see how much more mature are the radish plants than these slower-growing melons. Radishes make a protective—not to mention edible—border, keeping out accidental footsteps.

Harvesting the radishes interplanted in wide rows frees up extra space for the oncoming vegetables to develop. And the abundant radish foliage (first to appear in the spring garden) distracts insects from its tender younger vegetable neighbors. You'll see more ways I use my friend the radish as we proceed.

And I generally plant all of my root crops in wide rows on raised beds. Remember that for the largest, juiciest roots and bulbs you can add bone meal or superphosphate to the soil. To get this buried a half foot, I sprinkle it over the row on ground level, before pulling soil from the two sides to form the elevated platform.

Carrots in a 16-inch-wide row on a raised bed

I demonstrated building a raised bed last month (pages 57–58). As you could see, a raised bed automatically becomes an elevated wide-row platform. I've never grown straighter carrots or plumper, juicier beets than when I combined these two great planting techniques. Notice, I always mix my carrots with white icicle radishes.

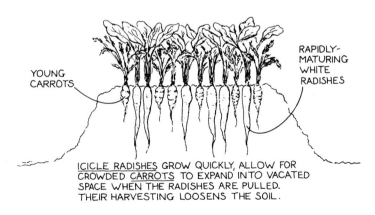

YOUNG CARROTS

RAPIDLY-MATURING WHITE RADISHES

ICICLE RADISHES GROW QUICKLY, ALLOW FOR CROWDED CARROTS TO EXPAND INTO VACATED SPACE WHEN THE RADISHES ARE PULLED. THEIR HARVESTING LOOSENS THE SOIL.

Summing up the advantages of wide rows:

- Grow two to three times the vegetables that you would grow in a conventional, single row of the same distance.

- Reduce the amount of cultivated garden taken up by walkways.

- Once established, this clustering of plants crowds weeds out.

- Wide rows of vegetables form their own living mulch, keeping soil cool and moist. They *conserve* water, slowing the moisture-evaporation rate.

- Wide rows make harvesting conveniently within arm's length. That applies to planting and all aspects of tending. Less tramping around in the garden means less compaction of the soil.

- Harvest is staggered because of the naturally occurring differences in maturity rates between larger and smaller plants. Even when all plants are the same size, harvesting some while they're young (always sweet and tender) allows remaining ones the shoulder room to expand. Variety in size means variety at the table. I often harvest the *larger* plants first, allowing the littler ones to catch up to good size.

- "Stretching the harvest" is another way to say the above. Instead of handling one large harvest of the same vegetable, more evenly grown in a single row, you can eat fresh from a larger, overall quantity of vegetables often right into the fall with the last to pick. Beets, carrots, and cabbages are good examples.

- There are always a few weak plants among a group of vegetables. In a wide row, the bigger, healthier ones fill out the row, so the skimpy plants do not waste space.

- I wouldn't swear on a Bible, but my experience indicates less insect hassle with wide rows.
  (1) For many of the above reasons, wide-row-planted crops grow healthier. Insects may attack more vulnerable, singly planted specimens.
  (2) With a greater quantity of any one crop, Jan and I have more to eat and store and share *even if* insects gobble some for themselves.

- The extra produce far outweighs in value the slightly greater cost for seeds. We may purchase 20 to 25 percent more seed, but the overall yield runs from two to even four times greater. (See wide-row versus single-row harvest results on pages 4–5.)

- Buy some seeds in bulk form (peas, beans, lettuce especially) and save on bulk rates. Or look at it

this way: I seem to have stopped throwing out or spilling partially used seed packets!

 • I grew wide rows in Tennessee, Texas, and Florida and found they kept crops *much cooler*, to the point where I could raise English peas and head lettuce in hot weather. Southern gardeners in all the Sun Belt states report great luck with wide-row planting. Plants take so much less watering.

Some crops are still best served by single-row planting . . .

tomatoes	the vine family (melons, cukes,
potatoes	and squashes)
corn	okra

More on my planting techniques for these vegetables is coming up.

Time to do final indoor transplant of tomatoes—

The only vegetables that I transplant twice

Peel off the old container—don't yank plant out.

Pinch off all but topmost leaf cluster. Leaf growth isn't as important to the tomato plant at this stage as its root system. By stripping off most leaves and burying former "stem," most of the length of the plant, now underground, will sprout roots and greatly strengthen the foundation.

Place the plant into the new container, then fill it with soil mix so that just the top leaf clusters are showing. The whole stem and root ball must be submerged. Otherwise, the plant will grow tall and leggy, with cramped roots. Here's the before and after of what we've just accomplished. Cut-off plastic jugs are good for this project, too. Now, back they go to my greenhouse. Or your sunny window. Or whatever.

The next transplanting step will be out into the garden!

My way to transplant tomatoes aims for the sturdiest, healthiest plants possible.

Using nice large containers like half-gallon milk cartons lets that young tomato plant have lots of room to develop a rugged root system.

Try to disturb root system as little as possible. The less shock, the faster the plant will take hold in new container.

Don't forget to firm the soil. And water regularly. Once a week add some ordinary houseplant fertilizer such as Miracle-Gro, or anything that dissolves in water.

A word on celery, leeks, and other small-seeded, slow-growing crops . . .

Celery needs lots of water as its roots are close to the surface. To force strong roots, I generally transplant celery somewhat deeper than it was originally. As for my onion plants and leeks, I keep the scissors handy and keep them trimmed to about four or five inches: I want those bulbs and lower stems to get fleshy.

It's time to plant more onions and their great-tasting cousins.

Did you realize that one pound of sets contains about 130 to 150 onions? Planted in a wide row (the 16-inch width of most rakes) it takes at most a section two feet long. When I want a lot of scallions picked early, I plant a pound in just one square foot. Sometimes I add some bone meal into a bed of root crops before planting. Bone meal assures me the biggest onions I can grow. It's expensive, so often I just use superphosphate. Not all gardeners will choose to do this extra fertilizing. Sometimes I don't myself, depending upon how busy I am. But I always side-dress later, with 10–10–10.

Planting red onions

Planting shallots

Onions are *so* easy to grow. I go for variety. The reds are not for storing, but for spicing up summer barbecues. I plant the big Bermudas three to four inches apart.

Break the garlic set into its cloves, just as you would when using them for cooking. Then plant each clove, broad side or root side down, every three to four inches apart. A foot of wide row is plenty. I use only the largest outside cloves to produce the largest garlic. Or buy the sets from a catalog or seed store; supermarket cloves are of varying quality, while sets sold for planting are top grade.

The cluster onions, to me, have a flavor all their own. The French swear by them. Plant four to six inches apart. Each set yields a cluster, good and hard, which means they store well for up to an entire year. I always plant a few feet of wide row to shallots, and sometimes a second planting if we use up lots of the first as green tops and in summer cooking.

Sometimes I think onions are my middle name. How can you cook without them? I've never had a failure when I've grown them. A little tip: I sprout onion seeds in wet paper towels to speed their germination, before sowing them in the garden.

Breaking garlic cloves . . .

. . . and planting them

While most gardeners are still dreaming, I'm ready to set out hardy young cabbage crops.

Here comes the payoff for starting some of my vegetables from seed indoors—I can now set out my cabbage, broccoli, Brussels sprouts, cauliflower—and head lettuces. If you didn't grow these indoors, you could try to find them locally. But don't worry, they'll be plentiful when we shop in May.

Pinch the leaves off all cabbage-family plants and the head lettuces, just as I demonstrated earlier for tomatoes. But to repeat: I do not *pick leaves off peppers, eggplant, or vine-family crops. That would weaken them, as they don't grow leaves as fast as tomatoes and cabbages.*

I said earlier that cabbages are hardy. But I treat all my seedlings with a baby-soft touch. If the roots can be jolted as little as possible, the plant will be set back to a lesser degree after transplanting. Into the hole for all transplants a gardener can place a *teaspoon* of chemical fertilizer or a handful of organic fertilizer or compost. Chemicals must be covered with an inch of soil so tender roots forming won't get too much too soon. This is an option gardeners can experiment with. When I fertilize at planting, *in addition to* that overall garden-soil fer-

tilizing at preparation time, I'm definitely boosting the plant's start. You'll soon see that I *always* add fertilizer when setting out my tomatoes, eggplants, and peppers—tender plants which thrive on extra attention. But with cabbages and lettuces and other hardy crops, this step depends on how much time I've got. That will probably be true for you, too. It's less rushed later, when I side-dress.

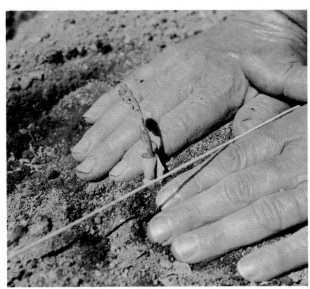

Add a "cutworm collar." Cutworms—soil-dwelling caterpillars usually an inch long and about a half-inch in diameter—are a menace to young plants (see page 107). This collar consists of a two-inch strip of newspaper which breaks down in the soil after its job is complete in a few weeks. Wrapped around the young stem, it protects these plants from being severed. I add a cutworm collar to all my tomatoes and cabbage-family crops. Firm the soil and water thoroughly.

But most important—
I "stagger-plant" my cabbages and head lettuce
plants in my 3–2–3–2–3 wide row:
13 heads in just three feet!

First, I stake out my row 20 inches wide—a few inches wider than most of my rows a rake's width. I plant three cabbages across the row, move down nine to ten inches, come in five inches from each side of the row, and plant two more. This leaves approximately ten inches apart each way. As the plants grow, the leaves will touch one another, shade the ground, and keep that soil cool and moist (not to mention weed-free). I space cauliflower, broccoli, and Brussels sprouts more like 12 inches apart but in a 2–1–2–1 pattern because these plants are larger. (See page 109.)

Leeks love wide rows.

Whether you've raised them or bought started plants—now's the time to get them in the ground.

This is what a trowelful looks like, from my plant bank where they were seeded.

I take the leek plant and, holding it against my index finger and secured by my thumb, poke my finger into the soft soil, with the little plant right along with it. I push my finger a good two to three inches deep, enough for the roots to get way down in there where they want to be, for plenty of loose, moist soil. I pull the plant back up, but bury it about an inch deeper than it had been growing, to encourage a sturdy foundation.

Firm it down, and water. I leave about four inches between plants, because they'll grow thick and fleshy stems in time. And I want to leave room for blanching the stems up several inches with the loose soil on all sides.

A section of wide row a few feet long will yield a lot of leek eating, considering it only takes one or two plump ones for a soup. So don't go overboard.

With hot caps, I plant some early vine-family seeds now.

Squashes, melons, and cucumbers love heat. I couldn't plant them before the end of May without taking this protective step.

To get a really early helping of yellow summer squash (or any vine crop), weeks before my neighbors, I use a section of raised bed. Squash like their feet warm, and this helps. After scooping out a ten-inch-wide hollow and dropping in the squash seeds, I scatter some radish seed.

My vine crops on a raised bed are cluster-planted, three to four seeds per mound, eventually thinned to the best two or three plants. Radish seed will produce good companions: they serve as nibble food for hungry leaf-eaters, which often haunt the vine-family members.

Firm down the seeds . . .
. . . cover with an inch or an inch and a half of soil . . .

. . . followed by a protective hot cap, which I anchor with a little soil around the rim. You can also get the same results under plastic tunnels described in March. I plant those in long rows. There is no need to water seeds and seedlings under these devices. Since soil is still so cool and moist, there is plenty of moisture for them—in addition to the condensation formed inside.

Cut-off plastic gallon jugs: great mini-greenhouses.

Early vine crops as well as tomatoes, eggplants, and peppers can be housed under sturdy, cut-off plastic gallon-size milk jugs. These jugs can be collected and saved for next year. And the open spout lets off excess steam during the day. (I save the caps, in case of a heavy frost.) It's just another idea for those interested in earlier starts.

Interested in Jerusalem artichokes? Now's the time to plant the tubers of this hardy perennial vegetable. Please see page 151 for my planting comments. I also show what a stand of these looks like by early summer. You may not have the space!

Reminders for April . . .

Indoors:
- Keep flats of seedlings watered and ventilated.
- Start hardening them off outdoors.
- Transplant tomatoes (twice), and the other vegetables once, especially eggplants and peppers. (The small-seeded onions, celery, and leeks can stay in their original containers for now, unless you have the time.)

Outdoors:
- Keep checking soil readiness.
- Begin spading or rototilling to dry up soil and to surface weed seeds.
- Begin planting hardiest seeds and started plants: lettuces, spinach, chard, onions, peas, potatoes, all cabbage-family crops.
- Gamble on some *protected* vine crops.
- Build raised beds for early root crops and heat-loving plants.

Brewing for May . . .

- Sprouting hard-to-crack melon seeds
- Corn planting and protecting
- My superharvest tomato-transplanting trick
- First helpings of lettuce, onions, and radishes
- Plant-shopping trip
- Planting my "pepper plantation"

- Planting a salad row
- Hardening off the last of the seedlings
- Shopping for the best plants and setting them out
- Understanding and outfoxing weeds from the start
- Speeding up melon "slowpokes"
- Transplanting tomatoes my way for the earliest ever

MAY

Prime time planting

EARLY MAY
Let's plant a salad row!

One of the first things I plant in my gardens—whatever their size—is a few feet of a wide row interplanted with five or more vegetables. I call this a "multi-row" or salad row. The head lettuce plants and others I'm raising indoors and in my greenhouse (or buying, perhaps, in your case) I set out in late April, and now will again in May. This row is an extra planting of looseleaf lettuce (three different kinds), radishes, and spinach—vegetables I can't wait to eat and that do just fine in cold spring weather.

Who says vegetables have to be planted by themselves, isolated from neighbors, each to his own? A salad row is *fun*. It's like creating your own outdoor salad bar.

The whole point to my wide-row planting system is to let the vegetables themselves do more of the work—shading and cooling the soil, keeping it loose and crumbly; "hogging" sunlight so weeds are choked out; catching rain with their shoulder-to-shoulder umbrellas of foliage; slowing evaporation of soil moisture because of that canopy of leaves. Of course, the biggest bonus of wide rows is the yielding of two to three times the harvest from a given amount of space. Wide-row gardens can be smaller, better tended, and more fun! Multicropping in a salad row really heightens these advantages. Please refer back to my 30- by 40-foot garden plan on pages 20–21 in January to see how this eye-catching section of wide row is the "cornerstone."

Sprinkle seeds *of each variety over a 16-inch band of a wide row very lightly. I also press in a few onion sets.*

Firm it all down and cover with soil. *In a multi-row there's always something different ready to harvest . . . and it keeps the salad bowl interesting.*

If I'm going to plant all my home-grown seedlings by the end of this month, I'm going to have to harden them off now. Here in early May, I keep taking my remaining flats and pots of indoor-started plants outdoors to harden off. The especially tender vegetables—my tomatoes, peppers, eggplants, and vine-family crops—need two weeks of hardening off before being set out permanently in the garden. Remember, the first week begins with just a few hours per day of fairly mild conditions, building up to all day by the end of the week. The second week, it's safe to have them out there all night. These eggplants are against my north-banked sunpit, so there is a good windbreak.

My rows of early potatoes in our 30- by 40-foot garden are up and growing. I planted them a month ago. It's time for their first hilling. The more loose soil I hill, or pile up around the plant, the softer and warmer the environment the plant has to sprout and grow new tubers. I cover the new growth completely. This also smothers weeds. The reason I left three feet between the rows was so that there would be plenty of soil for just this purpose. I'll hill them once again, later this month (page 111). Please refer to that section now for more know-how about this wonderfully easy and effective technique.

One nice sunny day, and that as-paragus doesn't need any more urging. You can almost watch it grow! Later this month, with the spears coming on strong, I share the harvesting techniques I like best, with advice on starting a new bed (see page 110).

Early tomato lovers

If you're brave, like me, you'll want to set a few plants of an early tomato variety out in the garden *now*, but under protection of hot caps or plastic collars. See pages 112–15 for my complete tomato-planting system.

IN DOUBT ABOUT HOW DEEP TO PLANT?

Depth planting guide

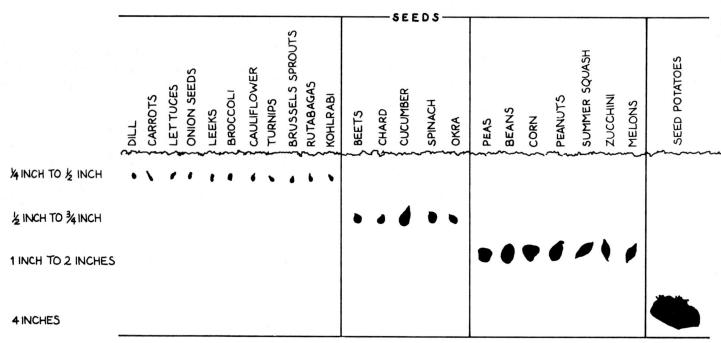

(GENERAL RULE: FOUR TIMES SEED'S DIAMETER)

MIDDLE MAY   Digging in

We grow potatoes for the whole family.

I offered a few potato pointers last month when I set out my early ones (page 72). Here are a few more tips as I plant my main crop.

- I avoid planting potatoes in a section where potatoes or tomatoes grew last year; they carry the same diseases so it's best to rotate. I also avoid sections I've limed within the past few years. Potatoes prefer a more acid soil, with a pH of around 5.0, as opposed to the rest of the garden which has a pH of 6.5. This reduces "scab" (a potato blight) and skin discoloration.

- It's been my experience that potatoes planted and buried in good, deep trenches grow larger than those resting atop the soil and covered with mulch. Since the new potatoes form above the seed potato, perhaps they get more protection from sunlight and air if they are well buried. Of course, weed seeds in mulch attract mice, and the mice attract snakes . . .

- Try a baking variety, and one that's good for boiling. I always grow some Kennebec here in the North. Each area has favorites. They *all* store well, given proper conditions.

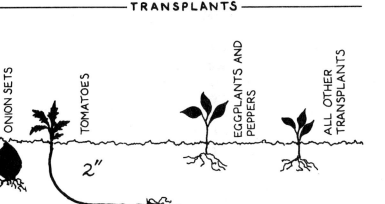

TRANSPLANTS

ONION SETS

TOMATOES

2"

EGGPLANTS AND PEPPERS

ALL OTHER TRANSPLANTS

Tomatoes and all transplants except peppers and eggplants:

Strip off *all leaves* except topmost clusters and bury the entire stem. We pretty much always kill some roots when we transplant. So this leaf-stripping helps to swing the plant's energy back to root formation. Strip off outer leaves of head lettuce; they wilt and die anyway. See pages 112–15 for my special tomato transplanting technique.

Eggplants and Peppers:

These slow growers I transplant at slightly below the level at which they were growing in containers. I do *not* strip leaves, unless they are yellowed and wilted.

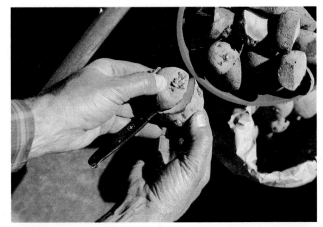

Cut the seed potato *into halves, thirds, quarters . . . so there are at least two "eyes" per section. I do this several days before planting so the ends can heal.*

See the difference in the healed cut? *It's formed a sort of callus. Now my seed potatoes will be much less apt to attract disease organisms, and they can begin a good and rapid growth.*

Keep in mind: *The three 30-foot rows Jan and I planted in the 30- by 40-foot garden in early April will yield two bushels or more . . . a nice-sized harvest for small family summertime eating.*

Middle May 97

Now That Grass Is Growing, So Are Weeds!

Once I've finished planting my garden, I'll be showing you the steps I take to control weeds—well before they get the upper hand.

Like most vegetables, most weeds are annual; they sprout, grow, and you try to destroy them before they go to seed and store in the topsoil the means for repeating the cycle later in the same season. But the original plant only lives once. Perennial weeds are trickier, living from year to year, and once you root them out be sure to shake the soil from the roots, discard them, and keep them away from the compost pile.

Every section of the country has its perennial-weed problem. One common type pictured here is called "witch" grass or "nut" grass or "quack" grass. If a gardener can rid himself of the roots of such weeds in the fall or at the start of the season, they should not be a problem again. One thing now you can do is to keep tilling or spading that garden section before planting. This breaks up that ornery network of perennial roots. Organic mulches don't really work, because perennial root systems like these push blades of grass right up through the mulch to energize their roots. Black-plastic mulch does work because it cuts off all oxygen.

Annual weeds continually reappear, carried in by the wind or by birds. Many gardeners, myself included, keep grass areas around the garden cut, as lawn. This makes for a neater appearance, but it doesn't really kill the weed problem. Nature is so persistent about reproducing plants that most weeds can set flowers and go to seed at just an inch and a half high!

But don't get discouraged. I've got several more ideas coming up to outwit weeds *without* hours of work. Simply raking your garden ¼-inch before planting destroys countless young weeds. Please see pages 122 through 125 in early June, especially my "Summary to a weed-free garden."

I've planned my garden so I can plant row after row, from earliest to last, with minimum compaction of soil.

I always retill or respade each row just before planting. Loose, well-aerated soil means transplants will take root quickly. And seeds will contact moist earth for faster germination in soil turned just prior to sowing. But the most important reason I do this is to bring more weed seeds to the upper levels and surface so they'll germinate and be destroyed by subsequent cultivation.

What I've planted:

- wide rows of early salad greens: multi-planted salad row, looseleaf lettuce, spinach, chard, and mustard greens
- early onions, from seeds, sets and started plants
- garlic, shallots, and leeks
- raised bed of early peas, cucumbers, squashes, and melons under protection
- cabbage-family crops and head lettuces
- beets, carrots, and turnips
- small early blocks of corn and potatoes
- main crop of potatoes

What I've yet to plant (later this month and in early June):

- tomatoes, peppers, eggplants, green beans and yellow wax beans
- main crop of sweet corn
- main crops of zucchini, summer squash, winter squash, melon, and cukes from seeds as well as plants
- repeat plantings of lettuce and other salad greens, for a continuous supply
- a few final tender crops, like lima beans, okra, sweet potatoes and beans for drying

THE CORN STORY

Early-maturing corn varieties start ripening in 60 to 65 days. Late-season (and to my mind, the sweetest) varieties take over 90 days. But I always try some early types.

I like to harvest my corn weeks before commercial growers do. After all, corn is one of the true taste treats of the whole garden. I like to start five to six weeks before final spring frost, or mid-April in my case. This year I planted some early corn on April 11, and it's not looking perfect but it will still produce some ears. When I replant now I know I'll get an outstanding harvest.

 Sun Belt gardeners also aim for early maturity, but their chief reason is to avoid as much of the drought season as possible.

Make a furrow. *Ordinarily, a corn seed need only be planted about one inch deep. But I want to get it a bit beyond the birds' beaks—they can somehow sense those nice corn kernels in the ground. I also want to anchor the corn seedling. If spring frost damages the topmost young leaves, the head of the plant will be buried and insulated.*

Next, sprinkle fertilizer *along the bottom of the furrow. Corn is a heavy feeder. I'll also be side-dressing this crop when plants are six to eight inches tall (page 135), and once again when the first tassels appear (page 175). Side-dressing, or adding more fertilizer next to the plant and working it in as an in-season boost, is explained more fully in June, page 135.*

As always, cover chemical fertilizer *with loose soil from the side of the furrow. A light, long-handled hoe makes these steps practically effortless.*

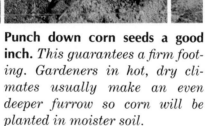

Drop corn seed along furrow. *I don't worry too much about spacing, for now. A few seeds, even though these are treated, will rot. And I can always thin to ten inches apart once the early-weather gamble is over.*

Punch down corn seeds a good inch. *This guarantees a firm footing. Gardeners in hot, dry climates usually make an even deeper furrow so corn will be planted in moister soil.*

Cover seeds with loose soil. *By now, the furrow is almost filled in, but not quite. There's still room for the first hilling (early June, page 131) to anchor the plant once it's a few inches high. Hilling corn (and potatoes, tomatoes, eggplants, and peppers, too) also smothers the weeds. Hilling is the easiest no-stoop method of weeding. More on this in June.*

Optional, for early birds—literally. *I fashion a "tent" of chicken wire. A long strip of bent chicken wire is the best idea I know for preventing the early, hungry birds from poking through the corn rows. Once the plants are four to six inches high, they're established beyond the point of bird damage. These wire strips roll up and store easily. The one-time investment, for me, has been worth the years and years now of the earliest sweet corn in town.*

Middle May   101

Progress in a block of peas . . .

They're a half-foot tall, not as thick and abundant as I'd like. But with a section of garden planted this way, and considering there's no weeding or staking involved at all, we'll be real pleased a few weeks from now at harvest time.

Progress of sweet potatoes on my windowsill . . .

I'll plant them late this month, after all danger of last frost has passed.

Don't forget to sprinkle (not *too* many) radish seeds in with seeded wide rows of:

looseleaf lettuce
kale, kohlrabi, turnips, and the other
    cabbage-family crops
carrots, beets
leeks, onions
spinach
any other leafy greens

I estimate I sow about 5 percent of the seeds in these rows as radish seeds. As you'll be seeing, I also sprinkle radish seeds in *single* rows of vine crops.

If any of your newly planted seedlings are a half-inch high . . . it's time to cultivate and thin the first vegetables you planted from seed—carrots, beets, and the salad greens. I do *not* take a tool to thin and cultivate my salad multi-row, with onion sets growing. Those vegetables I harvest-thin, as in the photo below. See pages 122–25 in early June for my complete cultivating and thinning advice.

ONION  KNOW-HOW

The small onion plants I buy or grow also get transplanted into a wide row. Onion plants (as opposed to sets) tend to produce the largest possible bulbs. I think this is due to their having one long, uninterrupted growing period. A set grown a prior season is stopped short when the bulb becomes marble-sized. It must begin all over again to establish a root system when planted in the garden. Of course, sets are more convenient because they are faster to plant.

Here's the same row of onion plants a few weeks later. They look skinny now, but I'll get hamburger-sized slices from these plants by September. We start harvesting the entire plant when the tops are pencil-thin. To be able to pull them continually in the scallion stage—the first two months—is the reason I plant my sets close together. I know we're going to thin these rows, leaving room for the remaining bulbs to expand. We've gotten in the habit of keeping a few handfuls of onion sets in the refrigerator where they won't sprout. This way, we can plant a small section every few weeks to spread our scallion harvest over half the year.

Here's the best way I can demonstrate how wide-row planting saves space. If I planted the 65 onion sets in this six-inch pot according to seed-catalog instructions (three inches apart in a single row), I'd have a row 15 feet long! As these potted sets sprout I'll pull most for scallions and let several grow to full size—a continuous harvest for over two months.

Snap off pods on onions when they're small. You have to check onion plants every few days at this stage. If they're successful, they will complete their earthly mission and the gardener will not harvest much of a bulb. Keeping those pods snapped means training the energy of the plant into bulb growth—and top growth. (The larger the green tops, the bigger the bulb.) More reasons to snap off the pods: The bulb where the seed pod has grown up won't grow as large; it doesn't keep as long in storage; and it's tougher and bland in taste. There's only a few days' difference in growth for these two pods, so you've got to be quick. The next thing I do with onions is to side-dress. I'll let you know when it's time.

PLANT SHOPPING

My advice in a nutshell . . .

- Look for *quality*, not size: dark-green leaves . . . no yellowed, purplish, shriveled or sickly leaves . . . thick stems.
- Look *under* leaves for tiny white clusters of insect eggs as well as for insects themselves.
- If leaves are purple underneath, they have a phosphorus deficiency and a poor root structure. If yellowed, they're undernourished. Avoid these flats.
- The best plants may not be the largest. Smaller plants are less developed, but will take root faster in your garden.
- Always harden off the flats of your vegetables before planting, whether or not they were outdoors at the garden center.

Which flat of head lettuce would you buy?

At right, too much energy in the flat of the larger head lettuces has gone into producing leaves. I'd select the other, more compact flat, which is likely to have a less-cramped root system.

Which flat of peppers looks best to you?

We want the shiny, dark-green leaves—in all vegetables. Ordinarily I'd choose plants smaller than larger, so I'd be less likely to wind up with spindly stems by the time I was transplanting. But in this case, the smaller plants are also on the yellow side, indicating they're in need of fertilizer. Don't grow just bell peppers—look for some of the other interesting varieties from yellow banana peppers to the hot chili peppers (see page 117).

Melons. Don't get them too leggy.

The leggy flat on the right probably wasn't getting enough light in the commercial greenhouse. It's been under stress already in its young life. The flat on the left looks more vigorous. This suggestion holds true for all vine-family crops.

Tomato talk

- Try three, four or five varieties of tomatoes popular or available for your region—but not a dozen. That many can be confusing in terms of keeping track of results and preferences. I recommend planting a few each of early, midseason, and late varieties to really stretch out the harvest.
- Plant a *marble-sized* or cherry tomato. One or two plants per family is usually plenty. They're prolific and super for snacking and salads.
- As I've mentioned before, Pixies are one of my favorites. They're golf-ball-sized, grow only 18 inches tall, and mature in 50 days from setting out.
- The *plum-shaped* tomato is especially bred for making sauce. It has fewer seeds and thicker flesh than most others. It's less tasty, though, for eating fresh.
- I prefer the *medium-sized, early-maturing* (60–65 days) varieties: Early Girl, Fireball . . . there are dozens of different ones. Huge "beefsteak" tomatoes are spectacular to slice and serve, but generally take longer to mature (three months after planting).

Jan and I agree that flowers belong in the vegetable garden.

The taller but *not* spindly tomatoes are the best bet.

The taller flat at left also happens to have thicker stems, greener leaves. I look for tomatoes about eight inches tall, with thick stems. Whatever the vegetable, starting out with the best plant stock has greatly improved the quality and length of my harvest.

Look under the leaves—don't be shy!

Be a fussy shopper. Why bring home egg clusters of white flies or aphids just because you didn't check under, as well as over, your plants?

No-Shock Transplanting

Here are my steps for setting out all young plants into the garden, whether I bought them or raised them myself. I have a special system for tomatoes, which follows soon on pages 112–15.

1. First I scoop out a hole about three to four inches deep with my hand or a trowel.

Transplanting Rules of Thumb

- Transplant on a cloudy, wind-free day or in the late afternoon when the sun has begun to set. Then there is less air-drying of roots.
- Soak the plant thoroughly before removing from its container so the soil and roots stay as "glued" together as possible.
- The longer the number of days or weeks the flats of plants have been parked outside, and overnight, the less shock the transplants will have to withstand. As I've said earlier, my plants harden off from ten days to two weeks. But because I'm out gardening *early*, a week is enough at this point in the spring. On the other hand, don't get concerned if you must leave them outdoors for up to three weeks before you can plant. They'll just get a little leggy, and you can bury much of the stem.
- Prepare the seedbed first, to make the transplanting process swift. Try to do this just before transplanting so the soil will be cool and moist. (It's always cool and moist a few inches down.)
- *Cradle* that little root ball! Keep as much soil intact as you can. That way fewer root hairs will get exposed to air and die.

2. Next I deposit a good handful of compost (if I've got a generous supply) or a teaspoon of 5–10–10 or 10–10–10 fertilizer. I always cover chemical fertilizer with some soil. Remember, this is in addition to that light broadcasting of fertilizer I added and tilled in earlier over the entire garden.

5. *My transplants get a good soak. I direct the water flow around the base of the seedling. I do not water lightly! Watering to the point of practically making mud ensures the best possible cementing of roots and soil, and the least possible delay in new growth. Young transplants need heavy watering the first three or four days until they become established.*

3. *I strip off most of the outer lettuce-plant leaves (which can be washed and eaten). I strip off most leaves of all plants—everything except eggplants and peppers. See my Depth Planting Guide on pages 96–97 for more details.*

4. *I set the root ball carefully in the hole, fill in with soil, and firm it well so roots make good contact.*

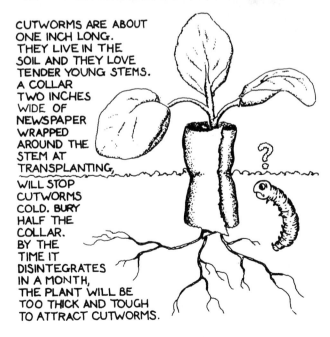

CUTWORMS ARE ABOUT ONE INCH LONG. THEY LIVE IN THE SOIL AND THEY LOVE TENDER YOUNG STEMS. A COLLAR TWO INCHES WIDE OF NEWSPAPER WRAPPED AROUND THE STEM AT TRANSPLANTING, WILL STOP CUTWORMS COLD. BURY HALF THE COLLAR. BY THE TIME IT DISINTEGRATES IN A MONTH, THE PLANT WILL BE TOO THICK AND TOUGH TO ATTRACT CUTWORMS.

Planting lettuce under *single*-row broccoli does great things for both crops.

Most gardeners have the problem of keeping broccoli and lettuce cool. They both can bolt to seed too fast. Besides clustering each of these crops in wide rows so that their leaves mulch the soil, I found I could utilize that idle space under broccoli if I planted them in single rows.

I sow looseleaf lettuce seed under and between my broccoli transplants. Or I transplant head-lettuce plants eight inches apart to form a wide row surrounding the broccoli running through the center of it. Either way, the broccoli serves as an umbrella over the lettuce to keep it shaded from strong sun. And the lettuce acts as a living mulch to keep the soil nice and cool. I like to eat my mulch!

When I'm purchasing supplies rather than using homemade, I favor these pyramid-style, molded flats called "Todd planters." They are filled with individual spaces shaped like a wedge, or a long, thin pyramid.

Instead of a root cluster growing in a ball formation, the plants in one of these wedgelike spaces "root-prunes" itself. The roots grow downward, heavier at the shoulders, slender toward the tip. The whole thing slides nicely out of the container, causing the least possible jarring of the roots, and with minimal drying out.

I've already planted head lettuces and some early cabbage-family crops. Remember how I "stagger-planted" them—13 heads in three feet of a wide row? To repeat that idea, please refer to the sketch at right. I simply mark out the 3–2–3–2–3 spacing by scooping out the soil with my hand. What about the other plants? In the case of eggplants and peppers, as well as the other cabbage-family crops, I stagger-plant them 2–1–2–1–2, and so on. As larger plants, they need a bit more distance. A variation on this I often use is simply alternating the plants as shown in the diagram. This final option can be a little narrower.

Transplanting in a wide row

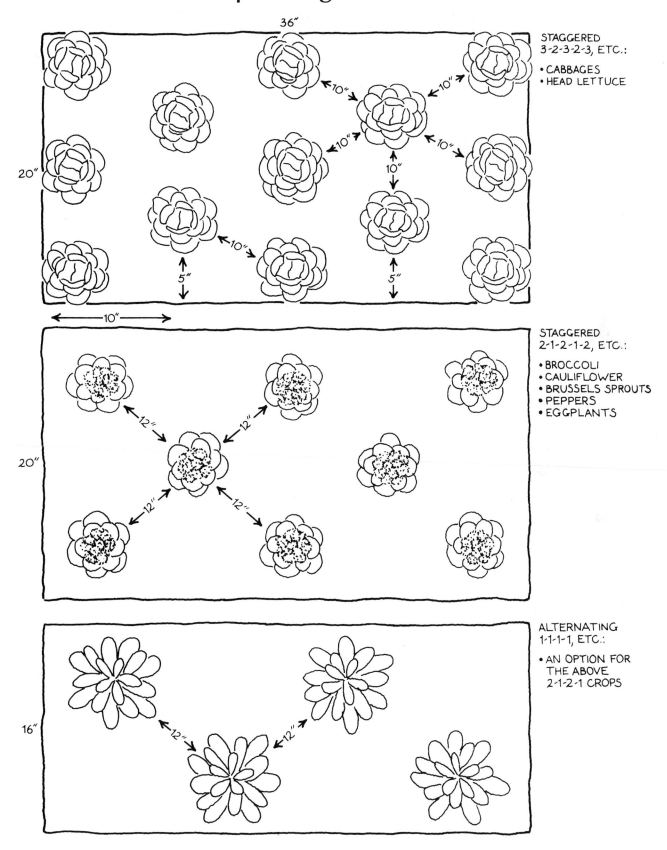

36"

STAGGERED
3-2-3-2-3, ETC.:

• CABBAGES
• HEAD LETTUCE

10" 10"

10" 10"

20"

10"

10"

5" 5"

10"

STAGGERED
2-1-2-1-2, ETC.:

• BROCCOLI
• CAULIFLOWER
• BRUSSELS SPROUTS
• PEPPERS
• EGGPLANTS

12" 12"

20"

12" 12"

ALTERNATING
1-1-1-1, ETC.:

• AN OPTION FOR
THE ABOVE
2-1-2-1 CROPS

12" 12"

16"

ASPARAGUS ESSENTIALS

Once asparagus season is upon us, we pick it. And keep it picked. This is the payoff of several years of mulching and tending . . . two solid months of this delectable vegetable.

To extend the harvest, plant crowns at different depths (by 2 inches), so deeper plants warm up later and stagger the harvest.

NOW IS A GOOD TIME TO PLANT A NEW ASPARAGUS BED.

As you've probably heard, you shouldn't pick newly planted asparagus plants—neither the season you plant them, *nor* the following year. You can begin the spring after that, but pick nothing smaller than the thickness of your smallest finger. I recommend buying two-year-old root crowns because they have many more roots than one-year-old stock. Keep the patch small; asparagus needs lots of hand weeding, especially in the early stages while getting established. They usually come in clumps of a dozen. Plant 25 crowns two feet apart—in one 50-foot row or two 25-foot rows —which is plenty for a family of three or four. Please see my earlier suggestions for asparagus on page 53.

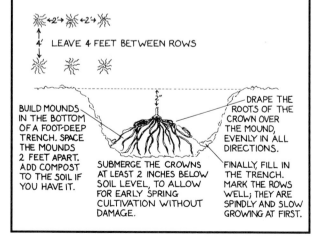

LEAVE 4 FEET BETWEEN ROWS

BUILD MOUNDS IN THE BOTTOM OF A FOOT-DEEP TRENCH. SPACE THE MOUNDS 2 FEET APART. ADD COMPOST TO THE SOIL IF YOU HAVE IT.

2"

DRAPE THE ROOTS OF THE CROWN OVER THE MOUND, EVENLY IN ALL DIRECTIONS.

SUBMERGE THE CROWNS AT LEAST 2 INCHES BELOW SOIL LEVEL, TO ALLOW FOR EARLY SPRING CULTIVATION WITHOUT DAMAGE.

FINALLY, FILL IN THE TRENCH. MARK THE ROWS WELL; THEY ARE SPINDLY AND SLOW GROWING AT FIRST.

Some people snap off spears at or near the ground and eat the top portion. This leaves a ragged end, often several inches high. It can invite insects and disease, and it looks sloppy. I prefer slicing spears close to the ground.

HILLING

The only way to weed corn and potatoes

In the case of potatoes, I'm also increasing the area of loose soil in which the tubers can expand.

Remember, potatoes form *above* the planted seed potato. Because I planted them in a trench, I'm already giving the new crop the benefit of lots of topsoil in which to form. But hilling soil to smother weeds increases this benefit even more.

I usually begin hilling when the potato plants are a few inches tall. I cover the plant completely, not even leaving the topmost cluster showing. The plant will keep right on growing and soon poke through the mounded soil.

The photo here illustrates the *second* hilling of my early-planted potatoes in our 30-by-40 garden. The first hilling was in early May (page 94). Early next month I'll be doing the first hilling on the later-planted main crop.

Hilling is not only an easy way to weed, but it's safer than using a cultivating tool close to the plants. By only cultivating out in the center of the walkways, down to an inch, I can make enough loose soil for hilling the vegetables. This limits the chance of cultivating too deep and too close to the plant roots.

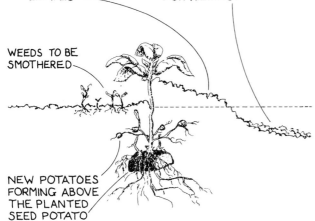

FIRST POTATO HILLING: PLANTS 3 TO 5 INCHES ABOVE GROUND

HILLED SOIL AROUND SMALL PLANT TO ALMOST COVER LEAVES

CULTIVATE SOIL BETWEEN ROWS TO LOOSEN AND PROVIDE EASY SUPPLY FOR HILLING.

WEEDS TO BE SMOTHERED

NEW POTATOES FORMING ABOVE THE PLANTED SEED POTATO

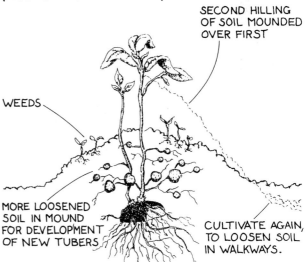

SECOND HILLING: PLANTS 8 TO 10 INCHES TALL (ABOUT 3 TO 4 WEEKS LATER)

SECOND HILLING OF SOIL MOUNDED OVER FIRST

WEEDS

MORE LOOSENED SOIL IN MOUND FOR DEVELOPMENT OF NEW TUBERS

CULTIVATE AGAIN, TO LOOSEN SOIL IN WALKWAYS.

NOTE: SOMETIMES I HILL UP POTATOES JUST AS SOON AS THEY POKE THROUGH. YOU DON'T HAVE TO BE TOO EXACT ABOUT THESE HEIGHTS AND TIMINGS. OFTEN I HILL THEM UP 3 TIMES, IF THE WEEDS GET BAD.

Middle May 111

LATE MAY

I plant tomatoes on their side!

My system for planting tomatoes ripens them two to four weeks early

When I think of tomatoes, I often think of spicy sauces and great Italian dinners. Most of us in this country don't have the growing conditions of those hot Mediterranean places. But your tomato plant doesn't know the difference if you capture more heat for it my way. The result is a much earlier, heavier yield. I've never heard any gardener who follows my system complain about plucking tomatoes off the vine, totally ripe, two to three weeks ahead of schedule!

After years of trial and error this is the best technique I've found to get a really early crop from these heat-loving plants. The basic idea is to plant tomatoes on their sides in a shallow two-inch trench. Planting the regular way, that root ball is submerged six or more inches into cold, damp spring soil, which can take weeks to heat up. That's okay for the Sun Belt. For all other gardeners, trench-planting my way means the roots will grow close to the surface and absorb more heat, which tomatoes love. Sun Belt gardeners, too, actually benefit from trench-planting, then applying a very heavy mulch. Lots more moisture is available to trench-planted roots, spread as they are over a much greater surface area than vertically planted tomato roots.

Trench-planting tomatoes on a *raised bed* speeds the heat-trapping process even more for us northern gardeners.

Just be sure you have passed the last frost date in your area (see page 36) unless you're using hot caps (see page 52). Now, let's begin.

"Trench-planting" a tomato

ONLY TOPMOST LEAF CLUSTER IS KEPT. STEM SOON STRAIGHTENS OUT. FRUIT BEGINS FORMING AT <u>GROUND LEVEL</u>, WITHOUT "WASTING" STEM GROWING ROOM.

STEM IS BURIED CLOSE TO SURFACE AIR AND WARMTH, WHICH TOMATOES WANT.

ORIGINAL ROOT BALL.

2"

NEW ROOTS AND ROOT HAIRS WILL SOON FORM, ADDING GREATLY TO TOMATO'S ABILITY TO TAKE UP NUTRIENTS AND MOISTURE.

CUTWORM COLLAR, HALF-BURIED, HALF-EXPOSED.

LEAF REMOVED.

STRIPPED "STEM," NOW BURIED TO BECOME EXTRA ROOT TRUNK.

1-INCH COMPOST IN BOTTOM OF TRENCH (OR 5-10-10, COVERED WITH 1 INCH OF SOIL)

IN DRY SUMMER PERIODS, ALL THESE <u>EXTRA</u> ROOTS (OPPORTUNITIES TO ABSORB AVAILABLE MOISTURE) MEAN THE DIFFERENCE BETWEEN MIDDLING AND SPECTACULAR RESULTS.

1. *First I scoop out a shallow two-inch trench and add a tablespoon of fertilizer along the bottom of the trench . . . 5–10–10 or 10–10–10—or I put in a handful or two of compost or organic fertilizer. For a heavy harvest, a tomato plant needs this extra supply of energy.*

2. *Covering commercial fertilizer with an inch or so of soil prevents tender roots from making direct contact and possibly burning.*

3. *My milk carton container has been peeled off and the ball of roots carefully cradled in my hands. Note: tomato varieties like Pixie happen to be "determinate": they grow to a set height, rather in the style of a bush, and then stop. Most tomatoes, however, are "indeterminate," and grow to six, eight, ten feet tall, if left unpruned. Their early plants can be leggier than this one in the photo. It's safe to assume you've purchased indeterminate vine types. I'll be advising you later on how to prune.*

4. *I've stripped off all the leaves except the topmost cluster. That good, thick stem is about to get buried and converted into root underground, encouraging the sturdiest foundation possible. Within a few weeks, the trunk will sprout root hairs and greatly expand the plant's ability to absorb nutrients and moisture.*

5. *Laying the young plant on its side in the hole, a few inches below ground level, will mean that much more "stem"—and eventual roots—will be close to the surface. This means more heat will be available to the plant and it will produce earlier tomatoes.*

6. *Next I wrap a newspaper cutworm collar around the stem and hold it in place with one hand. With my other hand I'm covering the root ball and the lower half of the paper collar. Cutworms chew along the surface, and this thin barrier will stop them from severing the stem. I form a little pillow of soil under the leaf cluster as I cover up most of the collar.*

7. *I gently press down the soil around the final section of the plant. It will still be at an angle as it comes out of the ground because of the horizontal position of the bulk of the stem and cutworm collar, but Mother Nature will soon straighten the plant out as it reaches for the sun. I firm the soil over the root ball and stem, too, for close contact and faster establishment of new root hairs on the buried stem. And then, of course, I soak the plant thoroughly.*

Late May 113

With longer, leggier tomato plants . . .

Lay tomato plant on its side in the furrow, but allow for about 18 inches to two feet between the upturned leaf clusters of the plants (18 inches distance, for staking; 24 inches distance, for caging.

On even closer inspection: See the thick, double trunk? It begins at the very base of the plant, at ground level. Next month, come tomato harvest, you'll see my staked plants begin producing ripe fruit very low on the plant—not just midway and up. So trench-transplanting offers the advantage of a true bumper crop.

See page 127 for details on tomato support options).

Strip off all leaves but the topmost cluster. Sometimes I think our national motto must be "waste not, want not." It is very hard for people to strip leaves at first. But results again and again prove this stripping to be correct. I'm about to show you a mature plant I dug up just to show the skeptics! Remember, tomatoes are vine-type plants and can easily put on excess foliage. For now, we want the plant's energy concentrated on root development.

Trench-planting a tomato on its side and burying all but the topmost leaf cluster pays off in many more roots—I dug one up to show you. In my right hand is the original root ball, much more fully developed, of course. Then there is another major root clump directly under the plant, plus the many fine roots and root hairs along the original buried "stem," which are less visible. This is one powerful foundation for a tomato. It is so much better able than the average plant to absorb moisture and nutrients, in both well-watered periods and extra-dry ones.

Tomato care tops my chore list

Why support tomatoes?

To save space. Most of us want to grow at least four or five varieties, a few plants of each. If we let them sprawl, the vines can take over. Since backyards are shrinking, supporting tomatoes is the best way to make room for them. If you do have the space, however, you may just prefer to let them sprawl (see p. 127).

You often hear that staked tomatoes grow cleaner. Yes, I find that's true. I support most of my tomatoes to simplify their tending. I can keep an eye on the developing fruit, better judge when to side-dress, spot the suckers to prune. Slugs tend to be a problem on ground-sprawling tomatoes. (See my suggestions for their control on page 132, next month.) I think supported tomato plants look a lot neater and more cared for. That counts, too.

I install the supports soon after I plant so I can remember exactly where the root ball is located (or I'll mark that spot with a few stones). This way I avoid danger of root damage. But this step isn't really essential until June. Tomato-support options, plus the pros and cons of letting them sprawl, are illustrated in detail at that time on page 127.

Here's the payoff in transplanting tomatoes twice indoors. I get a root system that is very well advanced and a plant that will soon be setting blossoms!

Early tomato cultivation tips (good for the rest of the garden, too):

- Cultivate *shallow*. Don't damage those young roots. You only have to go into the soil one-half to one inch to break it up so air and rain can penetrate. Since weed seeds are shallow-rooted, it doesn't take much depth with a cultivation tool to uproot them.
- Don't cultivate when it's wet. Disease organisms can be spread from plant to plant.
- Remember, the roots of plants extend out as far as the leaves. So as the plants grow, take more and more care with the depth of cultivation between plants—and walkways, too.
- Wait a bit before mulching tomatoes. On the one hand, you want the soil to warm up so the plant gets a good start. But, depending upon the strength of the sun, you want to conserve moisture. You'll see me mulching my tomatoes next month. Sun Belt gardeners should mulch early, as soon as they set out their plants.
- If you're itching for real early tomatoes, spray the flower clusters twice a week with Blossom Set, a commercial product that is derived from plant hormones and is perfectly safe. This product speeds pollination, since bees aren't yet very active. (Tomatoes are self-pollinating—once there are several clusters. But that first cluster can use some help.)

Here's my favorite setup for watering as I plant. This way I can really drench those transplants and seedlings. There are nozzles available for the end of your hose which include a nice long handle that is easy to grip and direct. The spray is released full-flowing but soft, distributed over dozens of holes. I really like it. In just one minute I can soak my new transplants or sections of seed-planted wide rows, as I plant my way through the garden. I just water the growing areas. There's no water wasted on the walkways.

I think regular watering is more responsible for my gardening success than just about any other factor.

Please remember to keep newly transplanted plants soaked until it looks like you're drowning them. This is an easy enough chore. Many gardeners overlook it. If air hits those tiny roots it can kill them. The new transplant needs lots of water the first few days to reestablish its roots. If the soil's well worked, it can and should quickly drain off rainwater. But after half a week, depending on the strength of the sun, plants get thirsty again, especially those seedlings in the topmost, first-to-dry soil. So keep the watering can handy.

Late May   115

I Plant a "Pepper Plantation"!

Here's how to plant peppers in a wide row:

In a wide row, there's plenty of space for several varieties. Do *not* strip leaves off peppers (and eggplants); they are slow growers, unlike the rapidly growing tomato vines.

Set the plants in a staggered double row, about a foot apart in all directions. As they grow, the leaves of the pepper plants will just touch, creating a wide mass of foliage. I've left about three feet between the rows. See diagram page 109.

1. When I say teaspoonful, *that really is the limit. Overfeeding is the chief cause of excess pepper foliage at the expense of fruit. Pepper plants (and those of eggplants) don't grow as big as tomato plants. If I fed peppers a tablespoonful, that extra dosage would encourage unnecessary, unproductive foliage. The scooped-out hole is a half-foot deep.*

2. Loose soil should always cover fertilizer, to prevent the young and tender roots from making direct contact.

From sweet . . . to hot . . .

Why grow just the same green bell peppers we can buy all year in the store? *Variety* **can spice a gardener's life.**

Many people think peppers other than the familiar green bell type are too hot to handle. Well, there's a whole world of peppers for the home gardener to discover. The yellow banana peppers are actually quite sweet. And, of course, peppers come mildly hot (Jalapeño and Cayenne) to wildly hot (Chile Tatony). "We have beautiful plants, but no fruit!" I hear this comment in just about every gardening class I've ever taught, when we talk peppers. Overfertilizing is the reason. Pepper plants can

only take a *teaspoon* of 5–10–10 at planting time and another teaspoon at the blossom stage. Spraying the plant with Epsom salts (1 teaspoon dissolved in an old window-spray bottle of warm water) can give pepper plants a boost of the secondary nutrient magnesium. Peppers require magnesium at blossom time. I repeat this trick ten days later, and by then the leaves have become dark green and glossy.

3. Peppers, too, get a simple cutworm collar. As always, I cup the root ball carefully in my hands so the soil stays intact.

4. Peppers (and eggplants) go into the ground slightly deeper than they grew in the container, so the roots are thoroughly covered. For a summary of how deep to plant all seeds and transplants, please refer back to my guide on pages 96–97.

5. I like to water each of my transplants right after planting. The more help I can give my plants at this critical point, the better performance I will get from them.

Now's the time to set out all tender plants . . .

eggplants and the vine-family crops. Vine crops can now be sown as seed, too.

Melons and cukes are especially slow to germinate. Their seeds are hard to crack open. So I came up with this way to "pre-sprout" them before sowing in the garden. It takes only a few days, and then these plants will start off much faster in the soil. (Works with onion seeds, too.)

1. Run three paper towels under the tap, then sprinkle the seeds evenly over the towels.

2. Roll the towels up and roll them inside a damp terry-cloth hand towel.

3. Place all this inside a plastic bag, and tie. Leave in a spot not subject to sudden changes in temperature, like the fridge top. Keep checking. Left more than two or three days, the sprouts will get too large, or the sprouted seeds will start to rot. Be careful not to snap or break their little shoots. If that happens the seed is lost—it won't regerminate.

I believe most vine-family members do best when planted in single long rows. I plant seeds six to ten inches apart in the row. I'll thin the seedlings to the best plants every four to five inches apart in a few weeks. Vine seeds get covered with an inch of soil.

Southern gardeners have the same goal of speeding these items, but for a different reason: They especially want to get melons (which take lots of water) to ripen before the worst of the summer heat and dry spells.

Sweet-potato planting

I prepare soil very thoroughly so it's easy to build raised beds. Sweet potatoes need all the heat they can get. For clay soil, raised beds are a must, as tubers need nice loose soil for expanding.

Beforehand, I broadcast fertilizer over the tops of the rows, and rake it in—about five pounds of 5–10–10 per 100 foot of row. I'm separating the slips, one per hole.

Easiest way to plant: Shove in a trowel, push to one side a few inches, slide in the plant. I plant sweet potatoes up to their leaf cluster, five to six inches deep every foot in the row.

Firming the soil is next. I'll give those slips a good watering right away. But thereafter, sweet potatoes can resist a dry summer pretty well.

Guess which sweet potatoes I raised indoors and which I bought by mail.

When planting the homegrown slips, I just "unplug" them from the starter seed potato, and plant the same way I've just demonstrated. You can also snap off these shoots from the potato and place in water. They'll form roots, and, when planted, they take off quickly.

It's time for all indoor-raised or purchased plants to be planted. While they're waiting for their turn, keep them in the shade.

Reminders for May . . .

- Harden off all flats of indoor-raised or pur-chased plants.
- Keep turning your unplanted garden soil as time and energy permit. This surfaces and destroys weed seeds.
- When weather is reliably settled, complete garden planting of tender crops. Refer to my depth-planting chart on pages 96–97.
- Lay that tomato on its side with the leaves stripped off. Refer to my diagram on page 112.
- Don't forget to use some fertilizer in the holes of transplants and really soak the plants afterward.
- Harvest early spinach and lettuces—don't let them bolt. Keep radishes picked.
- Cultivate and thin seedlings when they're ½-inch. See details early June.

Brewing for June . . .

- Easy "in row" weeding
- Cultivate now—less work later
- Cut-and-come-again greens
- Side-dressing: what, when, and how much
- Assuring a bumper tomato crop!
- My bug-control chart

- Cultivating, weeding, mulching, hilling, and watering—why, how and when
- Final planting
- The best way to harvest greens
- Simplifying insect control and fertilizers as side-dressing
- Pampering those tomato plants: supporting, tying up, and "suckering"

JUNE

Gardening care—done right—takes less time

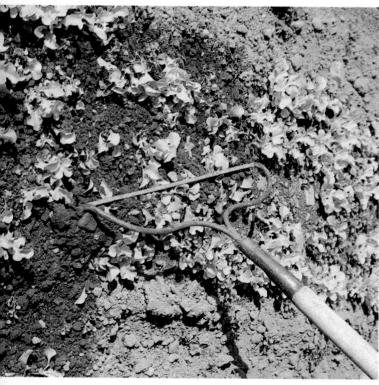

EARLY JUNE
Cultivating and thinning

When seedlings are a half-inch high, I do these two important steps with *one* simple stroke. It only takes a few minutes a week to get rid of weeds and keep a garden in top shape, my way. That's how I can keep cultivating the soil at this crucial stage every four to five days.

Aerating the soil is absolutely essential. Cultivating plants means allowing air to reach the roots and many forms of soil life that are busy at work. When we garden, we're not alone! It's more like being commander-in-chief of an army of organisms doing all sorts of good things for our soil and our plants. I use my hoe and rake. Sometimes I can get in and around my transplants best with a small hand tool.

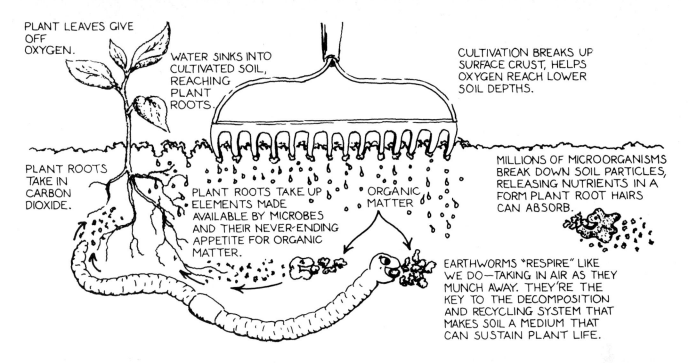

PLANT LEAVES GIVE OFF OXYGEN.

WATER SINKS INTO CULTIVATED SOIL, REACHING PLANT ROOTS.

CULTIVATION BREAKS UP SURFACE CRUST, HELPS OXYGEN REACH LOWER SOIL DEPTHS.

PLANT ROOTS TAKE IN CARBON DIOXIDE.

PLANT ROOTS TAKE UP ELEMENTS MADE AVAILABLE BY MICROBES AND THEIR NEVER-ENDING APPETITE FOR ORGANIC MATTER.

ORGANIC MATTER

MILLIONS OF MICROORGANISMS BREAK DOWN SOIL PARTICLES, RELEASING NUTRIENTS IN A FORM PLANT ROOT HAIRS CAN ABSORB.

EARTHWORMS "RESPIRE" LIKE WE DO—TAKING IN AIR AS THEY MUNCH AWAY. THEY'RE THE KEY TO THE DECOMPOSITION AND RECYCLING SYSTEM THAT MAKES SOIL A MEDIUM THAT CAN SUSTAIN PLANT LIFE.

If this seems brutal, don't look down.

I can cultivate *and* thin my newly sprouted rows with one pass of the rake. Any rake will do. This step is important because wide-row broadcasting results in vegetable plants so thick that they must be thinned. And, perhaps most important, this stirring of the top quarter inch also stirs up the germinating weed seeds exposing them to the surface so they'll die. Half of my weeding is accomplished right here.

But folks sometimes get squeamish about rake-thinning. And it does look awful for a few days, and gardeners hate to "waste" the plants. But I tell them they're doing the vegetables a big favor, and the overall yield will be greatly increased.

Here's what this same row looks like a few weeks after rake-thinning. The two thirds of the original seedlings that survived are really flourishing, with the competition from too-close neighbors and weeds virtually eliminated.

TOOLS TO DISTURB THE SOIL AND DESTROY SMALL WEEDS

Disturbed soil is dark because it's exposing the layer underneath the surface crust, which holds more moisture.

My favorite cultivating tool is a newly available "in-row" weeder with long, flexible steel tongs. They kick up the shallow-rooted young weeds but slide around the firmly anchored plants. And I don't have to bend over with this long-handled tool. If you can't locate one, don't panic. There are hundreds of small tools for the task. The key thing is to get in there to break up the soil crust, now that the sun is getting stronger and days are longer. Then oxygen and rain (or any watering you do) will sink to where they are needed. Without cultivating, rain can pack soil, sit on its surface and bake it, or run off with valuable topsoil. This makes the chores of cultivating and weeding ten times more difficult later on. Of course wide rows cut down on weeds in the first place, with developing foliage shading the soil and keeping it moist.

I like long-handled tools so I don't have to get down on my hands and knees. But many of my friends do—with one of a wide variety of hand tools.

A tool like this in-row weeder works even on young plants like this spinach. The springlike teeth get a grip in the soil but pass right around the plants. When using a hoe or hand tool of any sort, the idea is to break the soil surface while only slicing one-quarter to one-half inch deep. We do not want to reach down and damage plant roots.

This easy weeder is shaped like a pointed finger and called a "finger" or "poker" hoe. Because of increasing traffic through the garden, I need to break up really hard-packed spots here and there. This simple and easy handling tool has the leverage to break up soil with the power of a tiller. The finger can totally uproot a tall weed instead of slicing it off, which happens so often with a regular hoe. This poker or finger-shaped hoe is really better than a tiller because it can go shallowly in and around plants without disturbing roots, or it can go deep to lift out taller weeds without churning much soil. If I bump into my plants it won't cut them off.

Another new hand tool on the gardening scene is this "wing hoe." It's at an angle that lets me cultivate close up to plants, but just skimming the surface. The curved center glides in a little deeper, for walkways. A regular hoe requires more of a hacking motion, so please use that with care.

It only takes a few minutes to go up and down walkways to cultivate them with an ordinary rake. (This always seems like a bigger job than it is!) I work toward myself to avoid stepping on the loose soil. And I cultivate these walkways after I've done so in and around my plants, to avoid more compaction.

Summary of my plan to a nearly *weed-free garden:*

Weed seeds can sprout beneath the soil but they can't *grow* unless they are right near the surface. We want them to grow so they'll be destroyed by cultivation. Otherwise, with their hard shells, seeds can last for years in the garden. Although weeds don't amount to much now, and the garden looks tidy, this is the time to nip weeds before they're a problem.

Always cultivate shallow around plants . . . no more than a half-inch deep. It's easier, you'll do it more often, and it protects the plants. Between rows, an inch and a half.

- In spring, turn the soil several times before planting. This will bring weed seeds to the surface—their germination zone—where they will sprout and die. The soil will be too cold to grow very much. Later on they will sprout again, break through the surface, and be destroyed by rake thinning and shallow cultivating within the rows.
- Attack perennial weeds by deep and regular tilling before planting. In badly infested areas, combine this technique with the sowing of a thickly growing cover crop like annual rye grass or buckwheat, instead of gardening for vegetables, for

an entire season. This can weaken and choke out the weeds. (See an example of sections of my garden planted to cover crops on page 218.

- Regular disturbing of the soil after seeded vegetables are one-half inch tall continues to kill shallow-rooted weeds while leaving vegetable plants intact.
- Continue such cultivating every four or five days in rows of transplanted vegetables. These rows don't need thinning, but have developed root foundations strong enough to withstand the workings of a tool. Cultivating no more than one-half inch deep in walkways means saving vegetable roots, yet doing away with young weed plants.
- Don't let annual weeds flower and go to seed. Keep after the stray weed plants, on into the summer and fall.
- Keep adjacent areas mowed for the same reason.
- Avoid mulches with weed seeds, like most forms of hay and manures, unless very thoroughly composted or "cooked" for a few weeks.
- Wide-row planting crowds out most weeds. With block plantings of peas and beans, I don't do any form of weeding at all.

Mostly I cultivate with my rake, hoe, easy weeders, and hand tools, but a powered cultivator saves me time in my larger garden areas. With this machine, I can do shallow, precise cultivating in no time.

Early June 125

There are a few "skips" in my rows of early corn.

I just remove the wire and poke in some new kernels. I don't usually have empty patches in my wide rows. There I can be a little more generous with my seeds. I find, with my easy rake-thinning method, I'd rather overseed than underseed. But in my single rows, like this one of corn, I like to go back and fill the space left by unsuccessful seedlings. I only need to do this once. I planted this early corn a month ago (in early May, pages 100–101). In a week, this will be ready for removal of the bird guard and its first hilling. The newly planted seeds will make up some for lost time, and in fact stretch the harvest by staggering it.

When the leaves of my plants are brushing up against hot caps, it's time to unwrap them.

To dust or not to dust . . .

Despite my basic wait-and-see philosophy, I do practice preventive medicine with tomatoes, potatoes, and all cabbage-family crops. I know if I didn't dust I'd have a problem with flea beetles and blights. Practically every region has a local tomato pest. When I dust every ten days or so with a readily available product simply called "tomato dust," especially during this month of major growth, I know the plant is going to be much healthier than the average and set a bountiful crop of fruit. Early summer dusting happens way before harvesting, so it's safe.

Please refer to my easy bug-control "what-when" chart, coming up on page 133.

Progress in the family potato patch.

The main-crop plants have now developed vines and leaves above the soil. Because tubers form below ground, in a few weeks (pages 131, 138) I'll be taking my hoe or rototiller and hilling up these plants, just as I did my early-planted crop (page 111, in May).

To stake or not to stake . . .

I usually have in mind one of the tomato-support systems when planting. It's best to install it then. But as I said in May, I was so busy planting that I left this chore to now. And all my tomato stems are buried in the same direction so I can avoid damaging them.

Cages: *There's a variety of materials available for caging. I like the solid galvanized wire, commonly used as turkey fencing. Some holes the size of my fist have to be cut so I can reach in to harvest the tomatoes. Vines grow up inside the cages and the heavy foliage prevents ripening fruit from sunscald. I like a cage about five feet high and two feet in diameter, and secured at ground level by two wooden stakes so it can't topple.*

Wire Trellis: *Wire makes for the sturdiest support, yet doesn't block sunlight as wooden crates and posts do. But I'm more concerned with the choice of a soft material for tying the vines to the wire so the branches or stem don't get severed. I always add a wire-and-pole trellis tomato section to my garden. I know it takes more work to install and eventually to take down. And just about every week I find a heavy branch or two that needs support. But this system looks attractive and makes it really easy to tend and harvest the fruit.*

Stakes—*one per plant—take less room than cages, so plants can be set closer together. But stakes also mean tying the plant up a few times during the growing season. To prevent potential stem damage, I set my stake to the side* opposite *the prevailing wind, so that the stem can rest against the support rather than straining away from it. When driving the stake in, it's important to remember the location of that root ball and horizontally buried stem.*

Sprawling Tomatoes: *That's what I call my "no work" tomato patch. I have plenty of room, so I let much of my main crop of tomatoes sprawl, planted close together. It may look messy but this is what nature intended for the plant. Yes, I lose some of the crop due to rot or slugs, if it's too wet. And insects claim their share. But I don't need to mulch because the plants shade the ground. Actually, I don't do anything. And the final harvest tends to be larger than with pruned, supported tomatoes. So overall, it's an even draw.*

Last leg of planting: more green beans, corn, winter squash, plus beans for drying and delectable limas.

It's time now for me to plant my second, main crop of beans. I sow them in a block, just like I do my peas.

Please refer back to my diagram on page 71 in April, where this technique is fully explained for peas.

Basically I spade or till up an area at least ten feet long. Sometimes it's four or five feet wide; sometimes ten feet, to make an even square. I scatter the bean seeds so they're about three to four inches in all directions, then, with a tiller set at a depth of four inches, I work them right into the seedbed. This covers them with one inch of soil. Without a tiller, I sow a three-foot section, cover it by rake with soil from the next, still-unplanted section, and move this way through the block. Then, the only other thing I have to do is enjoy the harvest a few months later!

I plant my crop of supersweet corn (Silver Queen, the long-growing white variety, which birds don't like very much) and tomatoes (for storage) in larger plots of their own. But I use the same technique I illustrated in my 30-by-40 garden.

Planting parsnips in a wide row

As you'll be seeing this fall, many vegetables can stay right in the garden through winter and be harvested under snow. In the case of kale, it can be delicious a few weeks into the following spring, when it resprouts. But I can't really grow parsnips to full size *until* the following spring.

Parsnips require a very long growing season—up to 150 days. So, again, I add some radish seeds to mark the row. I'll harvest a few young parsnips this fall, but the bulk of the crop will not mature until early next spring, when I uncover the thick layers of winter mulch I'll put on this small section of garden in November. Parsnips are planted the same way as other small-seeded root crops, with a fine covering of loose soil drawn over the seeds from the side of the wide row.

If you'll refer again to my 30- by 40-foot garden plan on pages 20–21 in January, you can see I have lots of space to slip in two or three feet of wide row for parsnips—especially between rows eight and nine.

Storage food

It's early June. My soil is thoroughly warm. Now that I've planted lots of different vegetables in my main-crop 30-by-40 garden, it's time to plant some extra "storage" food for us, our daughters, and their families. We planted *bush*-style acorn winter squash in the 30-by-40 garden. But our favorite winter squashes for the root cellar are Blue Hubbard and Butternut. They need 6 to 10 feet between rows for the vines to travel, so they're getting a section all for themselves. Any gardener can plant these crops on a much smaller scale with just a few plants of each variety. I prepare the whole area thoroughly, then till or spade a few extra times for the seedbed rows. Next I'll make a long, shallow trench for the squash seeds with my hoe, or with my tiller's furrow attachment.

I've discovered drying beans and squashes are good companions planted in alternate rows. By the fall when the squash vines have died back and squashes are ready for harvesting, the bean plants are at the same stage.

Into the furrows for squash seed I first add compost or a thin line of 5–10–10 fertilizer . . . which I cover with an inch of soil by walking down the row with my hoe at the right angle. I don't worry if I sow squash seeds too thickly. I can always thin to one plant for every eight to 12 inches.

You can plant dry beans just as you buy them in the store. At the end of their growing season, dry beans become rock hard, and if kept dry, can store for ages. Yellow Eye, Soldier and Navy are our favorites. I simply plant these beans in a wide block, scattering broadly *over the entire area* between the squash rows. They'll sprout quickly and will soon "mulch" and "weed" this large stretch of garden before the squash vines get up steam. My rototiller simplifies the covering of bean seeds over this much space. The beans will be buried a few inches. Some won't make it, but most will. By hand, I would plant these beans as I showed you in my block-planting diagram earlier on page 71.

Time to plant rutabagas for fall storage. It's also warm enough now to sow my okra in wide rows, which I thin to stand in staggered fashion like my peppers.

Limas are last

Sow limas farther apart than ordinary beans—about six inches each way, in a wide row.

Firm into soil. The combination of heat and moisture will help these seeds and plants take off.

Rake loose soil from the side to cover and firm down once more with the hoe.

Lima beans finally get sown. They're tender, heat-loving, and take their (sweet) time.

If you haven't eaten homegrown limas, you're in for a real treat. They are about the most buttery, delicious bean of all. But there's a wait required—can't plant them until soil is really warm. And they take a very long growing season—up to 80 days. I stick to the shorter-to-mature varieties. I would have planted them two or three weeks ago in a drier year. But if we have a gentle September, we should have a fine crop.

And they get the *wide-row* treatment. More vegetables and narrower walkways still leave *ample* room for tending and harvesting plants.

First harvest: from our salad row

I've been pulling radishes for several weeks now. For the first time, there's really enough lettuce for a meal. Here's how I keep those greens producing . . .

Pull the whole looseleaf lettuce plant. It makes more room for remaining plants. I tug gently so I don't break the leaves apart. Also, I don't want to splatter soil on the other young lettuce plants.

Do the same with these tasty scallions. The space taken up by early "harvest thinnings," as I call them, means the remainder will have extra space and freshly loosened soil, too.

The crew cut: my *cut-and-come-again* technique

I take a bread knife and slice off looseleaf lettuce one inch from the ground.

Most folks get in the bad habit of picking the *outside* leaves of looseleaf lettuce plants, spinach, chard, and other greens. This actually causes the plant to grow more from the center, and go to seed faster. The seedpod comes from the middle of the plant—the process that's called "bolting." When these greens get to be four or five inches high, I recommend slicing off the entire crop from the base. In this way you can get two, three, four or even more cuttings from a single planting. With Swiss chard I can crew-cut it completely from four to six times during the season, way after frost. *Note:* I do *not* cut *head* lettuce this way; I'm growing that until there are mature heads to harvest.

CULTIVATING MY CORN BLOCK IS A LITTLE MORE INVOLVED

That doesn't mean that I have to spend all day pulling weeds . . . that's not my idea of fun.

When corn plants are four to five inches tall, it's safe to remove the wire, as plants are now too large to be uprooted by birds.

Just look at this mess of weeds.

Corn is shallow-rooted, and care must be taken with an ordinary hoe or with a powered cultivator so as not to go too deeply. Here I'm cultivating the walkways first just up to the plants. This is not my usual sequence. You'll see my reason in a moment.

I'm sprinkling some 5–10–10 alongside of the corn plants. This amounts to about a tablespoon per plant, or a cupful for each 15 to 25 feet of row. I do this first side-dressing when plants are four to six inches high. Since corn is a heavy feeder, I'll be side-dressing once again, at the tassel stage. (Please see page 135 for my simple side-dressing story.)

The soil I loosened in the walkways is now ready to be drawn against the young plants from both sides. This first hilling of corn anchors the plant, makes the stalk more rigid, to withstand strong winds when loaded with developing ears. It also covers the fertilizer. More important, hilling smothers all those weeds without my breaking my back! I'll be doing a second hilling a month from now, in early July.

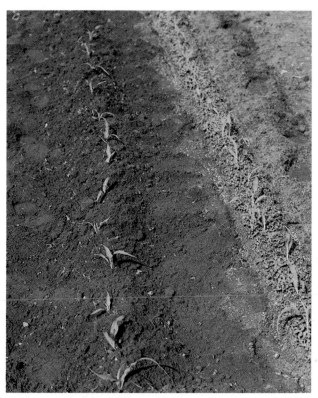

Before and After. Those little weeds that get buried aren't strong enough to push back up through a few inches of soil. See how much more energy is now directed into the vegetable greenery?

Here's a closer look at this process. It looks and is easy. If you really get to like this technique, you can do the same with okra, tomatoes, eggplant, and broccoli—but usually one hilling, not two as with corn and potatoes. Peppers don't want much of their stem buried.

Because the corn block is the tallest section, and the farthest north in the garden, the final row of the block is the place I like to add some sunflowers. They're great for color and for extra protein when we want to save the seeds—for ourselves or to feed birds over the winter. (Birds won't be attracted to the seed-filled flowers until after the corn harvest, so the corn is safe.)

How hilling helps corn

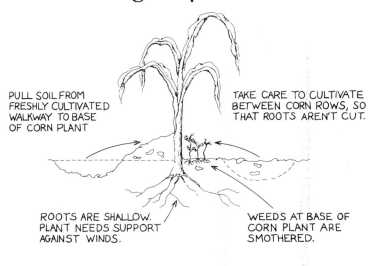

PULL SOIL FROM FRESHLY CULTIVATED WALKWAY TO BASE OF CORN PLANT

TAKE CARE TO CULTIVATE BETWEEN CORN ROWS, SO THAT ROOTS AREN'T CUT.

ROOTS ARE SHALLOW. PLANT NEEDS SUPPORT AGAINST WINDS.

WEEDS AT BASE OF CORN PLANT ARE SMOTHERED.

MY PRACTICAL APPROACH TO BUGS

I've already shared with you my basic garden-insect philosophy (March, pages 47–48). For the most part, it's a wait-and-see approach. The exceptions for my neck of the woods are tomato flea beetles, cabbage worms, cucumber beetles, and potato beetles. For these crops, you've seen me (and will continue to see me) dust or spray preventively, es-pecially through June and July. But for the hundreds of other insect possibilities, I prefer to keep a half-dozen commercial products on hand, which I introduced you to on that March supplies-shopping trip. I use these when the following home remedies don't work . . .

Some "home brews" for the bugs

- Sprinkled wood ash around cabbage-family plants tends to discourage the *cabbage worms*. Spreading scratchy materials like ashes and wood chips can deter *slugs*.
- Always use cutworm collars, especially when transplanting tomatoes and cabbage, to foil *cutworms*.
- Mild solution of soapy water slows down *aphids*. Solutions of garlic or hot pepper discourage *flea beetles*.
- Remove *borers* through a cut slit in the stem of damaged plant.
- Trichogramma wasps and ladybugs are great insect destroyers.

- Try covering plants with cheesecloth or fine netting to prevent moths from laying eggs.
- For *slugs*, some folks feed them beer in a pie plate. I prefer to drink the beer myself (most of it), then submerge the can sideways up to the hole in the metal top. The slugs can crawl in, drink, drown or be unable to get out. You can always buy slug bait, but I prefer putting down wet newspapers. Slugs crawl inside to keep cool during the day; then I can just dispose of them along with the papers.

Like the average gardener, I get frustrated when leafing through garden books that look like encyclopedias, hoping to pinpoint the *exact* cause of my plant damage. For one thing, it is often hard to see the actual culprits. And for another, in your region you'd swear yours have a black stripe but the book doesn't show it that way.

I'm successful limiting bug damage with a combination of prevention and cure. Usually my garden is so bountiful that bugs can generally take their share of nibbles without noticeable wreckage. Should bugs start getting out of control, I go to my supply of pesticides outlined on the following chart.

My simple bug control chart

USE THESE PESTICIDES, / WITH THESE VEGETABLES	CHEWING DAMAGE FROM BUGS AND BEETLES OF ALL SORTS — CABBAGE FAMILY, BEANS, GREENS, TOMATOES, CUKES, AND VINE CROPS	CHEWING DAMAGE THAT IS EVEN MORE EXTENSIVE	WORMS AND CATERPILLARS OF ALL SORTS — CABBAGE FAMILY (WORM), TOMATO (HORNWORM), CORN (EARWORM)	APHIDS, BORERS, LEAF MINERS, AND SUCKING INSECTS — PEPPERS, EGGPLANTS, TOMATOES	ROOT MAGGOTS — CABBAGE FAMILY, RADISH (MOSTLY), CARROTS, BEETS, TURNIPS, ONIONS	POTATO BEETLE — POTATOES, EGGPLANT
ROTENONE OR PYRETHRUM. NON-TOXIC. TRY ONE OF THESE FIRST.	X					X
DIPEL—SPRAY OR DUST. NON-TOXIC. ESPECIALLY EFFECTIVE AGAINST CABBAGE WORM.			X			
SEVIN—SPRAY OR DUST. MILDLY TOXIC. TRY THIS NEXT, IF FIRST PRODUCTS DON'T WORK.	X					X
MALATHION—SPRAY OR DUST. STRONGER TOXICITY, WITH LONGER RESIDUE INTACT.		X				X
"TOMATO/GENERAL VEGETABLE" DUST. ANOTHER GENERAL-PURPOSE, FAIRLY POWERFUL AND EFFECTIVE PRODUCT.		X		X		X
DIAZANON. GRANULAR (WORK INTO SOIL AT BASE OF PLANTS) SPRAY.				X	→X	

ALWAYS READ AND FOLLOW LABEL INSTRUCTIONS CAREFULLY. IF YOU DO, THESE PRODUCTS ARE SAFE.

Herbs are easy!

I always save a two-foot section of a wide row (above) for garden-fresh herbs. They take so little space. You only need a plant or two of each variety because a few sprigs pack so much flavor. After I harvest a handful of summer savory or basil it seems to have grown right back in by my next visit to the herb row.

I usually buy my herbs as started plants at a nearby garden center. These days the selections are getting better as people discover how trouble-free they are to grow. Whether the herbs are annual (like basil) or perennial (like thyme), I prefer to get them new each year so I can put them in my vegetable garden. You could, of course, raise annuals in with the vegetables or create an ongoing, permanent little patch of perennial herbs near the kitchen or as a border.

All of us have our personal favorites. The ones growing here in this small section (at right) of wide row are: parsley (there's a lot of that), red basil,

Try a hanging basket. These of parsley, basil, chives and thyme hang right outside our kitchen door. What could be more convenient? This way they really get used—often at the last minute. Herbs do well in pots, indoors and out.

chives, thyme, summer savory, and dill. Since we do a lot of pickling, I also sow a separate section of dill from seed in another part of the garden.

At a distance, our 30- by 40-foot garden looks like most is yet to come. And that's true. But as you've seen, Jan and I have been eating fresh salads for weeks.

MIDDLE JUNE
SIDE-DRESSING

If soil is rich in organic matter, plants start off with lots of available nutrients. But any garden makes demands—almost to an unnatural extent—on the soil. So I say: side-dress. Most soils need boosters. Just sprinkle the tablespoon of fertilizer around each plant, work it in gently just an inch deep with a hand tool and water well.

This is a step many gardeners tend to overlook. That's understandable—so often the plants look great as they are. And, if people garden like me, they've *already* spread and worked in some fertilizer over the entire garden in spring (see page 67 back in April).

I recommend adding some extra fertilizer to get the full potential from vegetable plants. That early dose over the entire garden helped get plants off to a good start and to build a strong root system. But midway through, as blossoms are being set, most plants can really benefit from an extra surge of nutrition . . . so they can fully develop as many of those blossoms into fruit as possible, and to yield really succulent sweet-tasting vegetables as well.

You don't *have* to side-dress. But if you do, I know you will be really pleased with the results. And it isn't a lot of work when you get in the habit.

MY RULES OF THUMB:

- One tablespoon per plant
- Don't guess: actually use a spoon to measure, so you don't overdo it.
- One large handful of good compost generally equals one tablespoon of 5–10–10.
- Draw a circle with your finger around the plant at its dripline (the distance from the central stem to the end of the widest lateral branches) up to one inch deep (any deeper and the roots might get disturbed). Sprinkle in fertilizer and cover.

Crops I *don't* side-dress:

- Peas, beans, *looseleaf* lettuce, spinach (although fertilizer *will* boost second, third, and multiple cuttings of the leafy greens)
- Root crops (beets, carrots, turnips) I add some bone meal for phosphorus—a root builder—at planting time.

Crops I side-dress once:

- Broccoli, cabbage and cauliflower: when they start to head
- Eggplant, peppers, tomatoes, okra: at blossom time
- Brussels sprouts: when sprouts are marble sized

- Cukes, melons, winter squash: just before they spread out their vines
- Summer squash, zucchini: blossom time
- Leeks: handful of compost per plant, when 12 inches tall (which also helps blanch stalks)
- Potatoes and sweet potatoes: before second hilling, so as to cover fertilizer with soil
- Chard: after crew-cut harvesting each time, for a vigorous regrowth. Sprinkle over wide row.
- Head lettuce: a few weeks after planting, to get largest heads.

"Big Eaters": Crops I side-dress twice:

- Corn and onions: one cupful of fertilizer per eight feet of corn row; or ten feet of wide-row onions. First, when plants are four to eight inches tall. Next, a few weeks later (for onions), and when tassels form (for corn). By the way, onions can be fed from the top (top-dressing). Just sprinkle fertilizer over the row like salt.

Ongoing Garden Care

Mulching . . .

Mulching is the layering of materials onto garden soil and around plants. It results in blocking out sunlight so weeds can't get a start . . . keeping soil cool . . . and conserving moisture. Some weeds are persistent enough to grow up and between the loose organic materials popular as mulch: grass clippings, hay and straw, leaves. In addition, many gardeners simply can't collect enough organic matter to cover their gardens.

When organic mulch is applied early in the season, often the soil microbes are so busy decomposing its bottom layer that fewer soil nutrients are available to the vegetable plants. The microbes are using them. And if the soil isn't *completely* warm, mulch will seal in *too much* moisture, attracting slugs and hampering the vigor of heat-loving crops. Personally, I'd rather cultivate the soil, for the most part. But in very dry conditions, mulching can be important. Now is the time to put mulch in place before plants get any larger and more difficult to work around. By the way, while black plastic raises some eyebrows, and it's not so pretty, it works. Some cover it with peat moss. The point is, it does do a complete mulching job.

Weeding . . .

This has been a bad year for weeds. When a patch gets this out-of-hand, I just till it all in and start over, perhaps with a new crop if it's too late to sow the original variety. But on the whole, I keep up with weeds, using my long-handled tools, tiller, and easy techniques more than I do my back.

Watering . . .

When to water? Every week, June through September, your garden needs an inch of rainfall . . . or water that you provide. Vegetables depend on water to absorb the nutrients required for growth. Leave a tin can in the garden. Check it after a rain (before evaporation) to get a rough idea of how much rain was of benefit to your plants. One inch means soaking the soil down to a depth of four to five inches, which reaches the majority of vegetable plant roots.

Please see page 115 for my favorite *hand-held* watering device, the soft spray wand which attaches to an ordinary garden hose. With this, it doesn't take long to cover a large garden, and only plants are watered, with little going onto walkways.

There are lots of good sprinkler systems, like this oscillating sprayer. To get that weekly inch for my plants I'll leave it on for at least a few hours. I set it up high on an old stool, for maximum reach. It saves time so I'm free to do another chore, or to relax. Always try to water crops in the evening or early morning when evaporation by the sun is low. After a hot day, we can expect plants to droop in the afternoon. But if they're still like that in the *morning*, we need to water—really soak down to a depth of four to five inches. Otherwise, roots will grow shallow and dependent on surface water, and be less able to resist droughts.

Ongoing . . . Some Particulars

Pixie tomato time! (well before the main crop)

The first sight of ripe, red tomatoes is always a thrill. The Pixies are the earliest variety I know of —the ones I grew indoors in winter to cheer things up. These were set out as started plants on a slightly raised bed the very first part of May. Not only are Pixies early, but prolific, too. These will produce now all summer—and they grow only to 18 inches high.

First hilling of main-crop potato patch.

I did this by hand in the much smaller potato block in our 30- by 40-foot garden. With a furrower attachment on my tiller, I can rototill the soil between the rows of potatoes and shove the loose soil to both sides.

This section of earlier planted potatoes has already had its second hilling. Whatever weeds weren't smothered by that hilling are pretty easy to spot— and pull—as I make my inspection tour.

Jan is harvest-thinning *sweet, crispy,* small *heads of Buttercrunch lettuce.*

I'd say this variety is my favorite. Harvesting some heads early keeps the supply lasting for months. Each head that is pulled leaves a pocket for its neighbors, so they can branch out. Don't pick out-side leaves! Enjoy the whole head: dark, crunchy outer leaves, blanched and sweet ones inside. Wide-row growing offers heads in various stages, as opposed to a single line, where the heads reach full maturity at the same time—that means more harvest than most families want to eat all at once!

Remember my cut-and-come-again crew-cutting way with *looseleaf* lettuce, where seedlings were thinned but still grow pretty close together, to form that blanket of greens you saw me harvest with a bread knife? But these head lettuces I'm growing as full individual plants, and they will be harvested as such.

Progress in my big bean and winter squash plantings . . .

Doesn't take long for beans to sprout. There is going to be one nice big mess of beans for the grand-kids to help me thresh this fall! Notice the slower-emerging winter-squash plants, to the sides. They'll catch up soon, with the strong sun these days. All we do is plant and pick. There's no tend-ing, mulching, weeding, or, usually, any watering in a thickly sown block planting of peas or beans. The patch is a little spotty just now, but as you'll see, it will quickly fill in.

Planting in containers

I can do this any time, because I'm in control of the environment.

Vegetables are happy to grow in containers. I wonder if, when gardening in them, we're more likely to keep the plants watered and fertilized, their being so dependent on us? Containers in sunny locations need watering just about every day, all summer. Other than that they are very easy. And what a conversation piece!

I'm planting one each of several vegetables—tomato, cabbage, lettuce (2 kinds), parsley, onions, radishes, spinach, broccoli—to demonstrate that anybody can garden, even without land. In the upcoming months you'll see me harvesting quite a bounty from here!

I thought a planter of green beans would look nice along the edge of our patio. I'm going to sow a few different kinds, plus a bush wax bean, too. The foliage will be large enough to be attractive very soon. And it's fun to watch your vegetables growing an arm's length away. I use a good rich mix of soil, compost for texture, and a handful of fertilizer. The other vegetables need fertilizer more than green beans do; this was for good measure.

With a container this size, you're getting serious. Eight cubic feet of soil can produce a lot of fully grown plants for eating fresh. All-day sun is a must. It contains all the vegetables in the circular tub, plus eggplant, carrots, beets, and chard.

Now for a whole salad garden in this circular tub.

Here's an eight-foot planter with over a dozen vegetables, including eggplant.

Now is the time to side-dress some of the remaining crops . . .

Tomatoes and eggplants when they are at the blossom point and **potatoes** before the second hilling

Time to dust for potato beetles.

Time to hill up the corn once more.

I dust potatoes because I *know* there will be beetles no matter what. And a light dusting now, followed up every ten days during the growing season, will greatly reduce the infestation and damage. Dusting or spraying also cuts down on blight, a common potato problem.

Please take my word: I move pretty fast through these chores. They often *sound* like work. Mostly,

it's grabbing my hoe and walking briskly up and down the rows. Sometimes I like to linger. But most times I like to *get through* these easy but essential steps of garden care in five or ten minutes. Frequent but short visits to my garden let me keep it almost weedless. If I thought each task was to take hours, instead of minutes, I know I'd put them off.

How I tie the tomato plant to its support . . .

Loose around the plant . . .
. . . but **tight** around the wire.

I generally rip strips of old cloth for this purpose—or I get some soft fabric roping, as pictured here. The support is secure to the wire while letting the plant move to some degree against winds and rain.

REMINDER FOR BEAUTIFUL, UNBLEMISHED TOMATOES . . .

Keep tomatoes well watered because blossom-end rot, that dark, squishy discoloration at the bottom of the tomato, is the number one source of tomato damage. It's due to lack of steady moisture (which carries calcium) as this rapidly growing plant speeds along in its growth.

One day I came upon a row of broccoli and lettuce that had become a feast for an uninvited animal. The broccoli and lettuce will return. But so will the rabbit. So I've got to install a fence around my 30-by 40-foot garden before the height of the harvest.

In fact, I've got some fencing along the borders of our entire homestead where we come up against the woods. So I've always had some problems with rabbits and other animals. But this year they've gotten a little too greedy. I find stringing an electric wire on top of my regular fence is the only real solution to raccoons. (Please see my animal pest-and-fencing suggestions back in March, page 49.)

Sun Belt gardeners

Either block planting or wide rows is the method to raise our regular, "English" peas, a cool-weather crop, in hot climates. The tangle of growth shades the ground and cools the plants themselves. This way, they take hardly any watering, which is a real breakthrough. It's as if peas grown in a block create their own air-conditioning. So give this idea a try.

This block of peas is four by 20 feet. Wait till you see the harvest. See how the vines are self-supporting? I figure we harvest 50 pounds of peas from a pound of planted seeds. (I get 50 pounds of beans, too, from a pound of seed sown by the block.) The vines are thick enough to block any sun from reaching tiny weeds, so weeding is no problem here.

These tiny weeds never amounted to anything thanks to the shade of the wide row.

LATE JUNE

I get more production *per plant:* I grew a special section of garden just to compare the results of wide versus single rows.

Head lettuces . . .

Cabbage . . .

Onions . . .

Although I usually *plant* my rows in 16-inch bands, of course they grow to over two feet wide, shrinking the walkways with vegetables as plants mature. Wide rows produce the greater quantity because there are simply more plants. But also,

I've noticed, as with my rows of lettuce, each plant is more productive. And one of the reasons for taller crops: wide rows keep the plants, as well as the ground, nice and cool.

Ongoing

White icicle radishes are helpers—they are cultivating my carrot row.

It took me some time to get used to white radishes. Radishes are red! But at all stages, the white icicles are crisp and tasty—milder than the reds. Because of their shape, they're easy to slice and serve. But their main purpose, for me, is to aerate the wide row of carrots. The soil is now loose where I've harvested the radishes. I may lose a few tiny carrot seedlings in the process, but that's fine, because thinning carrots is critical to getting a well-shaped crop.

I've got to weed, then mulch, asparagus.

As soon as we end the harvesting of spears, I weed the patch and side-dress with 10–10–10, which has plenty of nitrogen. I use one quart for every five feet of row. Then I cover the ground with a thick mulch. Asparagus plants need to start putting their energy back into their crowns and root foundation after a fine two-month harvest. That happens by letting the spears grow up into leafy ferns, where food for the plant is manufactured. The harvest season is short but intense. Now they need to rest.

JUNE 21—FIRST (OFFICIAL) DAY OF SUMMER

Suckering tomatoes . . .

All tomatoes form from blossoms that grow on the main stem. There are lateral leaf branches that shade the tomatoes from sunscald. Additional "main stems," or entire new plants, form at the V along the original stem or central trunk, and if left unpruned will continue to sprout more tomato fruits. It's helpful to slice some of these "suckers" off so the overall plant doesn't get top-heavy or produce more fruit than there is time or energy to mature. I always let a few of these extra main stems grow, especially within cages or on supports. I let *all* of them grow when I let tomatoes sprawl on the ground, unsupported (that's why sprawling tomatoes result in heaviest overall yield). Suckering is helpful, but you don't need to get uptight about it. I don't.

On larger suckers I use a knife.

Suckers can be pinched off. Generally I use my penknife for a cleaner break.

Mulching them . . .

If I didn't mulch already, now is about the time I would put down a good thick mulch around my tomatoes to conserve moisture in the soil for my plants (see page 112). Mulching vegetables with compost or grass clippings also provides additional food for the plant. It smothers weeds, too. A lack of moisture (to release calcium) is what causes blossom-end rot. In a dry year I'd also mulch around eggplants and peppers—less bushy than others; also, around my perennials. Mostly, I prefer *living* mulch—wide rows of vegetables! Ordinarily, I'd mulch in late June, but this year it's been raining so much, the ground is still very damp.

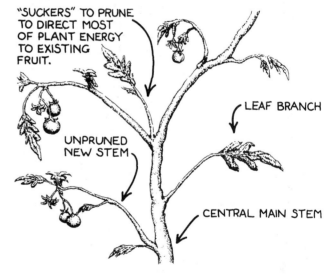

"SUCKERS" TO PRUNE TO DIRECT MOST OF PLANT ENERGY TO EXISTING FRUIT.

LEAF BRANCH

UNPRUNED NEW STEM

CENTRAL MAIN STEM

. . . And tying them up *where there are multiple main stems needing support.*

In the case of this tomato plant with one main trunk, a second tie was needed higher up, as the plant grew. Its burden is especially heavy—all on one main stem. A few weeks later it may need yet another tying up. So I keep a pretty close watch on these "gems of the garden." Remember that healthier, sturdier plants invite fewer insect and disease problems as well.

Progress reports in

My "pepper plantation"

Very few blossoms, but growth looks good. I have to be patient with peppers and eggplants—especially with eggplants. You often think eggplants are *never* going to set a blossom. Both crops need sun and heat. Remember: no more fertilizer on peppers until they blossom. And try my Epsom salt-spraying idea (page 117) at blossom, too.

My bean block

Beans don't usually turn in a poor performance. The last time I showed you this large block of beans, on page 138, much of the patch looked sparse. But, as in any wide row, the plants generally fill in gaps, and use that available sunshine. It's a sight to behold—a beautiful patch of thriving bean foliage in a section of one's garden.

In my patio planters

A few weeks after planting, the plants look small. But they're interesting—they draw your attention. You somehow still can't believe *full*-sized vegetables (cabbage, eggplant, tomatoes) can be produced without tons of soil underneath.

In my wide-row limas

By the time weeds realize they've sprouted, the so-much-larger lima-bean plants will spread those umbrellalike leaves, touch each other, and totally block all light. Limas are a plant-and-forget crop when sown in a wide row.

Reminders for June . . .

- Keep cultivating between and within rows to stay ahead of weeds.
- Replant "skips" in corn rows. Hill them when plants are four to six inches tall.
- Stay on bug patrol. Try my home brews (page 132) and, if necessary, see my bug-control chart (page 133).
- Plant last of the tender vegetables—all beans and remaining vine crops.
- Harvest-thin onions, head lettuce, beet greens. Crew-cut looseleaf lettuce, spinach, chards.
- Hill . . . one more time.
- Side-dressing starts this month (see page 135).
- *Water* . . . one inch per week.
- Give tomatoes extra attention: suckering, tying up, supporting, and mulching.

Brewing for July . . .

- Fall fresh eating from "succession planting" now
- Pea harvest!
- Robbing first new potatoes
- Harvest-thinning root crops
- Dry-weather gardening know-how

- ✓ Harvest-thinning more first pickings

- ✓ Spading under the earliest crops (lettuce, spinach, and peas) and planting new ones for the fall

- ✓ Harvesting broccoli and summer squash before they go to seed

- ✓ Side-dressing cauliflower, broccoli, tomatoes, eggplants, peppers and melons, at flowering stage for the best crops possible

- ✓ Watering without fail: My rules are simple but unskippable

- ✓ Mulching if it's really dry

- ✓ Patrolling for bugs

JULY

Pick 'em young, tender, and sweet!

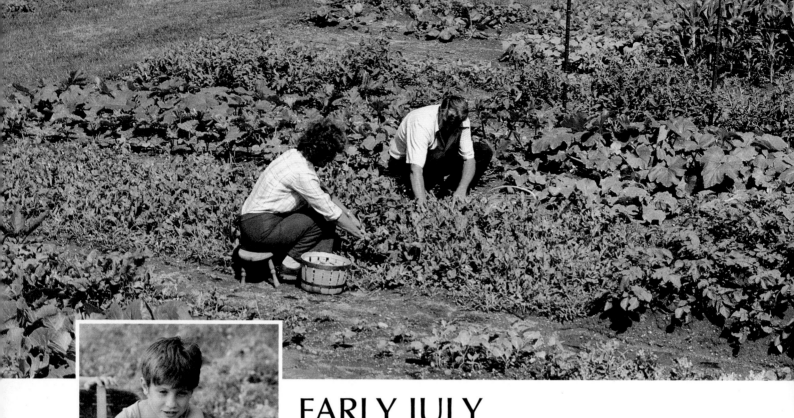

EARLY JULY
Peas are ready! Many hands make light work.

HARVEST TIP

Hold the pea stem in one hand near the base of the pod. Break the pod off with your other hand. Don't try to yank the pod off, one-handed, or you can snap the stem of still-standing pods or uproot the plant completely.

If there is any doubt about whether a garden is worth the time and effort, the first taste of home-grown peas puts that idea to rest.

When are peas ready? When the pods become full, about two weeks or so after they blossom. I break a few open each day to check. Even when they're small, it's nice to toss a few new peas in with buttered and boiled new potatoes, or just barely steamed bright green and added to a salad.

A few days later we can collect enough pods for real servings. But within a week, especially if the sun stays strong, it's time to call in help from other family members. Jan likes to bring a small wooden stool right into the patch to make picking easier.

I promised you a crop of peas that didn't take any weeding, watering, or side-dressing. This bonus, plus their wonderful flavor, should guarantee peas a spot in every garden. And wide-row or block planting yields a harvest large enough to satisfy everyone's appetite for them.

We can harvest edible-podded snow peas as soon as they're large enough to eat—the younger the better. As with so many vegetables, the more we harvest, the more they produce.

Peas start to lose sweetness as soon as they are picked, though not as rapidly as corn. It's a good idea to limit the time between picking and eating.

The patio tubs of vegetables *are keeping pace with those same crops in the garden. Since they sit close to the house, it's easy to give them a daily drink during this hottest of our seasons. The blossoms on these cherry-type tomatoes have just been set.*

The lettuce under the broccoli *almost looks like it's going to take over. In fact, it's providing ideal conditions for the broccoli, keeping the soil and main stem good and shaded . . . quite an accomplishment for early July!*

The broccoli crown and major leaves are exposed to full sun, and I'll get a tight, crisp head in a few more weeks. It's a gardening challenge to keep broccoli from bolting to seed in summer heat. A "carpet" of lettuce is one way to prevent this.

Spray/dust alert

Every ten days I'm going to remind you to spray or dust potatoes and tomatoes with Tomato/General Vegetable Dust and to dust or spray all cabbage-family crops with Dipel.

A stand of Jerusalem artichokes

I don't feature Jerusalem artichokes in this book because I figure the average reader doesn't have the room for them. If I didn't cut lawn area around this vigorous underground tubered vegetable, it would spread like wildfire. But I enjoy this hardy crop. If you think you might too, buy tubers to plant in the spring (or better yet, dig up some from a neighbor). Cut into pieces that have an eye, like a potato, on each piece, and plant them four inches deep and a foot apart. Harvest by digging in late fall after tops die back, or early next spring before they sprout again. They're crunchy, low-calorie, nutritious (and hard-to-clean, but worth it).

Early July   151

Succession planting is this simple.

Now's the time to turn under harvested spring crops and plant the space to new ones for the fall.

The lettuce I'm turning under was the first I planted a few months ago. We've had our fill of this variety; there are lots more salad greens coming along, so out comes the spade. Lettuce is soft and will decompose quickly. I bury the residues to the depth of the spade by completely overturning each shovelful. I rake the area smooth, broadcast a handful of fertilizer over the wide row, rake that in, then scatter the seeds of beets or carrots or spinach or more lettuce for harvesting this fall. (Please see the plan for my 30- by 40-foot garden on pages 20–21 in January. That gives a more specific idea of just what and where I "succession plant.")

Remember to cover the seed with soil to a depth of four times the seeds' diameter—about a quarter-inch for the tiny seeds, a half-inch for the larger ones such as beets. I pat down the planted seedbed with my palms or the back of a hoe and water well. All this takes less than five minutes.

Now that the corn is a foot tall, it's time to hill this crop a second and last time. In addition to burying any weeds in the rows, this extra hilling forms a good anchor around the base of the plants, greatly lessening the possibility of windfalls. My corn rows are 30 inches apart to allow for cultivating (less soil is needed for hilling corn than for potatoes, which I planted in rows 36 inches apart).

Blanch celery by hilling it. Hilling also comes in handy for raising milder-tasting celery. A few inches of soil mounded up against the stalks blocks sunlight and keeps the vegetable whiter and more tender. I'm not necessarily in favor of blanching homegrown celery. One of celery's real appeals is its dark-green crunchy stalks, so great in salads and soups. They have lots more "punch" than the watered-down commercial version. Since celery roots are near the surface, it's important to keep the soil moist. My best advice is to not apply mulch around plants too early in season; wait until about now when moisture retention is a real challenge. Hilling forms a good slug-free mulch that will do just that.

Last minute mini-gardens

This is the chance to plant for fall. Just for the fun of it, I'm planting some square-foot patches in my lawn. I'm setting out onion sets for scallions, an overgrown tomato plant that never made it into the main-crop garden, a variety of lettuces, and a half-dozen broccoli plants. One square foot is crowding the broccoli, but the heads will be small anyway since they'll be growing during the peak of summer. The only requirement is well-worked soil with a handful of fertilizer mixed in. And, of course, I'll make sure they get lots of moisture. The surrounding turf will, in fact, be like a mulch and will limit soil evaporation and compaction.

Over in the potato patch . . .

I inspect for beetles. It was easy to spot them in this case, since the larvae, adults and eggs were all right on one cluster. This is why we have to spray potatoes every seven to ten days. It's been over a week, so I'm going to have to keep after these potato beetles until they're under control.

By late June, I start poking into the soft soil under my early potatoes to see how they're coming along. These are too small to harvest, so I'll just replant the roots and tubers I disturbed. This doesn't harm the plant. In a week or two there will be some potatoes large enough to swipe, which I can also do without interrupting the plant's production (see page 165, coming up).

My dry-weather water-saving tips:

1. Water when plants need it: Late-afternoon wilt is one thing—that's to be expected in July; but after the benefit of a cool dewy night, if they are still drooping in the morning, then your plants do need a good drink.
2. Don't water midday. Too much water is lost to evaporation.
3. Cultivate the soil before watering so the maximum amount of moisture will soak in, rather than run off.
4. Put a small tin can in the garden when you water with an oscillating device over a large area to make sure you deliver up to an inch.

Or scoop down into the soil to see that water has soaked in four to five inches, good and deep. If not, plants are not getting what they really need, and more time and water are wasted on repetitive waterings that don't do that much good.

5. Mulch to slow down evaporation and choke out weeds competing for water and nutrients. Grass clippings (dried for a few hours so they don't get slimy), fall leaves, pine needles, and any organic matter free of weed seeds are good to use. But stay away from hay, unless it's been well composted. Mulch *after* plants have had a thorough soaking.

It's the season for thinning. With beets, everything's edible.

Even though I rake-thinned this wide row of beets back in June, they do have a tendency to fill out the space. That's fine, because we love cooked beet greens. When the beet bottoms are marble-size, as on the right in this photo, we think they're even tastier. We cook the young beets together with their greens.

Little known fact: As many as three beets (and chard plants) are produced from a single seed. So, to avoid overcrowding, early rake-thinning (pages 122–23) and follow-up harvest-thinning are important steps.

Harvest-thinning, of course, helps to cultivate the soil within the row, loosening the soil and making it easier for remaining root crops to grow. Like beets, fingerling carrots get harvest-thinned, too. I pick the largest ones, to let the smaller ones keep growing. You can tell the largest carrots because they have the darkest green tops.

Salad harvest tip: When harvesting single leaves of kale or collard plants for your salad bowl, don't pick haphazardly. Outside picking will force the crowns to become that much more productive. Try to pick before leaves get too large. All vegetables are sweeter, more tender and crisp, when picked small rather than large.

Outer cabbage leaves should definitely *not* be picked. They shade the ground and maintain the cool, moist environment cabbages need.

With *looseleaf* lettuce, spinach, chard, and all other greens which have a tendency to bolt quickly to seed, I recommend cutting off the *whole plant*, as it will regrow. It's my technique that I call cut-and-come-again and it's illustrated on page 129, when the rows are more fleshed out. If I've sown my greens and lettuces too thickly, for first harvesting I'll often pull whole plants—another way to harvest-thin.

Keep those early radishes picked.

They grow real fast. Before you know, they're all prickly upper leaves and stunted roots. Here's one that snuck by me in a salad row of interplanted crops (the bluish-green plant in the middle). When you see these, pull them out for compost, and give the others room.

Even the new gourmet supermarkets are hard pressed to offer the varieties available to home gardeners. Here, clockwise from top left, Ruby, endive, Salad Bowl, Black-Seeded Simpson, Prizehead, Iceberg. Actually, I prefer to cut and eat them when they're half this size, with darker outer leaves. But big heads are perfect for those large summer get-togethers.

Side-dress winter squash before runner growth.

There's not much more work left in handling winter squash. But first I'll side-dress with one tablespoon complete fertilizer per plant, and then they're pretty much on their own.

Top-dressing onions again: One cupful of 5-10-10 fertilizer for every ten feet of wide row. I start when the tops are six to eight inches high and fertilize them every two weeks. The taller I can get the tops to grow, the larger will be the upcoming bulbs (green tops make the food to swell the bottoms).

On the lookout to side-dress peppers and eggplants: One tablespoon per plant, when blossoms first appear. That may be a while yet, but it could be next week. It all depends on the weather. Peppers and

eggplants are slow growers, so be patient. (See page 37 for my drawing of a shallow circle around a plant and sprinkling in the spoonful.)

I train my pole beans, or runner beans, in two ways. I set tall stakes in the ground at three-foot intervals and tie string between them top and bottom. Then I attach additional string vertically every six inches, planting four or five beans at the base of each, and thin later to the best three or four. This method takes a bit more effort than the tepee I'm about to describe, but the extra harvest may be worth it. This string trellis will yield a bushel of beans from just a few square feet. Each garden tour, I wrap some stray tendrils around a string.

A tepee of four poles each, six or seven feet long and one to two inches thick, is easier to assemble and still a great space-saver. (See page 37 for how I've grown a hot-climate, shade-preferring crop of head lettuces underneath.) I put the poles on the ground and bind them together a foot from the top. Then the poles can be shoved six inches into prepared soil, four feet apart. I plant a half-dozen seeds about six inches from each pole, later thinning to the best three or four.

Pole beans, as you'll be seeing, make harvesting especially easy. They grow abundantly with this extra dose of light and heat. I'll side-dress these beans one time, a tablespoon per plant, once they start bearing.

MIDDLE JULY

Nature handles the delicate work. That's a bee pollinating this squash blossom. The pollen is carried from the male blossom, which only lives one day, to the female blossom, which forms the fruit. So don't be upset when you see squash blossoms on the ground. Pick female blossoms just for this purpose and sauté them—they're delicious. At this stage, picking will strengthen the plant, which will produce many more blossoms to replace those picked. (By the way, flies and other insects—good and bad—all pollinate vegetable flowers; so it gets done, with or without bees.)

Blanching for perfect cauliflower

Soon after the cauliflower head starts forming, the final covering of leaves spreads open to reveal the small and milky-white clusters, or curds. Just as soon as this happens is the time to take action. Once the strong summer sun hits those tender white buds, that's it. They turn yellow, tough, and start to separate and bolt to seed. They are very bitter to the taste, as a result. Don't fuss with strings or other materials. Tying up the leaves in a vertical position tends to trap rainwater, which can bead on the head and sometimes rot it.

The easiest and most effective method of blanching is simply to bend four or five of the large, outside leaves over the crown, partially snapping the leaf stem where it wants to break, then tucking the leaf tip into the opposite side. Do a few others the following week if the head needs more coverage as it expands.

There's only one head to harvest from each cauliflower plant, but, all snowy white and sweet-tasting, I think this spectacular garden vegetable is one of the most rewarding.

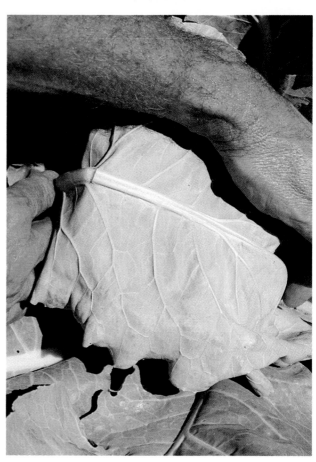

I left this cauliflower unblanched *to remind all of us what we don't want to happen.*

Reminder: Plants grow quickly at this time of year. When you combine heat and plenty of moisture—the foremost requirements—it doesn't take very long for cauliflower to swell and expose its center crown. So be on guard each day.

Kohlrabi is a first cousin to cauliflower.

If you sprayed kohlrabi (along with all cabbage-family plants) with Dipel last month, and every week since then, it should look like this.

Kohlrabi grows like an above-ground turnip. (To my taste, it's a cross between a turnip and an apple!) Cabbage worms can play havoc with its leaves, which is why I often repeat the above reminder about spraying all cabbage-family crops every five to seven days. Insects don't much bother the bulb. But remember: leaves generally are the plant's food-production units. Stunted leaf growth hampers the overall vigor of any plant, including the edible parts.

Harvest them when they are large enough to eat—a couple of inches wide. If you let them grow much larger than three inches across, the flesh gets woody. Snap off those flyaway stems and leaves, but the bottom must be sliced off with a sharp knife. Pare off the outer skin, which is fairly tender when the plant is young. The rest is all solid vegetable—for stir-frying, for grating into salads and slaw, or for slicing thin and serving raw with dips.

Middle July   159

Green beans are at their prime: young and pencil-thin.

Green beans, or snap beans, are one of the most prolific of vegetables. Once the blossoms appear, pods aren't far behind. Keep a daily lookout.

Pick the bushes clean of fruit. This encourages the plant to keep producing. Call in neighbors if you're pressed for time. Try not to let the pods get big with seeds. If they do, this signals to the plant that its mission is near complete, and production drops off.

I recommend block-planting beans, even if you don't do much canning, freezing, pickling or sharing, like we do here. That thick forest of greenery is putting an end to the weed cycle in this section of garden. Back in January (page 5), I showed you young bean plants coming up shoulder to shoulder and preventing sun from reaching any weeds. By this stage in the summer, weeds are no longer a threat.

Plus—all these beans have fertilized the soil with the nitrogen-fixing nodules on their roots. So, beans leave the soil better than when they were planted.

Harvest tip: As with pea pods, don't pull the beans off straight away from the plant. This could pull up the whole plant. Use two hands, one to hold the stem steady, one to pinch the base of the beans (usually there are two at the same juncture on the stem). Or snap and twist the pods in a downward direction, bringing pressure on the end of the pod rather than the stem on which it is growing.

Succession plantings of beans

Because beans are ready to eat about a month and a half after planting, my first harvest is always a reminder to plant them again for a continuous and fresh supply from the end of August right through September. Some years I've planted small sections every two weeks, but lately I've found that by keeping them picked, in combination with plantings of yellow snap beans and a few types of pole or runner beans, we have bounty and variety. Purple-podded beans are an interesting novelty. They speed picking because of their unusual color; they turn green in cooking. Of course, as beans have been such a staple over the ages, each region and climate has its favorites.

Keep the water turned on! Melons are among the thirstiest of our plants (they're mostly water themselves). Once the melons form, I'll show you what I do to speed their ripening by trapping more heat. In the north, we want to ripen them before cool nights and hint of frost threaten. In the south, you want to harvest them at their peak of flavor before the hottest weather prevents them from getting the water they rely on.

Feeding the melon patch

Can you see the bright yellow flowers dotting this row of watermelons? The muskmelons look the same way. The very first blossoms were my signal that these plants were about to go into overdrive and so I side-dressed them: one tablespoon of fertilizer per plant. They've become quite bushy, so this is the last chance I have to weed between the rows before the sprawling runners get any longer and more coiled.

Tomato department:

three essential midsummer steps

If I didn't tie up the newest growth on supported tomatoes before, I had better do it now. And for the largest-growing varieties, it's time to tie them *once again*, so as to train them within the support system and to balance the upcoming weight load. Untied, the rapidly growing vines can run out of bounds. As I discussed in June (page 140), I prefer strips of old cloth for this purpose. They are easiest on the stems. Remember: a tight tie around the wire or stake, and a loose loop around the stem.

Staked tomatoes now need mulching. They tend to dry out faster than plants sprawling more naturally on the ground.

I've found some first-cut hay for this mulching job, so the likelihood of bringing in many viable weed seeds is slim. Without mulch, vertically supported tomatoes run a high risk of blossom-end rot caused by insufficient moisture. I'm adding this mulch after the plants have had a good deep drink and the soil underneath has been well-cultivated.

Side-dress tomatoes once, when the plant has set blossoms, with *two* tablespoons of a complete fertilizer per plant. (Tomato plants are much larger than the others we fertilize.) You can side-dress before you mulch. Or, lift up the mulch if you have it already in place, and draw a shallow circle around the base of the plant out to the dripline. Sprinkle in the fertilizer and cover. Whether I use organic or chemical fertilizer, I'm equally careful to avoid disturbing roots.

Keep in mind my general rule for most vegetables that I side-dress: One tablespoon per plant. Please refer back to June, page 135, where I list the crops I do and don't side-dress, and when I do it.

This block of corn is like one big living mulch.

Here's weed-free gardening at work! Mulches I can eat are my favorite kinds. Although you can't tell from this photo, the corn block isn't much longer than it is wide—10 by 15 feet. Remember that we side-dress corn twice, since it's such a heavy feeder on nitrogen. I've already done this block when it was a foot or so high (see June, page 135). And I'll do so again when tassels or silks form on the ears (see page 175).

It's getting to be that stage of the gardening year that seems all pleasure, with very little work. I've won the battle of the weeds, thanks largely to wide-row planting and early rake-thinning. There's lots of good eating but most of the crops are still in the final growth period.

What better thing to do than stroll through the garden and look with satisfaction at one's plants that are flourishing and pretty much on their own?

Well, almost—I've still got several tricks up my sleeve to nudge things along.

I move my melons 400 miles south by setting them on tin cans.

Setting young melons on inverted tin cans warms them faster and more thoroughly than if they were left on the ground. Elevating them means exposing them to more rays of the sun—earlier in the morning and later in the afternoon. On the ground, melons are often in the shade of surrounding foliage. Also, they stay cool all day on their ground side. On cans, they can heat all the way through. I punch a hole in the bot-

tom of the can so water can't puddle under the melon and rot it.

Wherever sunshine falls on soil instead of plants, is, to my mind, wasting the sun's energy. I have walkways in my 20- by 20-foot garden, but much of the plot is reachable from the lawn areas.

Take a closer look at the right-hand rows in this 20- by 20-foot patch. The first row is actually a back-to-back "double-wide" row of lettuce, onions, root crops, and so forth. The second begins with 13 heads of cabbage in three feet. Since summer winds dehydrate plants, clustered vegetables lose a lot less moisture.

IN MID-JULY

From it, we've harvested

—head and looseleaf lettuce
—scallions, small onions
—parsley and herbs
—beets and beet greens
—baby carrots
—chard
—cauliflower
—early cabbage
—kohlrabi
—bush beans, green
—bush beans, yellow
—baby summer squash
—and squash blossoms
—spinach
—peas
—early Pixie tomatoes
—a few early potatoes

Mini-reminders

- *Spray or dust* tomatoes and potatoes, and spray or dust *all* cabbage-family plants with Dipel at the first sight of tiny holes in the leaves of broccoli, cauliflower, kale, kohlrabi, turnips, cabbages, Brussels sprouts.
- *Water* your weekly inch.
- *Side-dress* broccoli and cauliflower just as they start to head. (See page 171 for easy reference chart.)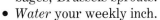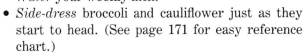

It's getting to be that stage of the gardening year that seems all pleasure, with very little work. I've won the battle of the weeds, thanks largely to wide-row planting and early rake-thinning. There's lots of good eating but most of the crops are still in the final growth period.

What better thing to do than stroll through the garden and look with satisfaction at one's plants that are flourishing and pretty much on their own?

Well, almost—I've still got several tricks up my sleeve to nudge things along.

I move my melons 400 miles south by setting them on tin cans.

Setting young melons on inverted tin cans warms them faster and more thoroughly than if they were left on the ground. Elevating them means exposing them to more rays of the sun—earlier in the morning and later in the afternoon. On the ground, melons are often in the shade of surrounding foliage. Also, they stay cool all day on their ground side. On cans, they can heat all the way through. I punch a hole in the bot-

LATE JULY
All pleasure, little work

tom of the can so water can't puddle under the melon and rot it.

Wherever sunshine falls on soil instead of plants, is, to my mind,

wasting the sun's energy. I have walkways in my 20- by 20-foot garden, but much of the plot is reachable from the lawn areas.

Take a closer look at the right-hand rows in this 20- by 20-foot patch. The first row is actually a back-to-back "double-wide" row of lettuce, onions, root crops, and so forth. The second begins with 13 heads of cabbage in three feet. Since summer winds dehydrate plants, clustered vegetables lose a lot less moisture.

Tomato department:
three essential midsummer steps

If I didn't tie up the newest growth on supported tomatoes before, I had better do it now. And for the largest-growing varieties, it's time to tie them *once again*, so as to train them within the support system and to balance the upcoming weight load. Untied, the rapidly growing vines can run out of bounds. As I discussed in June (page 140), I prefer strips of old cloth for this purpose. They are easiest on the stems. Remember: a tight tie around the wire or stake, and a loose loop around the stem.

Staked tomatoes now need mulching. They tend to dry out faster than plants sprawling more naturally on the ground.

I've found some first-cut hay for this mulching job, so the likelihood of bringing in many viable weed seeds is slim. Without mulch, vertically supported tomatoes run a high risk of blossom-end rot caused by insufficient moisture. I'm adding this mulch after the plants have had a good deep drink and the soil underneath has been well-cultivated.

Side-dress tomatoes once, when the plant has set blossoms, with *two* tablespoons of a complete fertilizer per plant. (Tomato plants are much larger than the others we fertilize.) You can side-dress before you mulch. Or, lift up the mulch if you have it already in place, and draw a shallow circle around the base of the plant out to the dripline. Sprinkle in the fertilizer and cover. Whether I use organic or chemical fertilizer, I'm equally careful to avoid disturbing roots.

Keep in mind my general rule for most vegetables that I side-dress: One tablespoon per plant. Please refer back to June, page 135, where I list the crops I do and don't side-dress, and when I do it.

This block of corn is like one big living mulch.

Here's weed-free gardening at work! Mulches I can eat are my favorite kinds. Although you can't tell from this photo, the corn block isn't much longer than it is wide—10 by 15 feet. Remember that we side-dress corn twice, since it's such a heavy feeder on nitrogen. I've already done this block when it was a foot or so high (see June, page 135). And I'll do so again when tassels or silks form on the ears (see page 175).

My Main-Crop 30- by 40-Foot Garden

The bare patches indicate where I've dug up old crops and replanted some for fall harvesting: namely, many varieties of salad greens, spinach, beets, carrots, and green beans.

"Stealing" potatoes

I dig up some early potatoes for a treat. Why leave all the potato crop to one big harvest at summer's end? I like to "rob" potatoes, as I've mentioned earlier, simply by burrowing my hand into the side of the hilled soil, reaching around and picking a few nice tubers, then firming the soil back. The plant will keep right on growing. In fact, that much more energy will go to speeding the smaller spuds along.

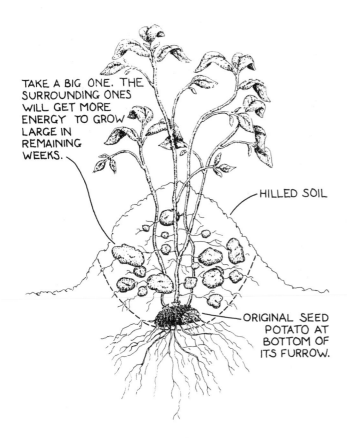

TAKE A BIG ONE. THE SURROUNDING ONES WILL GET MORE ENERGY TO GROW LARGE IN REMAINING WEEKS.

HILLED SOIL

ORIGINAL SEED POTATO AT BOTTOM OF ITS FURROW.

Are you going on vacation?

- Pay a neighbor or young person to water your garden. Compensation can often be fresh vegetables.
- Ask someone to come *every day* and pick. This is important if you want a few more months of vegetables at their best. Keep the garden clean of over-the-hill, soon-to-rot vegetables.

- Don't worry too much if you don't find a gardener to borrow. You'll lose some harvest, but plants are forgiving, and some will rebound with a burst of attention.

THINGS ARE POPPING IN THE SUMMER-SQUASH PATCH

There are few garden flags as bright as the yellow squash blossoms. This is good, because a day shouldn't go by without checking summer squash. As I said before, lightly fried or sautéed squash blossoms are a delicacy. Picking blossoms to eat in no way limits the upcoming harvest. It just triggers more.

Pick young. That's my motto.

The tiny developing squash on far left (in the group photo) and its shriveled (but not yet brown and dried) blossom are both edible. The next baby squash, about the size of my finger, is the way I like them best. The next two are at their prime for summer squash. All this applies to zucchini, too.

This is the "caviar" of the garden, to me. Squash that's picked before seeds form are all tender flesh, but crunchy-firm as well. It's harder to under- or overcook them. How many times have you been served limp, watery, seed-filled slices of yellow squash? Or pieces that, no matter how long cooked, are pebble-tough on the skin side and mushy in the center? It's not the cook's fault; it's the gardener's for not grabbing them when they're palm-sized and under.

With zucchinis you need to be even quicker on the draw.

The zucchini on the left is a little far gone, for my taste. The one on the right, with its flower barely collapsed, is perfect. Notice the one squash underneath, trying to hide in the shadows. Look for and pick those! If left on the plant, they signal that their goal is accomplished and the plant stops producing.

The same advice holds true for cucumbers. Pick, pick, pick, even this small. (Am I sounding like a broken record?) All I can say is, this is a good excuse to visit your garden every day. Eat or give away what you can. Preserve what you have the time and inclination to do. Compost the rest without feeling guilty, because unpicked fruit will limit overall yield.

If cucumbers are sprawling out of bounds, try training the vines to climb up a trellis of some sort. Mine here is made of chicken wire and a simple frame. I tilt the trellis back for better support, since the fruits create more weight as they develop.

Cut broccoli for tightness of center head—not size.

I have to keep an eagle eye on broccoli—so misunderstood at harvest time. The buds of broccoli blossoms are what we eat, and broccoli doesn't linger long at this stage, so we have to be quick to get prime eating.

This broccoli head is perfect. *It's small, because I got my broccoli in later than usual this year. If this were June instead of July, I wouldn't have to be so concerned about daily inspections. The hot sun will push the heads quickly to their flowering stage.*

This head is still compact but starting to flower. *Sometimes that happens before much separation. It will still taste good, but the texture won't be as crisp, and it will take longer to cook because it's a little tougher.*

This head is starting to separate its buds. *The buds are very swollen, and the flavor will be sharp, less palatable. We'd use this for soup.*

This head should be cut and composted. *Then the energy of the plant will return to producing edible sideshoots (small heads) if one is lucky. Sideshoots may produce a less extended harvest once the center head has reached flowering point.*

Remember to side-dress broccoli as heads are starting to form.

Harvest tip: Don't cut any more stem off under the center head than you have to, because a new and delicious sideshoot will be produced just on top of each lateral leaf.

I can grow six cabbages per plant!

These photos show how I begin the process.

I just harvested the cabbage on the left. It could grow a lot bigger, but it's already a good-sized head—really more than a family can use for one meal. Cutting it now will allow the neighboring heads (see center) in this wide row to keep growing with more shoulder room and a greater share of nutrients.

A cabbage is actually a seedpod. When picking the head small, the plant will keep trying to produce a "successful" seedpod.

But I'd prefer to harvest cabbages at this stage (see right), between the other two pictured and closer to a large grapefruit or softball in size. This will allow enough time and space for the tiny cabbage buds atop each main leaf (I'm pointing to one with my penknife) to grow into a fairly decent size, up to six additional heads per plant. I'll keep you posted on this progress in upcoming months. Most folks have to see my six-headed cabbage to believe it.

I hope you're following the theme that's being played. The more and the younger we pick, the greater the overall harvest. *The extent to which we exercise a plant's capacity to produce is up to us gardeners.*

Here's a patch of Brussels sprouts, looking healthy (thanks to regular five to seven day doses of Dipel dust or spray). I'm a month away from "ringing" the stems of leaves. A tiny bud—an eventual sprout—is just starting to form on the top of each branch where it connects to the main stem. When the buds are more fully developed, I'll be stripping the side branches and leaves off the plant to allow more sun and energy to reach the sprouts.

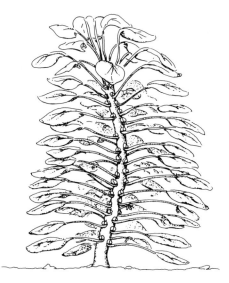

For now, if you inspect your Brussels sprouts up close, you'll see that just above the juncture of main stem and side-leaf branch a bud is forming. You are probably beginning to understand lots more about how the cabbage-family crops reproduce. Broccoli and cabbage produce multiple lateral heads, too—not as large as their central ones, but well worth encouraging midseason, while there's still enough time for them to grow to a decent size.

July reminders . . .

- *Spray or dust* cabbage-family crops, potatoes, tomatoes, and cucumbers every five days if these crops, or any others, are infested. Please refer back to pages 132–33 for my easy bug control.
- *Water every week* . . . soak the ground to depth of four or five inches, the result of delivering an inch of water.
- *Side-dress* broccoli, cabbage and cauliflower when they start to head; eggplants, peppers, tomatoes, okra, summer squash and zucchini at blossom time; Brussels sprouts when they are marble-sized; cukes, melons and winter squash just before their vines spread out; potatoes and sweet potatoes before the second hilling; chards, lettuce, and other greens after crew-cut harvesting.
- *Hill potatoes and corn* to kill weeds.
- *Pinch or slice suckers* off tomatoes.
- *Blanch cauliflower* when white heads appear.
- *Watch peas*, radishes, kohlrabi, broccoli, cabbages, and summer squash like a hawk so they don't get too large. Small is beautiful.
- *Tour your garden daily.* There's very little work, mostly good eating. Record first harvestings in back of this book, or elsewhere that's handy, to better gauge plantings for next year.
- *Plant fall succession crops* in place of completed spring ones. (See 30-by-40 plan, pages 20–21, for follow-up vegetable ideas by row.) Or plant a weed-choking cover crop of buckwheat.

Brewing for August . . .

- Vegetable plant pruning: the push for earlier ripe melons and tomatoes
- Still time for succession plantings of beets, carrots, greens
- Autographing pumpkins—purely for fun!
- My corn-ripeness test
- More prime-picking advice

- ✔ Following the steps of basic garden care even though it's prime-time harvest . . . watering, watching for bugs, outwitting animals

- ✔ Speeding the ripening of melons, Brussels sprouts, peppers, multiple heads of cabbage

- ✔ Enjoying the best specimens of each crop—cucumbers before they're seed-filled, eggplants and beans at peak flavor

- ✔ Time for more succession planting for late-fall fresh eating

- ✔ Sampling vegetables not ordinarily harvested for another month—potatoes, onions, celery, garlic, leeks

- ✔ Knowing when to pick corn and tomatoes—good and ripe!

AUGUST

The lush harvest month!

Sweet banana peppers are still developing, but we pick them as soon as there's something large enough to eat. There are plenty coming along. Like summer squash and eggplant, they're just as tasty when they're small.

EARLY AUGUST
Eating fresh is habit-forming.

I always bring a basket at this time of year whenever I take a look at the garden. I return to the kitchen and Jan starts meal planning. Though I don't believe that saving money should be the chief reason for gardening, we sure save trips to the supermarket when our vegetables become the main attractions.

To speed up peppers: Try my Epsom-salts trick. Mix one teaspoonful of Epsom salts in an old spray bottle you have handy, filling it with lukewarm water. This spraying at blossom time gives all pepper plants an extra dose of magnesium, an element that helps them set fruit. Do this once more in ten days.

I do only one side-dressing. I already side-dressed with a tablespoon of fertilizer per plant several weeks ago, when blossoms first appeared. Peppers can easily direct their growth into foliage instead of fruit if overfed.

When cukes arrive *in this quantity, pickling season is here, too.*

Pickles are even more delicious with homegrown garlic and dill.

One of the great things about pickles is that kids love them. When they're homemade you can always tell, because of the special crispness and flavor. What can beat garden-fresh ingredients?

The early corn is almost ready. *I have harvested first corn as early as middle July. Actually, this year it's late, due to a very cold and wet spring. But I'm still going to be a few weeks ahead of my neighbors.*

 Remember to side-dress corn a final time, when tassels first appear, as you can see here.

The block of green beans on the left is near to harvesting. Yes, we trample some of the plants when we get in the middle and pick, and come again to pick. But the extra harvest of a superwide row easily makes up for that. Plus, I've done no work at all between planting and picking.

The bean block on the right was planted last month for fall eating (for after Labor Day to as long into October if the frost holds back). Some years, a midsummer planting doesn't make it, due to early cold weather. But that doesn't keep me from trying. At the very least those beans are acting like a "green-manure cover crop." As a legume, they're adding more nitrogen to the soil than they're demanding. And I'll turn the plants under when still green as a valuable addition of organic matter.

Reminder: If I'm doing any more succession planting, now is the best time to do it. I can put some lettuce in as late as the end of this month, and I gamble with beets, carrots, and spinach, too.

A few more onion sets, if any are around, are nice to plant for green tops this fall. It's hard to pin down dates. Mostly it depends on the weather: how quickly spring crops grew and came to harvest, and how soon I'm able to spade under the residues and replant.

Don't forget:

Just because our harvest baskets are full doesn't mean garden-maintenance steps are finished.

 Regular watering (I'm a stickler about this!) means crops will stay greener, healthier, more productive, more resistant to insects and disease organisms, which could still get a hold this season and come back to plague us next year.

 Preventive dusting or spraying every other week. Insects are still active. If white butterflies still hover around cabbage-family plants, use Dipel every five to seven days, right through summer and into fall. Tiny holes chewed in the cabbage crops are a sure sign of worm damage. Don't let them get the upper hand.

 Yanking out that single large weed that sneaks into bushy rows of vegetables means thousands of weed seeds are prevented from infiltrating your garden soil.

Last month *when my early beets were finished, I sowed a crop of kale for late-fall harvesting (see 30- by 40-foot plan, pages 20–21). Kale takes a while to reach a decent size, so sprinkling in radish seeds has helped mark this row.*

How's this for a wide row of beets? *When I sow a crop of beets early, rake-thin them with a heavy hand, and keep harvesting them, marble-sized, for greens as well, I get a midsummer harvest of globes this large. It's based on continuous in-row weeding or cultivating, too, to keep the soil loose. Harvest-thinning the first beets large enough to eat breaks up the soil crust and allows shoulder room for remaining, expanding beets.*

Rabbits nibble, raccoons devour.

An August raccoon attack on my 30- by 40-foot garden meant I had to install some solid fencing. Raccoons seem to know exactly when the corn is ready!

Raccoons are fully capable of knocking over stalks and eating every kernel, as you can see they've done here. This corn was outside of my fenced-in 30- by 40-foot garden. It's too late to spread moth crystals (which does offend them) at the edge of the garden because now they've got a taste of the sweet treat that awaits them. Electrifying a fence is the only sure control. I've got enough corn planted this year to sacrifice some, so I won't bother.

A fence may or may not be a project for the gardener in the family. It's not too time-consuming, but it does require a sledgehammer, some muscle, and enough out-of-pocket expense to really want to beat the invading animals. It can be a permanent addition to your garden. Or, like this arrangement of metal posts and chicken wire, it can be taken down and rolled up.

If deer or woodchucks or skunks or other invading animals are known to be regular uninvited guests, go ahead and do it . . . the sooner the better. You need six to eight feet of fence for deer.

Fencing is a must for growing sweet corn if raccoons are around. For all other situations, it depends on how much harvest you're willing to gamble on losing. As I showed you last month, rabbits nibbled some broccoli but the plants recovered, so I didn't bother with fencing.

On my tour of the garden one early August day,

. . . a stunted cauliflower that wasn't blanched. I had to pick it because flower clusters were starting to separate. Left uncut, it would have been inedible within a day or so.

. . . a softball-sized cabbage that was perfect for harvesting. There's enough time for the tiny buds above the leaf connections to develop into some small heads for this fall.

. . . kale ready for harvest, now through the end of the year. I tend to pick the lower, larger, outside leaves, which lets the plant keep forming new leaves from the center portion of the plant. Kale is so prolific that I sometimes thin out a few mature plants in a wide row. This makes an especially rugged stand of the ones remaining, which will yield their highly nutritious greens through winter and another crop the following spring.

I found . . .

. . . green but soon-to-ripen tomatoes on their happily sprawling vines. I show this because we mostly stake our tomatoes. As I suggested earlier, the argument for staking goes: Fruits stay cleaner, free of slugs, etc. That's true. But for those who have the space, I say, Let 'em sprawl. It's so much easier. By midseason they mulch themselves. My experience is that I get a somewhat heavier harvest by letting them run. So a few more tomatoes in a plot of this sort makes up for any damage done by contact with the soil.

And look at these ripe beauties! Here's the early payoff for my trench-planting method.

An important step to hasten the melon harvest

I'm almost in a race with the clock when it comes to growing vine-ripened melons in New England. One of the most successful tricks I've learned is to pick the fuzzy ends off my melon vines.

I've got the developing melons on tin cans to trap heat and to speed ripening. I want most all the plants' energy going to this goal now. A fuzzy end is just more unfurling vine, foliage, and eventual fruit which will never make it on time. In this case, I'm leaving a blossom on while snipping off the remainder. The tiny melon forming might be harvestable if we have a mild autumn—so that's worth a gamble.

The squash in the baskets are headed toward the kitchen. The others are headed for the compost pile.

Summer squash and zucchini are in full production. Don't be squeamish! Take those baseball-bat squashes off the plants and compost them. That's the best place for them right now. The remainder of the nice ones we can't eat or freeze (our favorite method for preserving summer squash), we keep right in the basket in the shade of the breezeway by our front door. When we tell people to help themselves, they do.

General harvesting tip: When picking for preserving, try to do it in the morning—the earlier the better. Vegetables (especially leafy greens) are more crisp and contain more moisture then than they do later in the day after exposure to a hot sun.

All picked vegetables go downhill after harvesting in terms of flavor and crispness. They start to dehydrate, shrivel, and lose sugars to starch. It always helps to keep them in a cool, dark place until you can prepare and/or eat them.

Kitchen hint: Fresh-cooked cabbage turns emerald green in seconds and doesn't need anywhere near as much time to be boiled, steamed, or whatever as what you may be used to. Of course, this applies to all garden-fresh vegetables. They're simply more tender! So stand guard at the stove.

Not to worry if red cabbage is smaller than the white. It takes longer to grow.

Red cabbage, being somewhat coarser, better withstands harsh weather and resists insect damage. I love red cabbage for its special flavor; it's unbeatable sautéed with apples, spices, and vinegar. It holds up well in the root cellar and adds color and texture variety to fall coleslaws. It's worth the added wait.

Freezing suggestion: We use the smallest, crispest vegetables for freezing. They stand the best chance of being tasty and remaining firm as possible after processing for freezing and eventual thawing. (*Almost*-perfect specimens taste just as good as the perfect ones, when fresh.)

I usually cut a cabbage when it's small, just right for one meal's worth. But this one I let develop. See how the large outer leaves tend to hide the fact that such a sizable, mature head is perched underneath? This large one is perfect for a big summer-picnic slaw.

If this is your first experience with homegrown cabbage, I hope you're real pleased. Cabbages may *look* alike, but as for taste . . .

Don't wait until the onion-family crops are "finished."

Sample them early and throughout the season.

Garlic can be dug anytime. The bulbs are simply smaller than they will be when I harvest the main crop early this fall. At this stage, the greentops are perfectly edible, too. Fresh garlic has a special zing.

Shallots have stopped growing when the tops have turned brown and died back, usually by later this month. But I like a few clusters along about early August as we then do more cooking of vegetables and appreciate the unique flavor that shallots add.

Leeks are wonderful when big and fat. But since they're so slow-growing, I like to thin the wide row of these every now and then by harvesting a handful this size. As you've probably guessed by now, this also helps create room for the main and continuing crop to expand.

It's time for leek-and-new-potato soup, served hot or cold, garnished with chopped-up curly kale or parsley. (By the way, I do my share of cooking in our household. So don't get the idea I hand it all over to Jan—just most of it.)

Dill, sage, summer savory, basil, and some other herbs are welcome additions to the harvest throughout this entire month and next. I can eat green beans plain every night, but some gardening folks need to get more inventive as mid-August approaches.

Each week now, I pull up some carrots—those with the darkest-green tops. They're not much larger than my smallest finger, but this harvest-thinning is really helpful. Baby carrots are the sweetest.

Stay on bug patrol! Don't get overconfident amidst all the bounty. Bug-free, it can last for months longer. Refer back to my Home Brews on page 132.

MIDDLE AUGUST

RIPE TOMATOES AND CORN!

The very earliest tomatoes have made tasty eating for some time. They're good but I don't quite put them in the taste category of the larger, later varieties.

If I have the time, I keep pruning large suckers off my staked tomatoes to help produce bigger fruit. But it's not essential. I don't bother on the sprawling tomato plot. Remember, I'm up north and want lots of sun. In southern states, you don't want to remove too much foliage for fear of sun-scalding your plants.

Tomato-ripening trick:

Getting itchy for ripe tomatoes? One way I've found to speed along the tomato plant is to do some root-pruning. I take a large carving knife (not necessarily the family's best) and cut a semicircle around the plant, two inches from the stem and about eight inches deep. This severs some, but not all, of the root system—enough to shock it into forcing all its final energy into ripening its tomatoes. If I trench-transplanted the tomato, I slice along (not *around*) the main lateral root. If you're reluctant to do this, be patient and plant earlier-maturing varieties next year. Or just try one or two plants with this trick. (Most roots grow back, by the way.)

Tomato trouble-shooting:

- **"Cat-facing,"** or irregular shape and lines, especially at the top of the developing tomato, is caused by temperature shifts at blossom time. Nothing you can do about it. A ripe cat-faced tomato just gets sliced more creatively for the salad bowl.
- **Blossom-end rot,** which I've warned against, is due to lack of moisture. There's still reason to mulch in the hotter states. And all gardens should get that weekly inch of soaking, right through the harvest season . . . especially now, with *larger* plants and developing fruits consuming lots of water. Remove any rotting or diseased tomatoes.
- **Sunscald** hits many vegetables. If they are far from the ripening stage, chances are that the whole fruit will rot. Compost them, so you won't have to worry. Don't do any further pruning of foliage branches or even suckers. Their shade is now important.
- **Split skin** on cherry tomatoes is caused by accelerated growth, and their getting overripe. Keep 'em picked!
- **If there are bugs,** pick them off if they're in numbers you can control. Otherwise use the general tomato-vegetable dust or spray every week to ten days.
- **Dried, dead leaves** can be left on the plant: they're not drawing off any nutrients and moisture, and they actually create some partial shade for the fruit.

More advice on green beans

This particular block is at the north end of our 30-by 40-foot garden. We can easily pass up buying rubbery "snap" beans when they appear in the supermarkets off-season (they do snap when they're garden fresh). We've had the real thing for several weeks; they freeze well, too, for winter eating. Green beans are trouble-free in most regions—and what a lush, green patch of foliage they make in the garden. They're a welcome sight.

Remember the flexible plastic tunnels I used this spring to give my squashes and melons an early start? I may get them out again next month to protect a row of late beans to harvest at the end of September and even into October—well after frost in my area.

Bean harvest hint: I don't try to pick a block or a wide row of beans all by myself. I ask for help. It's not that often that I need it—only for peas and beans. And all the family agrees it's worth it to get them young and pencil-thin both for eating fresh and preserving. Pick every few days, at least twice a week, to keep the plants producing heavily.

Green bean troubles: The spores of bean-disease organisms are more easily spread when the plants are wet. So I don't touch bean leaves unless they are dry. Beans are basically easy to grow and are strong, so don't bother to rush to spray when beetles appear. I wouldn't give this advice for most other vegetables, but beans can stand up to quite a bit of damage. As with all crops, pull any diseased or insect-infested leaves, fruit, or entire plants. You *could* compost them if your pile is hot and fast (produces completed compost in two to three weeks). But it's safest to dispose of them.

Reminders . . .

- Keep those sideshoots of broccoli picked clean. If you don't eat or freeze them, toss them in the compost while they're still green and tender and easier for microbes to break down.
- Check fencing for any repairs. Tighten or patch where necessary.
- Keep any tubs or patio planters well watered right through final harvests.
- I keep up my regular doses of Dipel dust or spray on *all* cabbage-family crops. The cabbage worms would take over quickly if I didn't. In time you will certainly know (if you don't already) which vegetables are especially vulnerable to bugs in your area, so you can take a little extra care in spraying or dusting to protect them.

Here's the progress on a single cabbage plant when I harvested the first head softball-sized. True, these half-dozen "heads" are mostly leaves. They have a way to go before developing into something harvestable.

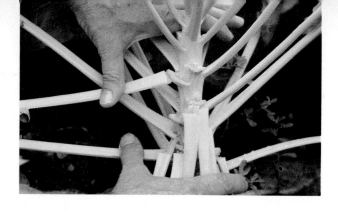

Stripping the leaves of Brussels sprouts

When buds begin to form on Brussels sprouts above each lateral leaf, it's my signal to prune the plant. Removing excess leaves channels the plant's energy into developing sprouts. I place both hands about a third of the way out on the lateral branches and press downward with a sharp motion. The branches snap right off, forcing the plant to grow in height and sprout more buds on yet higher branches in its mission to reproduce itself. I'll be snapping the new branches off, too. I also side-dress Brussels sprouts when the buds are marble-sized. Since leaves manufacture food for the plant,

it's important to supplement for this loss. Stripping off these leaves looks pretty cruel, but this will put the strength of the plant where I want it. I call Brussels sprouts the palm trees of my garden. They grow three to four feet tall with this treatment.

At some point I will want to stop the upward growth of the plant (and the formation of new sprouts) and direct the season's remaining activity into swelling the sprouts already started. To do this I just snip off the topmost leaf cluster, or terminal point. That does it.

The rows of sweet potatoes need no more attention. I dig up a few samples every week or so to see how they're doing.

Pole beans take longer to mature than bush beans. I'm looking forward to them. One tepee of four poles would provide a family of three or four with a generous amount of this carefree vegetable for eating fresh. It's fun to pick them as they hang in front of your face. This will be soon. They don't get as swollen and tough as quickly as bush beans, which is why I'm glad to have this harvest staggered with my bush varieties.

My cukes are in high gear.

These are kind of big. Remember to keep them picked. Then you'll have a continuous supply of just the right size over a much longer period. If you sprayed and nipped any beetles, other bugs, or borers at first sight, cukes should be in good shape. If some plants are badly infested, pull and dispose of them. Next year, stagger a few plantings to increase your success rate.

Bitter cucumbers? The skin can become bitter due to especially hot and dry periods. I don't know of any cure other than to recommend keeping them all picked. Later fruit may not develop this problem. And, of course, morning-picked vegetables taste sweeter in general.

If you've grown cukes on a trellis, remember they may need some extra attention. Sometimes I tie the ends of some out-of-bound vines to the wire support with cloth strips.

The okra flower is very distinctive and beautiful. It's time to side-dress this vegetable—one tablespoon per plant. If this is a favorite, make a note to side-dress it again in about a month to prolong the harvest. (This is only possible in the southern states, as okra is not cold-tolerant.)

Cool weather can cause okra to lose its blossoms. But if the soil is fertilized and hot weather returns, so will a good supply of blossoms and pods. I pick pods at four to five inches long, and I use gloves to avoid the prickly leaves. They can make your skin itch.

Constant picking means a steady production. Pruning some of the lower leaves also triggers additional pods.

Shallots are ready to harvest.

The tops have all died back, so the bulbs are as big as they're going to get. If I *don't* pull them, they'll start growing as plants and send up green tops, since the roots are still intact. This will soften and ruin the bulb, which is being tapped for its energy, and will leave a brown ring inside where first growth stopped and the next began. (This is true for regular onions, too.)

After pulling, I expose shallots bottom side up to dry out for two to three days. That gets the bottoms hardened and the roots will dry up and flake off. Next I spread them out in a shady but airy place. (I have a breezeway-style garage that's great for this purpose.) I leave them here for two weeks, turning them a few times. Again, this air

circulation is drying and hardening them. (The drier the bulbs, the longer they store over winter. Shallots, being hard and dense bulbs, can last up to ten months.)

I follow this same procedure for my larger, main-crop onions, so I won't repeat the advice for that upcoming harvest.

Next, I collect my shallots and hang them in a mesh bag in the kitchen or root cellar. Good air circulation is the key to keeping all members of the onion family in top storage shape: hard and dry.

I wish my corn-ripeness test was taught in school!

Please don't strip corn still on stalks to see if it's ready. I have a much better idea.

I sure hate to see folks go to the effort to raise corn, wait all summer for that glorious taste experience, outwit raccoons, then partially strip a growing ear to discover that it is unripe. Doing this is wrong on two counts: (1) it invites birds to come peck away and spoil the ear; and (2) the gardener is usually tempted to puncture a kernel, as if milky running fluid means the corn is ready. The fluid invites more birds, plus insects, and the ear can rot or turn sour.

Dark silks are *not* the gauge for corn ripeness.

Simply pinch the top, as I show here. If it's flat, as in this case, it's ready. The topmost kernels have all fleshed out. But if it comes to a point, don't pick it. There's still more growing to be done.

With these two ears I've just picked you can see that the flat or slightly rounded tops indicate they are ripe and ready for harvesting.

I always have the water boiling when I go out to get corn. The conversion of sugars to starch seems especially rapid with this vegetable, but maybe that's because corn can be so wonderfully sweet when absolutely fresh.

Kitchen hint: If you are forced to pick corn before you can husk and eat it, try this tip for preserving sweetness: immediately place the ears, unhusked, broken stalk side down, in a pail of water—just enough to cover the submerged stems. (We do the same with asparagus.) This helps slow down the loss of moisture and flavor. Take a pail of corn to friends where you're invited for supper. They'll be doubly impressed with this precaution and the great taste. You can also keep them in the refrigerator or a cool, moist place.

More than lettuce for the salad bowl!

If you take your salads seriously, no reason to rely just on lettuce. It's not bad for starters—but a gardener can grow such a wide variety of greens for salad. Here's what I picked out in my garden just past the mid-point of August.

First row, left to right: Boston loosehead lettuce, looseleaf lettuce, Ruby lettuce, spinach, and beets/beet greens.
Second row: kale, parsley, mustard greens, Ruby chard, regular Swiss chard.

I often hear people claim there's no way to grow lettuce in hot weather. That's partially true. But if I start lettuce real early in the spring, I get to harvest it in May, June, and all through July, because in wide rows the plants retain more moisture and are cooled at the soil level. By mid-July I've planted even more lettuce as a succession crop, for harvesting now through early October, with several cuttings in between.

With a little planning, I can have a steady supply. Then, beyond lettuce, there are several vegetables for salad making (collards, beet greens, onion tops, kohlrabi, chards) which are available all summer long.

The harvest goes on . . .

This is one of my favorite gardening chores. Don't these beans look inviting? It's like standing in a waterfall of them. As I said earlier, we can be more relaxed about pole beans than about bush beans—they take longer to reach the fat-seed stage. I think they're nuttier and crunchier than bush beans, but I love both kinds. Pole beans are perfect for gardeners who want to save space. I'll keep them picked (every two to three days) and do a side-dressing if I want to really extend the harvest.

This pepper is ready and one of the eggplants is, too. Can you tell which?

LATE AUGUST

HEIGHT-OF-THE-SEASON CHECKLIST

- Okra is ready, pods now forming under the flowers. Keep the okra pods picked.

- Enjoy the newly planted lettuce or spinach, which is much less apt to bolt and go to seed in this cooler weather. Slice off the crop one inch from the ground to force yet another cutting. If you are still harvesting older plants, it's best to side-dress.

- Top-dress onions once more, for the largest possible bulbs.

- Time to thin the root crops I sowed as succession plants. But first I've got to pull the white icicle radishes I added as row markers and ground cultivators in the carrot patch.

- Keep the garden watered. (I probably don't need to remind most readers, but just in case . . .) Speaking of watering, there's some harvest right at our doorstep where we've watered these tubs every day.

The cherry tomatoes have started to ripen. Most of them never make it into the house!

Eggplant harvest tip: I like to pick my eggplants when they're only a third their possible mature size. The taste, to me, is best then. I do this while the dark skin is nice and shiny. Once the skin is dull, the eggplant is past its prime. I left the dull-skinned eggplant on the plant here so you could see the contrast. I always use a knife to sever the tough stem. As with most crops, don't wait till they're large and turn soft. Pick small.

Many vegetables (succession-planted root crops and head lettuces) are just beginning their growth and will soon need to be thinned.

Now that the pumpkins are formed and grapefruit-sized, I like to autograph them.

I sign one with my name, and one with Jan's, and of course one for each of the rest of the family, especially the grandkids.

I just take a ballpoint pen and press hard enough to break the skin. You'll see how our personalized pumpkins turn out in October.

MY CARDINAL RULE OF HARVESTING:

When *first* harvesting a crop, reach for the biggest vegetables (although they are all quite small). This gives the very smallest ones more time to grow and come along. *I find many gardeners do just the opposite:* They harvest-thin the tiniest beets or carrots or lettuce plants so that the big can get bigger.

No! I try to avoid growing vegetables to full size, except—tomatoes, corn, melons, and winter squash that need to be full-sized before they're ripe.

Is that clear as mud? I hope the sketch further helps explain what I mean.

HARVEST-THINNING:
LOOK FOR THE LARGEST VEGETABLES AND PICK THOSE FIRST. THIS MEANS REMAINING ONES CAN GROW TO A GOOD SIZE, TOO.

THE LARGEST CARROTS HERE ARE ONLY "FINGERLINGS" BUT THEY'RE BIG ENOUGH TO EAT—DELECTABLE, IN FACT.

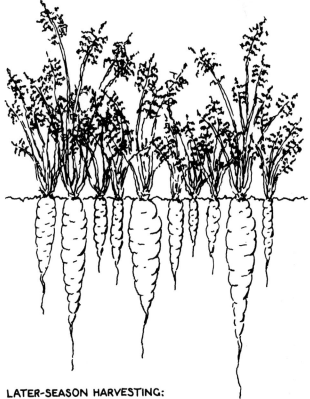

LATER-SEASON HARVESTING:
CONTINUE TO PICK THE LARGEST. I'VE SEEN SOME GARDENERS PULL THE SMALLER ONES UP TO LET THE BIG "SPECIMENS" GROW. "YOU WANT GOOD EATING," I SAY, "OR ARE YOU ENTERING THE COUNTY FAIR?"

My pepper production line

When I don't overfertilize, after a long, hot summer, my pepper plants should look like this one—small plants, large fruits. The strength has gone into pepper production. Pick the largest peppers to give the ones coming along the advantage.

If your pepper blossoms fall off . . . don't fret. It's due to a snap of cold weather. If hot weather continues, you'll get more blossoms. Then spray again with my Epsom-salts trick (see page 117). Keep picking peppers small, especially in warm-weather sections of the country. I've known of Sun Belt pepper plants that produced for over two years.

Cabbage-patch progress . . .

Squeeze your multiple-headed cabbages. Despite all that foliage, you may be surprised how hard and far along some of the half-dozen heads have grown these last few weeks. Red cabbage is developing slowly but surely.

If you live in milder regions, you can still plant some root crops and salad greens for end-of-year harvests.

 Late August is my last chance to sow a weed-choking cover crop in a section of the garden I am no longer using.

Buckwheat is especially good for a badly weed-infested garden area. It grows quickly and thickly, and really clobbers stubborn weeds. But it is not tolerant of heavy frost. I also sow annual rye grass for this job. Please see page 206 in September and page 232 in November for more on how cover crops work.

I've pulled the radishes from this row of July-planted carrots. Now I'd better get out the iron rake to thin them. I draw the rake across the wide row, letting the teeth sink in a quarter to a half-inch. This uproots most all the weeds and takes up half the carrots—more or less, depending upon how thickly I managed to sow the seed.

Here's a question I often get: "When to pick winter squash?"

Answer: When the skin gets thick and tough. They are then ready to pick for eating immediately, or storing in the root cellar. These Golden Nuggets are the first to ripen, as they are quite small. It's a month before our average time of first fall frosts, but I should mention that winter squash, despite their name, are not frost-hardy. They need to be picked before a killing frost comes along. But there's plenty of time for this harvesting chore.

A yard of . . .
onions . . . beets . . .
collards . . .
goes a long way.

Here's why I need help in picking beans (and peas).

Peas and beans freeze well. They hold up in texture, flavor, and color. So we like to put up several dozen pints. Gardening this way is easy, and does cut down on the grocery bill.

Warm-region gardeners: You can still plant beans and peas that will be ready to harvest in a month and a half. Peas will have enough cool weather at night now to get their choice growing conditions. And beans will still have the heat they need to flourish.

All other gardeners: You could try and gamble with fall pea and bean crops. But choose the fastest-maturing 50-day varieties.

The "inside story" of the vine crops

I figured that illustrating the stages of literally "going to seed" in the vine family would help us all to pick these vegetables when they're small, tender yet crisp, and immature in terms of seed development.

 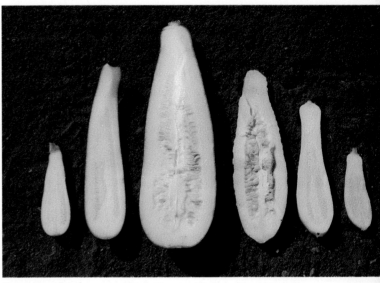

Left to right (outside, then inside): ideal zucchini, excellent zucchini, over-the-hill zucchini, over-the-hill summer squash, excellent summer squash, ideal summer squash.

Left to right (outside, then inside): rotting cuke, over-the-hill cuke, adequate cuke, excellent cuke, ideal pickling cuke.

Cracked cabbage.

When I let cabbages get too large, they can crack. Has this ever happened to you? The plant grows from the inside out. If conditions are good, it grows fast—often too fast—and the cabbage head splits open, inviting worms and spoilage. (Too much fertilizer can also result in this too-rapid type of growth. As a matter of fact, I overfertilized this cabbage on purpose, just so I'd have one to illustrate this problem.) Unchecked, cracked-open cabbages can send up a seed stalk. My solution: Take hold of the cabbage in both hands and revolve it a half-turn, 180 degrees. This will cause some of the roots to be ripped, shutting off much of the plant's water supply and food, so it will slow down the growth till you're ready to harvest it. It's like turning off a faucet. If the cracking doesn't stop, turn it again, a quarter-round this time, in a few days.

Tomato harvest tips: Wait to pick until the tomato is solid red, bottom to top. You've waited so long already—give it a few extra days and the taste will justify it. Don't strip off foliage branches to expose tomatoes to extra sun. In all parts of the country, the August sun is still strong enough to cause sunscald.

This is not the result of attack by some foot-long caterpillar! It's the mess a bird made, dive-bombing at a single ear and pecking away. It's an isolated event and no cause for alarm.

These muskmelons (or cantaloupes) are waiting patiently, and so am I. They're a few weeks off from harvesting. You can see they are still quite green. Closer to the harvest, in early September, I'll share with you my advice for determining exactly when a melon is ripe enough to pick. No one who grows these beauties wants to harvest them a day too soon!

This is the way I like to end the month of August!

Earlier in the summer would be better, I suppose, but vine-ripened tomatoes are sure worth the wait. I'm going to get a real heavy harvest on these staked tomato plants. The ones just starting to ripen are at the ground level. The fruit begins there because of the large proportion of the original transplanted stem that I buried to be converted into extra roots. So the above-ground plant will be solid tomato-bearing foliage.

August reminders . . .

- *Harvest* every crop when it starts to bear edible-sized vegetables. Keep it picked so the plant will keep producing.
- *Water* every week if it doesn't rain.
- *Stay on bug patrol*, although insects are less of a problem now. This month, the guard is more against animal pests.
- *Pick fuzzy ends off vines* to concentrate melon growth.
- *Strip* Brussels sprouts to speed sprout growth.
- *Enjoy* some onions, potatoes, garlic, shallots, leeks, cabbages, celery, eggplants, peppers, even though you may not be harvesting most of them until summer's end.
- *Do some more succession planting* as it suits you and your regional weather system, from a full-blown fall garden in the south to some spot planting up north. Spinach, all the greens, beets and carrots, peas and beans do especially well.
- *Keep track* of harvesting dates, for helpful reference planning next year.
- *Pray for hot weather* to make for the best corn and tomato season ever.

The more you pick, the more you get.

Brewing for September . . .

- The heat lovers finally make it: melons, main-crop tomatoes, peppers, eggplants, limas, Silver Queen corn
- Potato and sweet-potato harvesting, curing, and storing
- Readying the root cellar
- Continuous picking of cabbage-family crops and salad greens
- Winter squash ripeness test

EARLY SEPTEMBER
Melons—ready at last!

Cantaloupes are ripe when gently sliding my thumb against the vine easily separates it from the melon. I also smell them. Their aroma around the stem end is pleasantly strong when ripe. And the skin of several varieties turns from green to pale yellow or tan when ripe. The flesh of this cantaloupe variety happens to be pale . . . but it's dripping with flavor!

Watermelons are ripe when a small coil on the vine near the melon dries up.

There's a curly section of vine near the watermelon stem-end that turns brown and shrivels like a pig's tail when the melon has reached ripeness. I raise the Baby Sugar variety, by the way, which grows to this shape and color. But ripeness of all watermelons is difficult to judge. A trick I use is to knock on them. A sharp response, like that heard when tapping a door, usually means it's not ready. A dull thud, like that of tapping the floor, indicates ripeness.

Jan and I don't preserve melons. When they're ripe, we eat them or share them. The juice from homegrown, vine-ripened melons is something else. Although the growing period is long and the harvest season is pretty short, I think they're a taste experience every gardener should have.

All green peppers turn red if left on the plant.

Peppers are ripe and ready to eat as soon as there's something large enough to pick.

No reason red peppers should cost more in the stores than green, but they do. Don't ask me why. Within a week or so, full-sized green peppers turn red. This is true for all peppers except some yellow ones, which turn orange. Got that straight?

We're enjoying a wide variety of fresh peppers from our pepper grove. In another week or so we'll be up to our ears in peppers. We do a lot of preserving, and we also use peppers in many canned relishes and sauces. But a few plants of several varieties don't need to take up any more than a few feet of a wide row.

SEPTEMBER

The bounty

EARLY SEPTEMBER
Melons—ready at last!

Cantaloupes are ripe when gently sliding my thumb against the vine easily separates it from the melon. I also smell them. Their aroma around the stem end is pleasantly strong when ripe. And the skin of several varieties turns from green to pale yellow or tan when ripe. The flesh of this cantaloupe variety happens to be pale . . . but it's dripping with flavor!

Watermelons are ripe when a small coil on the vine near the melon dries up.

There's a curly section of vine near the watermelon stem-end that turns brown and shrivels like a pig's tail when the melon has reached ripeness. I raise the Baby Sugar variety, by the way, which grows to this shape and color. But ripeness of all watermelons is difficult to judge. A trick I use is to knock on them. A sharp response, like that heard when tapping a door, usually means it's not ready. A dull thud, like that of tapping the floor, indicates ripeness.

Jan and I don't preserve melons. When they're ripe, we eat them or share them. The juice from homegrown, vine-ripened melons is something else. Although the growing period is long and the harvest season is pretty short, I think they're a taste experience every gardener should have.

All green peppers turn red if left on the plant.

Peppers are ripe and ready to eat as soon as there's something large enough to pick.

No reason red peppers should cost more in the stores than green, but they do. Don't ask me why. Within a week or so, full-sized green peppers turn red. This is true for all peppers except some yellow ones, which turn orange. Got that straight?

We're enjoying a wide variety of fresh peppers from our pepper grove. In another week or so we'll be up to our ears in peppers. We do a lot of preserving, and we also use peppers in many canned relishes and sauces. But a few plants of several varieties don't need to take up any more than a few feet of a wide row.

August reminders . . .

- *Harvest* every crop when it starts to bear edible-sized vegetables. Keep it picked so the plant will keep producing.
- *Water* every week if it doesn't rain.
- *Stay on bug patrol*, although insects are less of a problem now. This month, the guard is more against animal pests.
- *Pick fuzzy ends off vines* to concentrate melon growth.
- *Strip* Brussels sprouts to speed sprout growth.
- *Enjoy* some onions, potatoes, garlic, shallots, leeks, cabbages, celery, eggplants, peppers, even though you may not be harvesting most of them until summer's end.
- *Do some more succession planting* as it suits you and your regional weather system, from a full-blown fall garden in the south to some spot planting up north. Spinach, all the greens, beets and carrots, peas and beans do especially well.
- *Keep track* of harvesting dates, for helpful reference planning next year.
- *Pray for hot weather* to make for the best corn and tomato season ever.

The more you pick, the more you get.

Brewing for September . . .

- The heat lovers finally make it: melons, main-crop tomatoes, peppers, eggplants, limas, Silver Queen corn
- Potato and sweet-potato harvesting, curing, and storing
- Readying the root cellar
- Continuous picking of cabbage-family crops and salad greens
- Winter squash ripeness test

My red cabbage is large enough to harvest. The white cabbage is ready, too, but it's larger than I usually let them get. But this one is going to end up as canned sauerkraut. Later still, I'll be harvesting large cabbages for the root cellar. The longer I can leave them in the garden, the later into the season I can store them (although cabbages only keep for one or two months).

Let's not forget the little guys, less showy but still putting out . . .

Broccoli kitchen hint #1: It's easy to blanch (steam) small broccoli shoots for a minute until they turn bright green, dry them, and toss them in a plastic bag as another portion for the freezer supply.

It still feels like summer, probably where you are, too. So the broccoli plants are trying hard to bolt to flowers and seeds. I don't let them, because there's a lot of cool, crisp weather coming up during which they'll thrive again. I still dust with Dipel every other week. That goes for all my cabbage-family plants. As you'll be seeing, we can harvest cabbages, kale, Brussels sprouts, and collards for *months* ahead.

I get in the habit of picking broccoli sideshoots, even if there aren't enough yet for a few servings. They'll hold in the fridge until there are. Or we chop them and serve them raw or lightly steamed in salads, soups, and casseroles.

Trench-planting gave my tomatoes an extra few hours of sunshine each day.

I stripped away the lower tomato leaves for the last day or two of ripening to bring tomatoes to an even riper stage. I don't recommend this when the tomatoes are still green or turning, because that increases the chances for sunscald. Leaf stripping is much safer in September than August. At this point I'm hoping for all the strong sun we can get to ripen even more of my heat-loving crops.

Without trench-planting, most gardeners' tomato plants don't bear fruit until halfway up the main stem. Now all of the aboveground stem is going to be very efficient, producing fruit the whole exposed distance. The lower or first fruit clusters to form, of course, ripen first.

Broccoli kitchen hint #2: In case you didn't keep up the spraying or dusting of cabbage-family crops, it's a good idea to soak broccoli spears in a dish of salted water for 15 to 20 minutes before you use them. If worms are clinging, invisible and underneath, they'll curl up, drown, and turn a yellow-brown. Sounds awful, but broccoli that's worm-free is better any day.

Tomato harvest hint: Pinch off the tops of all tomato plants. Break off that last six inches of foliage on each stem. We do not want more potential fruit-bearing foliage now; we want the plant's strength to work on ripening the larger tomatoes and swelling the rest.

Also refer back to my root-pruning suggestion (page 182) for speeding the ripening process.

Although in September the sun is less intense, plants still need to drink while they are growing. I water my garden weekly.

This is our youngest granddaughter, Janel. She thinks of gardening as all play, no work. So far, so good!

It's cherry tomato season, too. They go well with all kinds of vegetables, for instance, fresh scallions and Bok Choy.

What's a farm boy from Ferrisburg, Vermont, doing growing Bok Choy? Farm boys are resourceful and like to eat. I'm always on the lookout for interesting (new to me) vegetables. Bok Choy is a type of Chinese cabbage that resembles Swiss chard with its dark, vitamin-rich, crinkly leaf and broad celery-like stem.

Here's what I mean by getting a larger harvest when you let tomato vines sprawl:

I let these plum-style tomatoes sprawl, also. They, too, produced a good crop. We'll use both varieties of these tomatoes for making and canning tomato sauce, tomato paste, and, with the upcoming pepper harvest, a special spaghetti sauce. The plum type is thick-fleshed, less sweet, less watery, and has fewer seeds. It's been developed specifically for sauce making.

The tomatoes at left are a new orange variety. The taste is the same as others. They were supposed to be very prolific—and they were! I thought it best to try them out on a plot of their own and just let them sprawl, unpruned. As I said earlier, the loss you sometimes get from slugs or contact with damp earth is more than offset by a heavier yield.

I prefer rutabagas to turnips because of their milder taste. Rutabagas are also more of a fall crop. I'll have to harvest these big beauties right away. But in a wide row there are always some seedlings that get a later start to stagger the harvest. The surplus we begin to store in the root cellar. I like to place rutabagas (as well as other root crops) in plastic bags with some holes punched for circulation. The bags keep them clean, at a steady temperature, and seal in an even moisture level. We'll have the last of the fresh rutabagas for Thanksgiving dinner.

But I'm getting ahead of myself. It's only early September. There are still months ahead of garden-fresh vegetables to eat immediately, protect, harvest, some even to store over winter in the ground.

When the tops turn brown, potatoes are ready to dig.

As we head toward fall, the early potato plants from our 30- by 40-foot garden begin to look over the hill. The healthy foliage fades and some leaves turn brown, so I know that they've stopped manufacturing food to feed the growth underground.

When I dig up my potatoes, I'm going to store them in the root cellar right off. So I want their skins to be fairly tough. The more developed the skin, the longer the potato will store. If I can still rub the skin off with my thumb, then I postpone this project for another week or so.

Most of the potatoes are growing at about the same level in the ground. After I determine this level, I'll bruise or sever only a few in the process of digging up the row. For this task I like my wide-gap pitchfork. On the farm, it's called a manure fork. But you could use any fork or shovel. Just go slow, dig deep enough to get under the hilled potatoes, and lift gently. The potatoes I do damage in any way we wash, put in the fridge, and use up fresh.

Once I harvest a row I let the potatoes dry out, but just for an hour or so. Otherwise, they'll turn green. A little outdoor drying is just to let the excess soil flake off.

Potatoes need a dark, cool, well-ventilated spot for storage. We reserve some of the lowest shelves in our root cellar for potatoes. They can go in slotted boxes or bins or in baskets that allow some circulation. I stack the potatoes carefully (and that's true for all stored vegetables). If the skin is cut, this permits disease organisms to get to work, and rot will set in. So I always handle root-cellar vegetables like fresh eggs. This extra care pays off.

Ongoing . . .

The Brussels sprouts are ready for stripping again.

The lower sprouts are harvestable, although I'm letting them get a bit larger. Stripping off the next-highest set of side branches will help to accomplish this, plus triggering upward trunk growth and faster development of the next set of sprouts. The flavor of Brussels sprouts *improves* after frost. They are one of the staples of the fall garden.

Harvest time is ANY time there's something big enough to eat.

The fall carrot harvest begins with the "fingerlings." Harvest time does not mean just eating large and fully mature vegetables. Carrots this size are one of the real delicacies of the garden.

Sunflowers dominate the garden at this time of year with their color and size. Bees are attracted to sunflowers, of course. But so are the birds. I like to harvest the seeds for winter bird food, so I wrap the heads as they're bending and the seeds maturing in a light mesh bag—the kind onions usually come in. (Birds have trouble poking through this.) Heads can be cut and strung up to dry until used.

It's easy to remove the seeds once the heads are dry by scraping two heads together. You can also use a stiff brush. The challenge comes in shelling. We've tried a grain mill at the coarsest setting, with good results. Lightly roasted sunflower seeds are so delicious we rarely have them left over to store. But when we do, they keep for months in tightly closed jars.

THE GREAT TOMATO WATCH

Will they make it or won't they? Now's the time of year to watch my tomatoes and wonder how much more of the crop will have the hot sunny days necessary to ripen them. My experience has taught me to be patient. A fully ripe tomato is worth waiting for. And it ripens from the bottom up, as well as inside out. So I let it stay on the vine unless I'm willing to slice off the top third.

Green tomato reminder: Try my speed-ripening, root-pruning trick (page 203) if you haven't already.

The corn harvest is at its peak. I try to keep it picked.

Every other day we're eating fresh corn on the cob. The kernels are full and juicy. But there are extra ears just right for freezing.

Corn-freezing kitchen tip: We steam the ears for a minute, splash in cold water to stop the cooking, then slice the kernels off the cob. We do this by holding the ear vertically by its pointed end in a large bowl or on a board with one hand, then slicing off a few rows of kernels with a sharp knife. It's very quick and easy to do this. Pack in containers and freeze. That's it.

Root Cellars Simplified

Root-cellar cleanup: At some point in September, I take all the storage bins from the root cellar and let them air out in the sun all day. I sweep up the cellar itself so there are no molding particles around. It's a good extra measure to spray the area with disinfectant as well. Soon we'll be hanging the onions and setting in boxes of carrots and beets, plus lining up the new jars of tomato sauce and other preserves.

People can expend lots of money and effort on a root cellar. How much effort you put in depends on how much food you have to store, and how long you want crops to keep in good shape. A section of cellar closed off for this purpose is ideal. Then the environment can be controlled. Insulate the ceiling and exposed walls. The floor and outside walls are already earth-insulated. More on this later, but for now, here are the basic factors to keep in mind, whatever the situation:

—45 degrees in a dark, dry place is the goal. Too warm a space and many vegetables will sprout. If too much light reaches them, the same could happen. Too moist or humid, and vegetables will soften and eventually rot.

—Stored vegetables need to breathe. The storage space and containers themselves (potato boxes, plastic bags, onion bags) should be ventilated.

—My best advice is to try to keep vegetables out in the garden for as long as possible without danger of frost (to limit time in storage).

—Use up the vegetables with shorter shelf life first: green tomatoes (see page 211 for how to store for indoor ripening) . . . large, sweet onions . . . celery . . . cabbages. Root crops vary in storage life from two to four months, depending on conditions. I put my beets, carrots, parsnips, turnips, and rutabagas in plastic bags or in slightly moist and clean, fresh sawdust, in trays. Onions, potatoes, and winter squash can last up to half a year or more. (Pumpkins only half that time.)

—Check all stored crops regularly for signs of rot. Discard blemished vegetables or cut up and use the good parts.

—Experiment! It's fun and rewarding to know you have a supply of homegrown food at hand. Each year you will improve on storage life as you gain experience (kitchen beams may be best for onions, garlic, and shallots; boxes of potatoes can go in a little-used room in winter).

SOME ROOT-CELLAR ALTERNATIVES

- A clean garbage pail submerged in the ground, layered carefully with vegetables, a thick mulch on top of lid to insulate and mark the spot.
- Leaving root crops (parsnips, carrots, beets) right in the garden under a very thick mulch, also to insulate and identify.
- An above-ground "box" of hay bales topped by an old door, and then more hay insulation. A variation of the hay-bale cold frame, pictured last spring on page 76.

Remember: *gourds and winter squash are ready for harvesting when the skins are tough—also, when the plants and vines are starting to droop and die off. They should be picked before heavy frost—so I've got a few more weeks.*

Are you a radish nut like me?

Last chance to sow some black radishes, also called winter radishes. They take about eight weeks, have a superstrong flavor, and grow to the size of apples. They won't store in the ground long into winter without becoming pithy. But I do pull some to store in the cellar as I do my other root crops.

Keep the whole garden watered. There's still a lot of hot weather this month, and ripening vegetables need to drink.

The early September view of our 30- by 40-foot garden is showing some signs of age, but there's lots of life left in it, as you'll see over the next few months. Heavy frost is about two to three weeks off, and soon I'll be listening more carefully to weather reports. If greens and root crops were planted in midsummer for the fall, then the harvest goes on for many, many weeks—into November.

MIDDLE SEPTEMBER—Pepper Season!

Peppers come in all sizes, shapes, flavors, and colors. Peppers continuously change color, but that doesn't affect the flavor. I hope you feel encouraged to grow a small pepper orchard yourself next year if you had a limited selection this year. Jan likes to try different combinations for relishes.

This damaged section of green pepper is due to sunscald. The hot sun blisters the skin every now and then. It's unpredictable. I don't know how to prevent it. But I just cut out the blemish and eat or preserve the rest.

My cuke-in-a-bottle trick

A great gift from the garden is a dilled cucumber pickle in a bottle, the cucumber seemingly too big to have been placed inside it. I slip a bottle over a young and forming cuke as I've illustrated here, then shade it with a paper bag to keep it cool. The vegetable will grow to the limits of the bottle, then must be picked, still inside its bottle. (Otherwise it would continue to grow, squash itself, and rot.) It can be pickled in a hot brine and the bottle sealed. The pickle can be removed by cutting it up in chunks with a knife while still inside the bottle, then removed. But how it got in there is a puzzle that stumps the recipient!

Starting to put my garden to bed . . .

I've mentioned cover crops before. Here's what a sowing of annual rye grass looks like in a section of my 30- by 40-foot garden where I've already dug up and harvested my early potatoes. It was too late in the season (earlier this month) to plant a succession vegetable crop for the fall. But I did sow annual rye grass to protect the soil and produce some organic matter. It's already up a few inches and may reach a half-foot by next month. I do this when time permits and space becomes available. It's like putting my garden to bed under an organic blanket. Next spring, it will be seedbed-ready in this section under a thin, dead mat of grass that easily crumbles into the soil and doesn't interfere with any planting activity. Annual rye-grass seed is available at the larger garden-supply centers.

Cornstalks get composted. Corn borers are not a problem for me. They could be if I let these cornstalks stand over winter—the residue could offer various insects and their egg clusters a perfect winter shelter. When each crop is finished bearing, I yank up the remains and haul them to the compost heap. If they're shredded or broken up, they will compost faster.

However, the important thing is to get crop residues out of the garden (unless they can be chopped and tilled under by machine). Fall cleanup is a good habit that takes very little time. More on this next month.

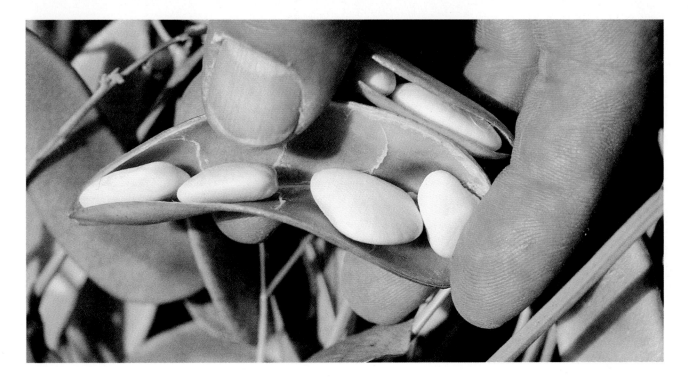

Limas!

The last of the summer crops that went in provide some of the finest eating. I've harvested a few servings of the early limas. But this is one vegetable I pretty much let mature to full size. Early pickings are not going to encourage an extended harvest—our season's too short for that. So I save the pods up for one prime harvest period.

"Lima" is a name that doesn't do this bean justice. "Butter" is more like it. Garden-fresh limas truly melt in your mouth.

The pods with beans large enough to harvest will feel quite full, and they're easy to spot. If I rush this vegetable and try to pick much before this point, I split open a pod with beans way too thin. That's disappointing after the long 11-to-12-week wait.

> **Lima bean kitchen hint:** Steam the *pods* for a minute or so, if you find them too hard to shell. This will soften them.

Dry beans

This variety is called Vermont Cranberry. But I handle all my dry beans in the same way.

- Wait till the plants are thoroughly brown and dry, with pods starting to split open. The beans will be hard.
- Gently pull the plants up and string them upside-down in the garage for a week or two, or more—it doesn't matter. This will help them to become totally dry and hard—all the better for long-term storage.
- Then wait for a breezy, pleasant day to "thresh" them—separating beans from the pods. This is simple, and fun, and can be done any time the beans are dry. I just hold the plants upside-down in a clean garbage can and whack them against the sides. The brittle pods easily split open and the beans fall to the bottom.

The "chaff," or small, broken bits of the plant, still remain, which leads to the next step. On a windy day, I spread a blanket on the ground and slowly pour the beans and chaff into the center. The chaff blows off, leaving the beans free of dried plant material after a few rounds of this step.

Fresh eggplant is at its prime.

We like harvesting eggplants when they're small. Sliced or diced, the skin is more tender, as well as the flesh. By mid-September we're harvesting beauties this big that demand to be featured in a meal or casserole of their own—fine with Jan and me. Eggplants don't preserve well, so we enjoy the fresh-eating season. (Sometimes Jan freezes extra amounts of cooked eggplant dishes.)

Gardeners make the best spaghetti sauce.

Tomato kitchen tips: I can't take credit for our spaghetti sauce. That's Jan's expertise. But I provide the best ingredients I can: tomatoes, peppers—sweet and hot—onions, and garlic. She lets her sauce simmer long and slow (overnight, or boiled down to about half) before canning. She also uses extra peppers in soup stocks. You can chop tomatoes to cut down on their cooking time. Always stir sauce frequently so bottom layer doesn't stick, burn, and spoil flavor.

Jan also freezes tomatoes whole or sliced. She scalds them for one minute to skin-breaking point (this stops enzyme action, like blanching other vegetables to be frozen). Then she places them, whole or sliced, on oiled baking sheets in the freezer for an entire day. When frozen solid, tomatoes can be bagged or boxed and returned to freezer.

Tomato frost watch

It's still early here for a frost. But what I do if a light frost is threatening is to take some newspapers out to the garden mid-to-late evening and drape them over my tomatoes. The dew at this time of year quickly makes them cling to the plants so the papers don't need anchoring. I uncover the plants in the morning. This is sufficient to keep the foliage protected. But even if the foliage is darkened or wilted or killed, the tomatoes will still be good on the vine—perhaps another month before a heavy frost comes.

I like to harvest most vine-family crops by the end of this month. Pumpkins and gourds can wait till early October, but all melons and summer and winter squash have to come in before frost.

I've just dug up the first row of our large main-crop potato patch, which is now ready. We only harvested a few bushels earlier this month, from our 30-by-40-foot garden. The main-crop harvest is more for our daughters and their families. They'll be coming over to make this digging a speedy one.

Does your lettuce or chard need another crew cut?

Even if I'm not eating all the lettuce that's out there, I keep it trimmed when it gets to the bolting point. This way fresh salad greens will be coming for another several weeks. Please refer to page 129, to review my cut-and-come-again harvesting tip.

LATE SEPTEMBER

Hubbard squash get the thumbnail test.

These Hubbard squash are large and take longer to ripen than the Acorns and Golden Nuggets. Butternuts are somewhere in between.

A Hubbard is ready for harvesting and a good, long storage life when its skin is tough. I try to penetrate the skin with my thumbnail. You can see the print I made on the squash on the right. I'll leave this one on the vine for another week or so—right up to frost if necessary. Then it's got to come in and continue ripening in the root cellar. But the larger, more bumpy-surfaced squash on the left is too tough to break. That one is ready for harvesting now.

To harvest, I take my penknife and slice the stem two inches away from the squash. This leaves a short section of stem intact on the squash. I do this with all squashes and pumpkins. If the stem breaks off, the vegetable is more apt to get infected at that point, and it will start to rot. I take care in handling squashes even though they look like pretty tough characters.

When I harvest squashes I place them in a row, bottom side up from the way they were growing. A day or so like this dries up the side that had rested on the ground. They'll be cleaner in the root cellar without slugs and cakes of soil and, of course, will last much longer in storage.

These vitamin-filled vegetables were harvested from the long rows of sprawling squash I interplanted with dry beans—all of this to share with my daughters and friends.

I'm not taking any chances with my sweet-potato crop.

I want it out of the ground and indoors before frost. Frost can harm sweet potatoes buried under their hills. And the top growth doesn't begin to die back, as with regular potatoes. So about this time of year I dig them up.

As with all my vegetables, I take care not to bruise them in the process of digging or yanking up the plants. After letting them dry out for an hour or so, I sort them by size in boxes to cure. Damaged goods we eat right away. The boxes are then put in a dark, well-ventilated, but *warm* and *humid* place for two weeks. This cures the sweet potatoes for storage in the root cellar.

This set of precautions is a little trickier than those taken for regular potatoes. And sweet potatoes don't last anywhere near as long for us. So we prefer to cut them into chunks, cook, and place in the freezer.

Down south, sweet potatoes can stay on the plant until most tubers grow to full size. But I'm real happy with my harvest, which includes many small tubers. They're every bit as tasty.

Root cellar reminders:

- I don't wash off vegetables. Washing is unnecessary and can bruise the skin.
- I try to handle vegetables as little as possible. This lessens the chance of nicks and tears.
- I don't bother to dig up parsnips—they taste even better when stored in the ground.

Parsnips

We've been harvesting some of the new crop of parsnips especially for soup stock. They've taken all summer to grow to a harvestable size. But I like to leave them right in the ground to harvest as we need them under a layer of mulch, which I put down after the first frost. The mulch will leave the soil soft and make it easy to pull parsnips as we want them. The ones we don't get to, we'll harvest early next spring when the ground has thawed. They're absolutely delicious at that point. But they must be harvested within a few weeks before they start to sprout tops again and turn the roots into soft pulp, as with all roots allowed to regenerate growth and go to seed.

These turnips are perfect *for harvesting now. Jan likes to mash them with butter in a big batch, then put them into freezer containers. Notice there will be lots more turnips to pick after frost, well into October and November, to eat fresh or store.*

Turnip kitchen hint: Sometimes turnips can taste bitter. Adding a single potato to the pot makes the whole dish a lot more mellow.

These carrots are too small *to dig up and store. I'm going to try them again in late October. They're frost-hardy, and still have several weeks to keep growing.*

Rescuing my tomatoes

At some point in late September, when a frost can come, I take a cart to the tomatoes and pick all the healthy ones—semiripe to green. Ripen green tomatoes indoors *my* way—not on the windowsill. Tomatoes ripen from bottom to top, but also from the inside out. So it's not really necessary to plaster your windowsills with them. That turns them *red* but not *ripe*.

What works best for me is to place them in a warm, dark spot and cover them with a single sheet of newspaper. These are the conditions the tomatoes most need to continue the ripening process, which is internal. The light—necessary for growth —is not important now.

Don't bring in more than you can use or want to use. The best of the harvest has been consumed or preserved. Compost rotting tomatoes as you inspect them for ripeness every few days.

Emergency tomato frost prevention: I often set up my sprinkler and water my tender plants starting the late afternoon before a predicted heavy, killing frost, and leave the system going all night and early next morning. Quite often this trick works to keep the plants too wet to freeze and be killed. It's worth the try if there's a good chance of a few more weeks of above-freezing weather.

Before the frost hits, pick off and pot a tomato sucker for starting a fresh indoor supply. For avid tomato fans, it's fun to slice off a six-inch sucker and place it in a jar of water for a few hours. Strip off the lower leaves and bury as much of that stem as possible in a six-inch pot filled with your best soil mix. Water regularly and fertilize a few times with liquid houseplant food. Pixies do especially well for this project, since they're the fastest-growing tomato variety. I leave the pot outdoors on sunny days for an extra boost, but otherwise keep it in a sunny window. There will be red, ripe tomatoes for the holidays.

My favorite thing to do with hot peppers: string them up to dry.

I like to crunch up a dried hot pepper into spaghetti sauce or a deep-winter stew to spice things up. One easy way to do that is to have a string of them hanging right in the kitchen.

In this photo, I have a basket of assorted peppers in one hand, and in the other a whole plant of hot peppers (they're either Cayenne Hots or Anaheim Hots).

I just take a needle and thick thread and string peppers together. They last indefinitely. Or I hang the entire plant upside-down in the root cellar. A word of caution: The juice from these peppers is *hot*, so keep fingers away from eyes and mouth while stringing with a needle.

Late September   211

Don't neglect this powerhouse producer.

These sideshoots have grown since the last cutting, which was the second and third from these plants. Provided I side-dressed the crop at first heading and kept up with regular doses of Dipel, my broccoli plants can keep going well into the fall. I have to keep an eye out for spindly shoots going to seed. I just snap those off, hoping to encourage a more compact and edible flower stalk for its next growth.

Bath sponge from the garden: the Luffa squash.

The Luffa summer squash has a fibrous interior which serves as a sponge or scrubber. It's fine enough for use in the bath. I wait until the plant is fully grown—from ten to 20 inches—and harvest it when the skin is green.

I just peel the skin layer off, soak the sponge under running water to get rid of its oily surface and let it dry completely in the sun. When dry, the remaining seeds will fall out. Luffas make great gifts from a gardener.

These final weeks in our area before frosts begin are very precious. The last of the limas, okras, peppers, eggplants, corn, and tomatoes are ripening. The pace is much slower, but the harvest is still at its best-tasting.

I pick only the fleshed-out lima pods. If they're flat, it's not worth the effort of shelling them.

Saving seeds

It's always interesting to save some seeds from vegetable plants, store them properly, then plant them the following year. It's a great project for kids to learn to understand how plants work. For flavor, though, stick with new seeds each year.

Frost-shield ideas: Sometimes I toss an old blanket over a three-foot section of wide row with lima beans in early evening. I'll do this if the plants are still loaded with developing pods. Or I'll cover a large block of beans or peas with a sheet of plastic held down with rocks. We've usually had our fill of the vine-family crops but blankets, plastic, newspapers, any light and easy-to-manage covering, could save some plants. Often the large foliage of squash, eggplants, and others will be killed by frost, but the shielded, lower fruits remain untouched. As these have no leaves to manufacture food, I go ahead and pick them because they won't grow any larger. And, of course, eggplants and summer squash are edible at *any* size.

September reminders . . .

- Ready the root cellar.
- Let melons, limas, tomatoes (the slow growers) ripen naturally. They take more time this month than last month.
- Keep broccoli sideshoots, large cabbages, shiny eggplants harvested. Repeat cutting of greens to stimulate new fall growth.
- Dig sweet potatoes just before frost threatens. Dig regular potatoes as late as possible, so root cellar will be as cool as possible.
- Pick all tomatoes, peppers, beans, vine crops, winter squashes, and other tender vegetables before hard frost.
- Keep garden watered. Late onions, celery, peas, greens, and cabbage-family crops are still going strong.
- Spray or dust cabbage crops with Dipel once or twice. Worms are still out there, even though they are getting sluggish.
- Begin garden cleanup—composting tough residues, spading or tilling under the softer, greener ones whenever you can.
- Record keeping: dates of final harvest, notes for next year.

Happy harvesting!

Brewing for October . . .

- Pumpkin time; collect last of squash
- Fall treats: sugar snap peas, spinach, crinkly lettuce
- Onion, beet, and carrot harvest and storage
- Hardiest fall crops, mostly in the cabbage family
- More root-cellar know-how

- Prolonging the fresh harvest with some simple protective devices

- Final harvesting of the hardier vine crops

- Root-cellar organizing; storing of main-crop roots

- Fresh fall pickings of greens and root crops

- Making compost of all residues right in the garden, or in separate piles

OCTOBER

I don't let my garden get away with early retirement!

This one is from my brag patch. The little ones make better pies. At least they're easier to cut, cook, and handle seeds.

It took my grandkids all of 60 seconds loose in the pumpkin patch to discover the ones with their own names inscribed in the pumpkins.

EARLY OCTOBER

Pumpkins and gourds need to be picked. Killing frost due any day.

The important thing is to first bring inside the tender squash—the winter squash. Pumpkins are a little tougher and can withstand a few initial light frosts. I like to stock the root cellar at the last possible point in time for each crop, as I've said before. This helps extend their "shelf life."

I harvest them carefully, always leaving a few inches of stem. Sometimes, however, stems snap off at the base. Just use these vine crops first.

Reminder: Crop residues harbor insects and disease organisms over winter.

Last month I mentioned pulling up cornstalks so they wouldn't provide easy winter shelter for garden pests and plagues. This common-sense garden hygiene applies to all vegetables. I'll be discussing soil building in more detail next month . . . why all soils need ample and regular doses of organic matter. But for now, know that I think it's important to spade or till under all crop residues when plants are finished bearing. When they're still green and tender, it's easier to chop and bury them, as well as for soil organisms to decompose them. Coarse material I yank and haul to the compost pile.

Here's where succession planting pays off.

It's early October and most folks, at least up north, are thinking about putting their gardens to rest. Not me. I'm not ready to go back to canned and frozen vegetables (even though they're from my own garden!). I'd rather eat fresh.

I used to think of peas as just an early-summer treat. But they're relatively hardy and grow super at this end of the season, too.

It took very little time to prepare and plant this block of peas a few months ago. We should be able to pick for a while longer. As long as the peas are starting to mature, they can withstand a few light frosts.

"One garden a year is enough for me!" I often get told. Fair enough, I reply. But since I garden with wide rows and block plantings, stretching the fresh-eating season is no more work.

What's left in the garden? All these frost-hardy vegetables: all root crops (including turnips and parsnips), cabbages, broccoli, Brussels sprouts, kale, radishes, kohlrabi, chard, and more.

I leave a good half-inch to an inch of stem on beets for storage. This way they won't "bleed" so much during cooking. (If the skins of beets are cut, they bleed badly.) As I do for turnips, parsnips, and carrots, I either place beets in perforated plastic bags or in shallow boxes packed in moist sawdust. I don't snip off the root ends, either, for the same reason.

Can beets get too large for storage? No. I'd be happy if all my beets reached tennis-ball size.

Again, after pulling any root crops, I leave them to dry off in the sun so the excess dirt will drop off. But I don't wash vegetables for storage, as I've

These main-crop beets are about as big as they're going to get.

already mentioned. Not only might washing bruise the skins, but water carries new bacteria. So I like to leave them in their natural condition.

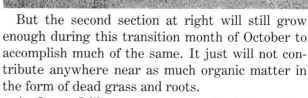

Why let any section of the garden during the growing season lie idle? It's just an invitation to weed seeds.

Once sections of my garden are finished bearing vegetables I like to sow a cover crop. As I've mentioned before, annual rye grass is great for this because it grows so quickly. "Annual" means that it will grow for as long as hard freezes hold off this year. Then it will die. Under the mat of dead grass the following spring, I'll find the soil loose and crumbly—practically seedbed-perfect.

Sometimes I plant strips of just a few sections. Obviously I don't spade or till up my whole garden, because many crops will keep bearing for months into the fall. And I leave my parsnips and kale in place, right up to next spring, so the garden gets to look like a patchwork quilt. In this photo, the taller, thicker cover crop of annual rye grass was sown three weeks earlier. At this time of year, a few weeks can make a big difference. I got the garden section on the left tilled and planted early enough last month to have this good foot of growth. Because the soil is so well insulated, it will stay warmer longer into late fall and winter. This will keep the earthworms more active in the upper soil layers, doing that much more good in building fertile soil for next year's garden.

But the second section at right will still grow enough during this transition month of October to accomplish much of the same. It just will not contribute anywhere near as much organic matter in the form of dead grass and roots.

As I say, I like to cover as much of the garden this way as I can. It means less crusting, less compaction (since I'm not as apt to walk over newly planted grass), less erosion from rain and wind, and less likelihood of harboring autumn weed seeds.

A rototiller makes very simple work of this, but I also spade up small sections by hand. A light mulch is also a good soil cover. What the worms haven't eaten by next spring can be spaded under (early) or raked off to compost or to reuse later as mulch.

Greens thrive in cool weather. Wide rows of tender, sweet spinach and looseleaf lettuce will add flavor and texture to October salads.

Spinach and lettuce won't grow to full size, and I'll only get one cutting from them. But with some decent October sun, these crops will produce three- to six-inch leaves. Low-growing, clustered plants in wide rows are more protected from the frosts. I should be able to pick from them into early November.

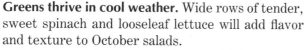

Kale is coming into full maturity.

A few plants like this one will keep us supplied with crunchy, nutritious greens through the end of the year and well beyond.

I find most people don't eat large portions of kale. It's strong, and to most tastes needs a flavorful dressing or to be mixed in with other salad greens. A few kale plants are plenty because it's so darn prolific.

Cold and freezing weather gives kale a sweeter flavor. I even harvest it under snow, as you'll see in December.

Rugged, dependable, vitamin-packed kale is truly the backbone of our fall garden.

Still growing strong . . .

The cabbages are starting to slow down in their growth rate.

Just when to pick them is up to you. However, for storage purposes in the root cellar, I try to leave cabbages outdoors as long as I can (easily until Thanksgiving). This will keep the heads fresh and crisp when finally placed in the root cellar.

Allowing any vegetable to rest on the ground for a really long time invites some amount of spoilage due to slugs and damp earth. I just toss any damaged outer leaves in the compost heap.

The last of the onions have to be pulled, dried, cured, and stored. For storage purposes, it's very important to get onions to dry. It takes two to three days with onions upended and on the ground for them to get nice and hard. I know they are dry enough when the bottom-side roots are brittle and break right off. Then it's two to three weeks of curing, either braided or in mesh bags, in a shady but warm and dry place before stringing them up for the root cellar. If I'm going to *braid* the onions, it's best to select those with the largest tops. If any onions have especially thick necks, we eat those right away rather than store them. Such a bulb produces a seedpod which drains it of energy so it won't store good and hard.

MIDDLE AND LATE OCTOBER

The "fall garden" is really just a small section of our 30- by 40-foot garden.

But it offers plenty of good eating. I think most Americans are practical people and hate to throw good food away. My grandmother said this about *everything:* "Use it up, wear it out, make it do, or do without." So it's hard to squander the generous harvest possible each fall.

Don't forget to record the dates of *final* harvests from your garden, as well as the *first* and *prime* ones. You'll probably be surprised how much good eating is possible (thanks to the hardiness of the cabbage family) right up to the holidays at year's end.

Remember last month when I mentioned leaving my sprinkler on to protect from frost kill? I did do that a few times, and it worked—for light frost. But with this real heavy one, the bean plants finally froze solid and are now done for. Well, nothing gambled, nothing gained!

FALL PROTECTION CHECKLIST

I use the same things to shield my plants from heavy frosts in the early fall that I do in late spring.

- newspapers
- cardboard boxes
- collars of roofing paper
- paper bags
- old blankets
- sheets of plastic
- old cloth
- the plastic tunneling (page 52) I used for starting vine crops and tomatoes.

The critical time for avoiding frost is from late afternoon to the following morning. Sometimes I just hate to see that one special pepper plant or eggplant quit. So, to stretch the harvest, I'll take one of these precautions for a week or so.

Two rutabagas: Is one better than the other?

No, they're both good. The smaller is hard-ball-sized; the other, the size of a golf ball. The flesh of each is sweet and firm. Conditions of storage, rather than size, will determine how long they'll last. You can store them all.

- I don't put potatoes (or any vegetables) directly on the floor, but a little elevated. They need good circulation. Also, potatoes do best on the coolest (lowest) shelves of the root cellar.
- The winter squashes also need active circulation, so I keep space under and over them, on slotted shelves. I try not to layer them too deeply.
- We cook up and freeze some of the squashes and pumpkins, as a kind of insurance. Besides, a full freezer runs more efficiently than a partially empty one.
- Cabbages are wrapped in newspapers, and brought in at the last possible time (same for celery). Their storage life is pretty short—one to two months—so autumn is boiled New England dinner season, complete with turnips and potatoes and dry beans (and salt pork).
- Hot-pepper plants, bags of onions and shallots, braided garlic, some corn for meal and for popping . . . are all hung on nails near the ceiling. They need the most ventilation.

Root cellars need *some* degree of moisture or the vegetables will dry out. Sixty-degree humidity is ideal. I sprinkle some moist sawdust on the floor and redampen it occasionally.

Carrots can stay in the ground *for harvesting through winter under heavy mulch. They've stopped growing but are content to stay put. This is a little risky if the mice find them.*

I actually prefer to dig up some carrots as I need them throughout the fall and store them in plastic bags in the root cellar. When one supply is near finished, I go out and get some more. The garden— up to January and real deep winter when the soil is frozen solid—acts like a "holding tank" for mulched carrots. The longer I can have them in the garden, the better. When I do bring them in, I cut off the carrot tops and leave them in the garden where the extra organic material is always welcome.

hot peppers . . .
popping corn . . .

. . . and showoffs!

October reminders . . .

- Heavy frost watch. I keep a few plants going by protecting them: peppers, tomatoes, eggplants, beans, peas—just to see how long they can make it.
- I gather lingering vine crops early in the month.
- Root-cellar cabbages get stored as late as possible because of their short shelf life.
- Spade under or compost-pile crop residues to destroy winter quarters for insects and to prevent any weeds from going to seed.
- Record final harvest dates for reference next season. Note varieties that were family favorites or especially insect- or disease-resistant.

Brewing for November . . .

- Soil building: giving the garden some well-deserved food of its own
- Fall leaves: "gold" to gardeners
- Tool and equipment care
- Root-cellar inspection
- Enjoying the harvest!

- Collecting leaves, grass clippings, odd bits of brush

- Improving soil with organic matter

- Turning and building up compost piles: boost for next year's garden

- Keeping fall crops picked

NOVEMBER

Shape up garden soil

November's my month to relax. But I do keep tabs on my garden.

There's not a whole lot I *have* to do—so there's no point, in these final months of the gardening year, in dividing them into early, middle, and late, to indicate what activity takes place at which time.

Replenishing my garden soil

See how loose and crumbly is the texture of this soil? If our garden soils were this perfect, we'd be lucky indeed. This excellent soil happens to be under a blanket of leaves in the woods right next door to my place. Nature has a very efficient system to recycle waste and nutrients. The leaves are insulating the soil; the soil stays fairly warm so the earthworms and other forms of soil life can stay busy munching and digesting well into winter. The result of this constant supply of organic matter as food, and its decomposition into fine particles, is a soil rich in nutrients. And the texture makes an ideal growing medium—one where roots can sink in deep and make close contact with moisture and available nutrients.

Gardeners can and *should* create similar conditions. The concentration of vegetables growing in one relatively compact area means I'm taking out more in the way of plant food than I'm putting back in. So mid to late fall is my big chance to do my garden soil a favor.

I like to till or spade in a half-foot of leaves.

To cover the entire garden may be too large a task, and it's sometimes difficult to collect that many leaves in one season. Also, I have many sections and parts of rows still producing vegetables, and they will be producing for many more weeks. So I do a few sections one year, a couple more the next. I try to cover as many leaves as I can with some topsoil during this process so they won't blow away. By next spring, the leaves will be mostly decomposed (earthworms are nonstop snackers). Any leaves intact on the surface I rake off for use as mulch. They would interfere with making a smooth spring seedbed.

I keep an eye peeled for organic matter all year round.

Coarse material, like yard trimmings, I just stack and let partially break down. Such brush is too coarse for including in a compost pile just yet. Grass clippings I collect fresh after they've dried an hour or so and use as mulch. Crop residues, like the leaves broken off Brussels sprouts, generally go in the compost pile. The main thing is, I try not to let these good soil-building materials go to waste. I find a use for them eventually—as mulch, as ingredients in a compost pile, or as organic matter to be spread and dug directly into the garden soil come fall, like I do with leaves.

The greener the plant material, the more tender it is and the quicker it will break down. That's why I like to chop and bury vegetable-plant leftovers right into the soil. The ones I let go by—or *had* to in the case of beans for drying and storing (which have to stay on the plants until the fall and whose pods are brittle and brown)—cannot easily be tilled or spaded into the soil unless I use a power shredder first.

Compost making can be simple and satisfying.

Composting doesn't have to be a messy project. Nor does it have to be very time-consuming to make more when you're running low on this wonderfully fertile stuff. (See page 31, back in February, for more discussion of compost as a fertilizer.)

I love to use it for potting plants and for giving garden transplants an extra boost. When I set out a transplant in a hole filled with a few handfuls of dark, moisture-holding compost, it's like giving it all the foundation benefits of the rich forest floor—plus full sunshine! As the compost breaks down into a finer texture, even more of its nutrients are released, giving my transplants a light dose of fertilizer without harming or shocking young roots.

Here's my checklist for easy and quick compost:

1. The ingredients for fast-heating compost piles are organic matter, air, and moisture.

2. Never pack down a compost pile. Just firm it. Without continuous circulation, the microbes working to break down the material cannot get the oxygen they need to breathe, and the pile will become slimy.

3. To allow for these other important ingredients, I always make compost in layers—a few inches of whatever organic material, and then a handful of "activator," which I'll explain in a moment. It's like building a multilayered cake. I spray each layer of the pile with water. Layering builds in the necessary air spaces for good circulation.

4. I make compost inside a standing container, preferably circular, and about three feet in diameter. If it's much larger, the pile can become too heavy and dense in the center, cutting off air circulation. In a *square* container, it's hard to get the corners to heat up. A container also "organizes" the pile so it doesn't spread out all over the place and get too compact and airless in the center. Organized, it's more attractive for everyone who sees it.

5. An activator is some source of nitrogen and protein, like alfalfa meal, bone meal, blood meal, or composted manure. Alfalfa is wonderfully rich in nitrogen and the cheapest for those without manures. This activator assures that the microbes clinging to the organic material to be composted will have an initial source of fuel to trigger the chain reaction of breakdown. Otherwise, the pile could sit there and decompose in time over months on its own, but by then the bulk of the released nutrients would have leached out the bottom of the pile into the ground. The resulting compost would still be nicely textured, but would have lost its fertilizing value. So . . .

Rich compost is compost quickly produced.

6. Once the pile has begun to heat up, in two weeks or so, I slip off or remove whatever wire cage or container I have used, and turn the pile upside-down as I place it back into the container. This fluffs up the pile and gives me a chance to put still-coarse material from the edges into the center of the newly built version. It, too, can now "cook" where the microorganisms are most insulated and active. I also again wet the pile at this time. Composting my way—start to finish—only takes a few weeks.

7. I do not compost animal garbage such as meat scraps and bones. That attracts skunks, raccoons, dogs, and other creatures to make a mess of it all. Keep in mind: Banana and citrus peels, eggshells, and such can be composted. But the tougher the material, the longer it will take to break down.

   Compost I make this fall season will soon freeze, so I certainly won't have any nutrient-leaching problem before it gets used next year. In fact, there's very little leaching when making compost piles this small. Rain is simply shed by the top crust (rather than sinking through a large pile which eventually becomes concave).

   I'll turn these piles again in early spring for a good supply by next gardening season.

I'm collecting some compost *I will use this winter and early next spring for potted plants and seedlings. I'll store this in a plastic bag in the cellar. First, though, I spread it out to dry. This prevents "damping off" of tiny seeds and seedlings when used in a seed-starting medium.*

Some cheery sights under darkening skies . . .

Most vegetables get sweeter after frost.

This is purple kohlrabi, in case you didn't recognize it.

A vegetable named for the coming season—winter radish.

Turnips: We can even harvest these after snow.

Spinach—crisp and delicious in the fall.

Chinese cabbage—perfect for stir-frying.

Last call for onions.

Buckwheat—the ultimate cover crop to smother out weedy garden patches.

This project is optional, for gardeners who like the idea of cover crops. I've described using annual rye grass for this purpose. Buckwheat, available in farm seed or supply stores, is also outstanding as a cover crop which grows *thickly*.

Late in August (page 190) I decided to sow fast-growing buckwheat in those sections of my garden that weeds had begun to monopolize. Ordinarily, buckwheat is killed by the first frost or at the beginning of October. This fall I got a few extra weeks of growth beyond that. This densely standing crop interrupted the weed cycle and blocked sunlight from those lingering weeds. Last month I rototilled this "green manure" into the topsoil. Next spring, these sections will be nearly weed-free, with very light and workable soil. I gambled planting buckwheat so late, but in many parts of the country there's a chance to get a good stand by early fall for tilling in.

The toolshed shutdown

- If anything needs repair, now might be a less rushed time to attend to it—for myself or a repair shop as well.
- I take a clean paintbrush and pure vegetable oil to the toolshed and coat all my hand tools. I wipe off any excess the following spring. Oil lightly coats the metal parts and prevents rusting. It reconditions the wooden parts, too.
- Power equipment should be drained of gasoline. This cleans out the carburetor. I simply let the machine run in the yard until the tank goes dry.
- I also make a mental note of which tools were most helpful. Time to sort through supplies and tidy up. It's nice to end the season feeling organized. Then in spring I don't have to walk into clutter and search all over for things.

This is my last chance to build a raised bed for some real early planting in drained, warmed-up soil next spring. There have been some heavy frosts, but no snows as yet. The soil is still dry, crumbly, and easy to till and spade. (Please see page 58 for my step-by-step technique for making raised beds.)

The raised bed difference

These pictures explain it all. Carrots in clay soil struggle to grow, and become twisted and stunted (as well as difficult to clean). Root crops in well-conditioned soil, especially soil piled and mounded in a raised bed to double the topsoil depth, produce a crop like the one you see in the second photo. By the way, the varieties pictured here are fully developed specimens of the Kinko, Nantes, and Imperator carrot types.

A final gamble

I've experimented with sowing spinach seeds and onion sets at this time of year to grow over winter for extremely early spring growth next year. I plant them a bit deeper than usual. In a section of a wide row, some or many of them are going to make it through the freezing, thawing, and drastic weather swings in the next four months. I would recommend this for a raised bed to limit chances of sets and seeds getting waterlogged. I'd also suggest it be in an odd corner of the garden so as not to interfere with spring soil preparation. Use stakes to mark the row, and make a note so you'll remember. It's a fun way to gamble at gardening—tangy green tops and dark-green spinach popping up with the rhubarb and other signs of spring.

ROOT-CELLAR INSPECTION

Jan and I try to check the root cellar regularly. We bring to the compost any cabbages, carrots, beets, potatoes, or squashes that have spoiled.

- The green tomatoes are still ripening under newspaper cover. Some are spoiled. We'll cut and fry or add to other cooked dishes the better tomatoes or tomato parts that are *almost* ripe. You can't expect them to get garden-fresh this way.
- We always eat the "worst first" . . . a potato with a blemish, a cabbage or celery plant getting a bit limp.

- I look for evidence of mice. They're trying their darndest this time of year to get inside, especially to a food source. I set traps. I don't like poison spread around my food.
- If the humidity seems low, I sprinkle the floor with moist sawdust, or wet the sawdust already there. If the cellar seems too damp, I need to ventilate for a while.
- If there's a window in your root cellar, be sure it's covered with something opaque to block out light. Light will sprout stored vegetables and turn potatoes green.

Jan Raymond's tried-and-true root cellar serving tricks . . .

- Add a large potato when cooking strong turnips and rutabagas. It helps mellow the flavor.
- Combine apples with squash in cooked casseroles. This lowers dependence on butter and sweetener.
- Try stir-frying coarse vegetables—collards, Brussels sprouts, leeks, kale, outer cabbage leaves—in a little oil or butter, or some of each.
- Experiment with herbs and spices. Cinnamon and carrots we like. Also ginger and cabbage, dill and squash.
- Use a variety of cutting styles to add interest to the November-through-April hardy vegetables —diced carrots, julienne strips of kale, finely shredded cabbage, grated beets, and so on.
- Make a soufflé of turnip by folding egg whites beaten stiff into the cooked, mashed, and seasoned vegetable, then baking it.
- All vegetables can be cooked and pureed to form the basis of a creamed soup (adding milk and/or cream, flour, onions, and butter).
- Use stored onions in everything. They make the flavors richer and more satisfying.
- Cook and chill root crops, steam and chill leafier vegetables. Then slice them very thin and toss in a light marinade of seasoned oil and vinegar. Make creative non-lettuce, deep-winter salads.

- Make hearty soups and meat stews with combinations of most all the stored vegetables, whether or not recipes call for them. Add a package of frozen, greener vegetables, like peas or beans or asparagus, when fall-garden chard and kale supplies dwindle.
- Serve chilled and thin-sliced vegetables with dips: carrots, kohlrabi, turnips, rutabagas, radishes. People will nibble kale gladly with a dip.
- Spice up dull leftovers with dried hot pepper. Never fails to work!
- Substitute squash for pumpkin in pumpkin pie, bread, and dessert recipes.
- Dip slices of vegetables in a seasoned egg-and-breadcrumb mixture, then fry. This will make them deliciously crunchy.
- Serve those homemade pickles and relishes both at lunch and dinner. They're not on the shelf just to look pretty, and they perk up a winter meal.
- The same advice goes for jams and jellies. Use them as glazes on root crops and roasted meats.

Waiting for snow . . .

The asparagus looks dead to the world but in fact the ferns are still making food and transporting it to replenish the crown underground. It's a mistake to cut asparagus ferns now. I always wait till spring to cut and shred or remove the dried top growth. Then I know for certain that the ferns are finished with their work. Please refer to page 53, in March, for more detail on first-of-season asparagus chores.

There will be many frosts by the end of this month. The hardy collards, sprouts and other cabbage-family crops have slightly wilted outer leaves now from the repeated freezing and thawing. (For some reason, this has only *improved* the texture and flavor of sprouts and kale.) But the vegetables themselves, or the leaves in the middle and center zones, are great for harvesting, and still delicious.

November reminders . . .

- Scout in the garden for edible plants. Compost those that are not.
- It's now time to mulch the parsnips. A six-inch layer of mulch will help to "mark" the patch and to remind us next spring that this sweet root crop is ready for the pulling.
- A light mulch of dry fall leaves protects carrots for fresh harvesting well into winter. Even up here, the ground doesn't freeze hard till the first of the year. I could put a heavy layer of fall mulch down and insulate them further, but I prefer to pull most of them in late fall for the root cellar.
- Become a saver of organic matter that could break down and be converted fairly easily to "soil food." My rule of green thumb: If an earthworm could munch on it, it's worth composting in a pile or simply stacking and saving for next year's mulch supply.
- Monitor the root cellar. Use the coolest spot near the floor for root crops, and the warmest near the ceiling for onions. Don't get too fussy or discouraged. All vegetables spoil at some point. Think of your stored crops as bonuses. It can take a while to get a feel for root-cellaring.
- Spread a blanket of fall leaves on your garden. Spade some earth over as much of it as you can, to anchor them. You can rake off the undecomposed remainder in the spring for mulch. The soil will be in much better shape by then because of the added encouragement to earthworms.
- Bag a sample of completed compost or potting soil for indoor seed starting in early spring.
- Continue to make notes in the back of this book. The "final harvest" column dates may surprise you.

My most often quoted statement, so I'm told:
Feed your soil, and it'll feed you!

Brewing for December . . .

- Nothing, really, in the way of gardening chores
- Holiday garden gifts
- Mental list of do's and don'ts for next year
- The garden-fresh harvest goes on, even under snow!

DECEMBER

I don't quit!

Snow serves as an insulating blanket.

When heavy, killing frosts arrive they destroy most foliage on plants. If I'm lucky, snow will fall early in the season and act as a mulch to protect my vegetables from further severe conditions. Gardeners in regions without snow can always accomplish the same with loose straw or fall leaves.

The cabbages with their multiple layers make their own protection. The red cabbage I just harvested finally grew to a decent size. The fall-planted carrots didn't grow very large, but they taste supersweet at this time of year. The Crisphead lettuce is perfect right now, after this nice,

fluffy blanket of snow with the temperature in the high 20s and low 30s. But I've got to harvest the rest soon. It's not *that* hardy. The onions are. Those I could leave under snow, or under a mulch if the snow melts. The scallions from the last of the sets I planted are a good size to harvest now and throughout the winter. I've also got leeks in the fall garden about this same thickness.

I don't want to bore you, but I thought I should include a few more snapshots of harvesting under snow, for proof that stretching the garden season is possible and very satisfying!

Chard

Scallions

Carrots
Head lettuce

Brussels sprouts
Turnips

GIFTS FROM THE GARDEN

- Luffa squash sponge
- Baked Hubbard squash pie
- Any canned goods topped with a stick-on bow
- Indian corn
- Popping corn
- A half-dozen dried hot peppers, tied in a bunch
- Gift basket of choice root-cellar samples: acorn squash, Golden Nuggets, Baby Sugar pie pumpkins, etc.
- Decorative gourds, dried and shellacked
- A braid of garlic or onions
- A nice container of potato-leek soup

Dick's quick potato-leek soup

Sauté chopped onions and leeks in butter. Add sliced, peeled potatoes (plus or minus turnips, carrots, rutabagas, and squash) and a can or so of chicken broth. Simmer till just tender, and put it all through a blender or food processor. Add cream or milk, plus seasonings to taste. Serve hot or cold. Garnish with fresh parsley or kale. I vary the amounts of vegetables as it suits the moment. The more vegetables, the thicker the soup. It's always good.

December notes . . .

- Indoor tubs of parsley and Pixie tomatoes and herbs get the sunny window treatment, weekly doses of houseplant fertilizer, and lots of water as needed. The important thing is to keep the edible parts picked!
- We *use up* our canned goods. Caps can rust, if kept in fairly moist areas for long periods.
- I make some final notes in my record books on quantities, dates, flops, favorites, and so forth.
- It's *almost* time to get the new year's seed catalogs. But first, Jan and I take plenty of time to enjoy the harvest and the holidays with our family and friends. We wish the same for you, too!

INDEX

Page numbers in italics denote illustrations.

19__ GARDEN RECORD: DIMENSIONS (__ X __)

VEGETABLE / VARIETY	AMOUNT OF SPACE	DATES		PLANTED IN GARDEN	HARVESTED	COMMENTS
		SEEDED INDOORS	SEEDED OUTDOORS			

19__ GARDEN RECORD: DIMENSIONS (__ X __)

VEGETABLE / VARIETY	AMOUNT OF SPACE	DATES			HARVESTED	COMMENTS
		SEEDED		PLANTED		
		INDOORS	OUTDOORS	IN GARDEN		

19__ GARDEN RECORD: DIMENSIONS (__ X __)

VEGETABLE / VARIETY	AMOUNT OF SPACE	DATES		PLANTED IN GARDEN	HARVESTED	COMMENTS
		SEEDED				
		INDOORS	OUTDOORS			

19__ GARDEN RECORD: DIMENSIONS (__ X __)

VEGETABLE / VARIETY	AMOUNT OF SPACE	DATES SEEDED INDOORS	DATES SEEDED OUTDOORS	PLANTED IN GARDEN	HARVESTED	COMMENTS

19__ GARDEN RECORD: DIMENSIONS (__ X __)

VEGETABLE / VARIETY	AMOUNT OF SPACE	DATES SEEDED INDOORS	SEEDED OUTDOORS	PLANTED IN GARDEN	HARVESTED	COMMENTS

19__ GARDEN RECORD: DIMENSIONS (__ X __)

VEGETABLE / VARIETY	AMOUNT OF SPACE	DATES				COMMENTS
		SEEDED INDOORS	SEEDED OUTDOORS	PLANTED IN GARDEN	HARVESTED	